THE
CHRISTIAN
DOCTRINE
OF HUMANITY

PROCEEDINGS OF THE LOS ANGELES THEOLOGY CONFERENCE

This is the sixth volume in a series published by Zondervan Academic. It is the proceedings of the Los Angeles Theology Conference held under the auspices of Fuller Theological Seminary in January 2018. The conference is an attempt to do several things. First, it provides a regional forum in which scholars, students, and clergy can come together to discuss and reflect upon central doctrinal claims of the Christian faith. It is also an ecumenical endeavor. Bringing together theologians from several different schools and confessions, the LATC seeks to foster serious engagement with Scripture and tradition in a spirit of collegial dialogue (and disagreement), looking to retrieve the best of the Christian past in order to forge theology for the future. Finally, each volume in the series focuses on a central topic in dogmatic theology. It is hoped that this endeavor will continue to fructify contemporary systematic theology and foster a greater understanding of the historic Christian faith amongst the members of its different communions.

LOS ANGELES
THEOLOGY
CONFERENCE

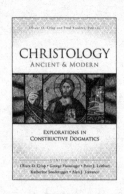

**CHRISTOLOGY, ANCIENT
AND MODERN:**
*Explorations in Constructive
Dogmatics, 2013*

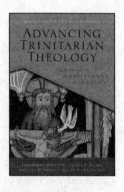

**ADVANCING
TRINITARIAN THEOLOGY:**
*Explorations in Constructive
Dogmatics, 2014*

LOCATING ATONEMENT:
*Explorations in Constructive
Dogmatics, 2015*

**THE VOICE OF GOD IN
THE TEXT OF SCRIPTURE:**
*Explorations in Constructive
Dogmatics, 2016*

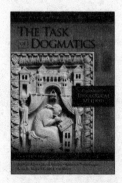

THE TASK OF DOGMATICS:
*Explorations in Theological
Method, 2017*

Oliver D. Crisp *and* Fred Sanders, Editors

THE
CHRISTIAN
DOCTRINE
OF HUMANITY

Explorations in
CONSTRUCTIVE DOGMATICS

——————————— CONTRIBUTORS ———————————

Marc Cortez • Hans Madueme • Ian A. McFarland
Richard J. Mouw • Lucy Peppiatt • Frances M. Young

ZONDERVAN

The Christian Doctrine of Humanity
Copyright © 2018 by Oliver D. Crisp and Fred Sanders

This title is also available as a Zondervan ebook.

Requests for information should be addressed to:
Zondervan, *3900 Sparks Dr. SE, Grand Rapids, Michigan 49546*

ISBN 978–0–310–59547–2

Cover design: Gradient Idea
Cover photo: Duomo, Monreale, Sicily, Italy/Bridgeman Images
Interior imagery: © CCallanan/Shutterstock

Printed in the United States of America

18 19 20 21 22 23 24 25 26 27 28 /DHV/ 15 14 13 12 11 10 9 8 7 6 5 4 3 2 1

With grateful thanks to Revd. Dr. Stan Gundry,
our editor-in-chief at Zondervan Academic,
for believing in the LATC from the start.

CONTENTS

ACKNOWLEDGMENTS

THE EDITORS WOULD LIKE TO THANK Dr. Marianne Meye Thompson, Dean of the School of Theology, and the faculty and administration of Fuller Theological Seminary for their support for the Sixth Los Angeles Theology Conference (LATC) in January of 2018, out of which these published proceedings grew. Without the assistance of Allison Wiltshire and Chris Woznicki, who both oversaw the practical side of the event, this conference would not have run as smoothly as it did. We are very grateful to them. Thanks too to Biola University for its ongoing support of LATC. As with the previous volumes in this series, the editors wish to record grateful thanks to our editor and colleague, Katya Covrett, for her invaluable assistance before, during, and after the conference proceedings. Thanks too to the Zondervan Team (aka "The Z Team")—Stan Gundry as editor-in-chief, Jesse Hillman, Kari Moore, and Josh Kessler.

CONTRIBUTORS

Marc Cortez—is professor of theology at Wheaton College. He holds a BA from Multnomah Bible College, an MA and ThM from Western Seminary, and a PhD in divinity from the University of St. Andrews.

Matthew Y. Emerson—is Dickinson Chair of Religion and associate professor of religion at Oklahoma Baptist University. He holds a BA from Auburn University, and an MDiv and PhD from Southeastern Baptist Theological Seminary.

Joanna Leidenhag—is a doctoral candidate in systematic theology at New College, University of Edinburgh. She has an MA from the University of St. Andrews, and an MA from Princeton Theological Seminary.

Hans Madueme—is associate professor of theology at Covenant College in Georgia. He holds a BS from McGill University, an MD from Howard University College of Medicine, an MA from Trinity International University, and an MDiv and PhD from Trinity Evangelical Divinity School.

Ian A. McFarland—is Regius Professor of Divinity at the University of Cambridge. He holds a BA from Trinity College in Hartford, Connecticut, an MDiv from Union Theological Seminary in New York City, a ThM from the Lutheran School of Theology at Chicago, and a PhD from Yale University.

Richard J. Mouw—is president emeritus and professor of faith and public theology in the School of Theology, Fuller Theological Seminary. He holds a BA from Houghton College, an MA from the University of Alberta, and a PhD in philosophy from the University of Chicago.

R. T. Mullins—is a research fellow in the Logos Institute, University of St. Andrews. He holds a BS from Point University, an MA from Trinity Evangelical Divinity School, and a PhD in divinity from the University of St. Andrews.

Faith Glavey Pawl—is an adjunct professor at the University of St. Thomas in Saint Paul, Minnesota. She holds a BA from Wake Forest University, and a PhD in philosophy from St. Louis University.

Lucy Peppiatt—is principal of Westminster Theological Centre in the UK. She holds a BA from the University of Birmingham, a BD from the University of London, an MA from King's College, London, and a PhD in theology from the University of Otago.

Ryan S. Peterson—is associate professor of theology at Talbot School of Theology, Biola University. He holds a BA from Moody Bible Institute, an MA from Biola University, an MTh from New College, University of Edinburgh, and a PhD in theology from Wheaton College.

Rev. Gabrielle R. Thomas—is a postdoctoral research associate in the Department of Theology and Religion, Durham University. She has a BA from the University of Bristol, an MTh from the University of Chester, and a PhD in theology from the University of Nottingham. She is a priest in the Church of England.

Aku Visala—is a research fellow of the Finnish Academy of Sciences. He has a PhD from and is a docent in philosophy of religion at the University of Helsinki, Finland.

Rev. Frances M. Young—is Edward Cadbury Professor of Theology Emeritus at the University of Birmingham. She was also the dean of the Faculty of Arts, and pro-vice-chancellor of the University of Birmingham. She earned a BA from Bedford College, University of London, and an MA and PhD in theology from Cambridge. She was awarded an OBE for services to theology in 2004, is a Fellow of the British Academy, and is an ordained Methodist minister.

ABBREVIATIONS

ANF	*The Ante-Nicene Fathers.* Edited by Alexander Roberts and James Donaldson. 1885–87. 10 vols. Repr., Edinburgh: T&T Clark, 1989.
Carm.	*Carmen de vita sua.* By Gregory of Nazianzus.
CCC	*The Catechism of the Catholic Church.* New York: USCCB, 1995.
CD	*Church Dogmatics.* By Karl Barth.
C. Gent.	*Contra Gentes.* By Athanasius.
De Inc.	*De Incarnatione.* By Athanasius.
Dem.	*Demonstration of the Apostolic Preaching.* By Irenaeus.
Haer.	*Against Heresies.* By Irenaeus.
IJST	*International Journal of Systematic Theology*
Inst.	*Institutes of the Christian Religion.* By John Calvin.
LW	*Luther's Works.* Edited by Jaroslav Pelikan et al. Philadelphia and St. Louis: Fortress and Concordia, 1955–.
Or.	*Orations.* By Gregory of Nazianzus.
PG	Patrologia Graeca. Edited by J.-P. Migne. 162 vols. Paris, 1857–86.
PL	Patrologia Latina. Edited by J.-P Migne. 217 vols. Paris, 1844–64.
SC	Sources Chrétiennes. Edited by Jean Daniélou, Claude Mondésert, and Henri de Lubac. Paris, 1941–.
ST	*Summa Theologiae.* By Thomas Aquinas.
WBC	Word Biblical Commentary

INTRODUCTION

What are human beings that you are mindful of them,
mortals that you care for them?
PSALM 8:4

THE QUESTION THE PSALMIST ASKS GOD is primarily about the relative importance of humanity in the midst of the rest of God's creation, especially the vastness of the heavenly realms. But it is also phrased as a straightforward question of definition: What are human beings? Precisely what is the thing that a human being is? The task of theological anthropology is to answer that question.

In offering answers along the lines of "constructive dogmatics," as all the essays in this volume do, theologians can take a *direct* or *indirect* approach. The direct approach is to consult the Bible for the terms, categories, and schemas found in the layers of its manifold witness. The same sacred volume that asks, "What are human beings?" also answers the question: human beings are a single unified race of creatures, each one in the image of God, created male and female, given life by the divine breath, and so on. Any one of these categories offered by the biblical witness could be the subject of an expansive study in its own right; each has received such treatment in the history of doctrine, and each is taken up by the authors of this volume.

Often these biblical accounts have been subsumed in theological categories for the divine image so that today there are at least three broad approaches to which one can point. The first is the structural account of the divine image, represented in this volume by Aku Visala's chapter and that of Faith Pawl, as well as (to some extent) in the essays by Hans Madueme and Marc Cortez. On this way of thinking, the divine image found in Scripture is to be understood as something substantive in human beings that sets them apart from other creatures. Often this is identified with human

15

reason or possession of a soul. Then there are those who think that the *imago Dei* is more of a function of human beings, giving rise to functional accounts of the divine image. On this way of thinking human beings bear the divine image in virtue of acting in a particular way—that is, as God's viceroys on earth, imaging the deity in virtue of a benevolent caretaking role over creation. A third approach to the divine image thinks of it relationally, as something that human beings bear together as a community of creatures. There is something of this view in the contribution from Ryan Peterson, as well as in the chapters by Frances Young and Ian McFarland. Another ancient approach to the divine image is to identify it with Christ as the archetypal image, and human beings as ectypes. We image God as we image Christ. This way of thinking about the matter is prominent in Cortez's work. Christological considerations also make an appearance in the chapters by Lucy Peppiatt, Gabrielle Thomas, and Joanna Leidenhag and R. T. Mullins.

In addition to the more direct approach to thinking about humanity dogmatically, there is an indirect approach to answering the question about human beings. This involves considering the implications of other doctrines and approaching theological anthropology through them. Each tract of systematic theology has implications for the Christian doctrine of humanity, and the indirect route takes its bearings from doctrines nearby (creation, sin, salvation) and doctrines farther afield (Christology, pneumatology, eschatology). The indirect approach to theological anthropology has the advantage of tracing the many connections that unite the doctrinal system, ensuring that the resulting doctrine of humanity is explicitly Christian. In this regard, one interesting subtheme that runs through several chapters has to do with how attending to a particular aspect of traditional Christology may help us understand some aspect of divine action in human beings better. For example, Peppiatt examines how Spirit Christology bears upon the work of the Holy Spirit indwelling human beings, while Leidenhag and Mullins seek to demarcate the difference between the indwelling of the Spirit in human beings and the manner in which God the Son is said to be incarnate in Christ. By contrast, Ian McFarland's essay presses in a rather different and more apophatic direction with a more skeptical account of what we can say about the image in human beings in light of wider theological considerations. Another broader theological concern on display in this volume is the current debate about the constitution of human beings. Do we have souls distinct from our bodies? If we do, how should we think of such things? If we do not, what important implications follow from such a claim? The essays by Rich Mouw, Hans Madueme, and Matthew Emerson all touch on these matters in important ways.

There is also an interesting interplay in these essays between the retrieval of ancient doctrine for contemporary dogmatics and the correlation between contemporary philosophy, science, and theological construction. This creative tension is quite evident in, say, Young's desire to recapture Athanasius for moderns or in the ways Mouw, Madueme, and Visala worry about the relationship of theology to wider intellectual concerns of a more philosophical nature.

Ideally, a satisfying theological anthropology will be engaged in all these things at once: direct and indirect accounts of human beings in relation to God, the careful plotting of a route through the various accounts of the divine image, and attention to the development of doctrine in this area as well as the pressing need for correlation with our current state of knowledge about our relation to the wider created world—including our place in a creation full of many other creatures that are also subject to God's divine care. The chapters of this volume delve into all these areas, providing the reader with a rich smorgasbord of dogmatic explorations on theological anthropology. Whilst not a systematic account of the doctrine of humanity, these are rich and rewarding studies that repay careful reading towards a more systematic-theological understanding of humanity's place in God's creation.

Overview of the Chapters

Marc Cortez has written much on christological anthropology, and his chapter opens this volume by pressing for clarity on Irenaeus's teaching that "the image of God is the Son, after whose image man was made." Cortez puts several questions to Irenaeus: Is it the embodied humanity of Christ that makes him the image, or is it his eternal identity as the Son? In what sense can one of Adam's descendants be the prototype of Adam's being? In a wide-ranging discussion that in many ways sets the scope of the whole volume programmatically, Cortez argues for an ontological and epistemological priority of Christ over Adam, as well as pneumatological considerations that keep nature and grace from being merely bifurcated.

In chapter 2, Faith Glavey Pawl locates the human creature among the other animals with whom we share the world and does so by defending an admittedly unfashionable notion: hierarchy. Drawing on Thomas Aquinas, Pawl argues that we can affirm that humans are superior to nonhuman animals and that in fact creation is ordered toward the good of humans. Yet we can do this without relegating nonhuman animals to the status of irrelevance for either humans or, more significantly, for God. Where conventional accounts of the good of animals tend to discard hierarchy as early as possible, Pawl argues that hierarchy can serve as a valuable metaphysical tool for ecological theology.

In chapter 3, Richard J. Mouw considers the implications of Christian belief in the afterlife for a Christian account of human composition. Must Christians who believe in an afterlife believe that humans are composed of bodies and souls? It is not quite that simple, according to Mouw. Cognizant of neuroscientific findings and alert to the reasons why moderns are skittish about any Platonist dualisms, Mouw nevertheless insists that our affirmations about human composition should comport with our control beliefs about eschatology. A judicious use of theological imagination, he counsels, will also consider pastoral implications such as speaking about the intermediate state, or of failing to do so.

Hans Madueme, in chapter 4, likewise considers the way our view of human composition should be determined by outlying control beliefs. The beliefs he has in mind are Christian affirmations about sin, which require that we be morally responsible for our actions before God. "Dualism makes better sense of human sinning than physicalism," he says, because mere physicalism enmeshes human agents too completely in chains of physical causation. What Scripture presupposes is moral accountability that is most consistent with body-soul dualism. While physical determinism crowds out moral accountability, Madueme argues for a form of divine determinism that is compatible with human responsibility and thus comports with Scripture's presuppositions about sin.

In chapter 5, Aku Visala considers the challenge that recent cognitive science poses for any doctrine of the image of God that locates the image in human cognitive abilities. Visala believes that modern cognitive scientific findings, far from erecting insurmountable obstacles, actually point to human uniqueness in a new and helpful way for theology. Humans have several unique cognitive capabilities: flexible reasoning, the ability to adopt moral norms and to follow them behaviorally, and the most flexible social cognition of any animal. Visala argues that there is much to be gained from developing an account of the *imago Dei* that is informed by current cognitive sciences.

Gabrielle Thomas, in chapter 6, considers the *imago Dei* from another perspective, arguing that human nature is open to influence from two directions: contact with God on the one hand and contact with spiritual enemies on the other. For her project, Thomas appeals to Gregory of Nazianzus, whose theology, spirituality, and poetry set forth a classic Christian conception of humanity in terms considerably more holistic and dynamic than most modern theologies have been interested in. One of the advantages of this retrieval of a patristic witness is, perhaps unexpectedly, greater attention to the actual lived experience of being in the image of God. This contrasts with merely structural or even merely relational accounts of the *imago Dei*, which are more concerned with identifying the image than illuminating the experience of being in the image. To be human, on this account, is to stand between the cosmos and God in an active and dynamic relationship with both. The *imago Dei* is not only vulnerable to God because of its intended purpose of union with God, says Thomas, but also vulnerable to "the world, the flesh, and the devil" as it moves toward its destiny.

In chapter 7, Ryan Peterson examines humanity's use of the category of identity, which has in recent decades become a pervasive and important way of talking. Peterson is interested in the relation between constructed identities—racial, ethnic, national, religious, and sexual identities, for example—and what he calls biblical-theological identities, such as creaturely, covenantal, redeemed, and eschatological identities. As he points out, the novel category of identity has entered contemporary usage without much clarity or definition, so it is ripe for some theologically guided conceptual scrutiny. Extending his earlier work in this field, Peterson argues that biblical-theological identities have a certain priority. They should constrain and shape constructed identities, keeping them from some evident idolatrous tendencies. But within proper boundaries, a range of constructed identities can serve human flourishing by enabling people and communities to find and name their distinct places in the world. Peterson recommends using identity talk alongside of, but not in place of, more traditional categories like nature, ends, faculties, and habits.

Chapter 8, by Frances Young, is an ambitious project of considerable scope. Young opens up the world of patristic Christology, tracing the thought of Athanasius of Alexandria with special attention to the way he could build arguments about redemption on the presupposition that there is such a thing as humanity. Strong patristic notions of human solidarity, whether they drew on a Platonic conceptual background (a world-soul) or some other ancient metaphysical schema (any sort of realism about universals), enabled thinkers like Athanasius to make sense of biblical language about Adam and Christ as the locus of an old and a new humanity, respectively. If we as moderns do not share these ancient underlying metaphysical assumptions, Young says, we nevertheless have the same need to make sense of the biblical way of speaking about humanity as a coherent entity. In pursuit of a contemporary appropriation of patristic anthropological holism, Young offers a catalog of thick collectivities: slime mold, an oceanic feeling, a collective unconscious, interlaced narratives, emergent unity, and social forms of solidarity such as the shared life produced by the stresses of a labor camp. Young announces an agenda for theological anthropology: since we need to make good sense of shared sin, shared guilt, and shared judgment, we need to articulate in contemporary terms an account of real human unity.

In chapter 9, "Life in the Spirit: Christ's and Ours," Lucy Peppiatt puts some hard questions to the proponents of Spirit Christology, particularly those who emphasize the role of the Spirit in the life of Christ in order to show that Christ's life is enough like our life to serve as a model for Christian experience. Peppiatt shows how these accounts of Christology tend to run aground on questions of agency in the incarnation and especially on the question of how to manage the difference between our willing and doing and Jesus's willing and doing. Deeply informed by the theology of John Owen and (to a lesser extent) Thomas Aquinas, her constructive account is more attentive to the analogical difference between Christ and us in this regard. The result is not an entire rejection of Spirit Christology's contribution to theological anthropology but an account of how a pneumatic christological model, with its attention to the empowering, guidance, and comfort of the Holy Spirit for Christ and for us, is the most promising matrix for a view of human development and spiritual formation.

In chapter 10, "Flourishing in the Spirit: Distinguishing Incarnation and Indwelling for Theological Anthropology," Joanna Leidenhag and R. T. Mullins consider the biblical portrayal of human flourishing as being somehow related to the incarnation but also as being filled with the Spirit. They are especially concerned to offer a clear conceptual distinction between incarnation and indwelling because they want to account for how Christ's humanity unlocks flourishing for the rest of humanity. By distinguishing the work of the Son from the work of the Spirit, they show that the special, divine, and personal presence of the Holy Spirit is what brings about transformative sanctification, and thus it provides the best model for understanding indwelling and the necessary condition for the flourishing of humanity.

In chapter 11, Matthew Emerson looks to Christ's descent to the dead as a crucial testing ground for both the Christian understanding of the afterlife and its distinction between body and soul. In Emerson's retrieval of the traditional theology of the descent, Christ's body went into the earth as his human soul went to the place of the dead. Christ, in other words, experienced an intermediate state between his death and resurrection. Because Christ's humanity is paradigmatic, human beings must also be capable of experiencing an intermediate state between their deaths and the final day, and one of the key conclusions to be drawn from this is that we should confess humanity as being composed of body plus soul.

Ian McFarland's chapter closes the volume by directing our attention to a very large question in theological anthropology: the relation between nature and grace. In some classic ways of describing the relation, it seems that humanity can only have one or the other but not both. If humans were created to reach the end of union with God in glory by grace, then grace seems to be built into the nature or definition of what it is to be human— but then it is not a matter of grace. On the other hand, if we preserve the gratuitous character of union with God, then we have to define human nature as being complete in itself without such an end, in which case grace is supplemental and in no way a natural end of humanity. McFarland proposes the category of vocation as a solution to this problem of "the oddness of human nature." To be called by God is to be summoned to an end that is compatible with human nature but is beyond it and not intrinsic to it. With this account of human nature as open-ended, McFarland is undertaking to resolve a theological conundrum that has usually been posed in updated Thomist categories by the judicious application of a Lutheran category.

May these essays extend discussion of the task of dogmatics, *ad maiorem dei gloriam.*

Oliver D. Crisp and Fred Sanders, April 2018

CHAPTER 1

NATURE, GRACE, AND THE CHRISTOLOGICAL GROUND OF HUMANITY

Marc Cortez

THE AUTHOR OF HEBREWS articulates several vital truths that form the core of any orthodox Christology, namely that in the incarnation Jesus was "fully human" (2:17) such that we are all a part of the "same family" (2:11), but that Jesus exemplified this humanity in such a way that he remained without sin (4:15) so that he could serve as our unblemished sacrifice (9:14).[1] Such claims immediately draw Christology and anthropology into intimate dialogue with one another, raising questions about the extent to which either should inform the other. Indeed, to some it will seem simply obvious that such incarnational claims establish Christology as the basis for understanding what it means to be human. If Jesus is truly and perfectly human, why would we look anywhere else?

Yet we should not draw such a conclusion so quickly. To see this, let's consider my daughter's hedgehog, creatively named Hedgie. As far as I can tell, Hedgie is in fact fully hedgehogian.[2] Yet that does not mean we should somehow view Hedgie as the exemplar of hedgehogianity upon which we can ground our knowledge of hedgehogs in general simply because she happens to be a true hedgehog. And we cannot even address this by claiming that Hedgie is a perfectly flawless example of a hedgehog. Even a

---

1. Scripture references in this chapter, unless otherwise indicated, come from the NIV.
2. Yes, I have officially decreed this to be a real word.

perfectly flawless hedgehog would not be able to actualize all the potentialities of hedgehogianity. Hedgie will never be as big as some hedgehogs or as fast as others. No matter how flawless she might be as a particular instantiation of hedgehogianity, it is difficult to see why we should view Hedgie as paradigmatic for understanding hedgehogs in general.

The same holds true for Jesus's humanity. Merely claiming that Jesus is both fully and perfectly human will not suffice to establish the precise role that Christology should play in understanding humanity. In this brief essay, I will not attempt a comprehensive argument for why anthropology should be grounded in Christology.[3] Instead, I will offer Irenaeus as a dialogue partner, using his reflections on the nature of the *imago Dei* as a way of explaining why someone might think that Christology should ground our understanding of humanity and highlighting a number of important issues that must be addressed in any such christologically informed approach to theological anthropology.

In *Demonstration of the Apostolic Preaching*, Irenaeus makes a statement that is notable both for its theological simplicity and its anthropological significance: "For [God] made man the image of God; and the image of God is the Son, after whose image man was made: and for this cause He appeared in the end of the times that He might show the image [to be] like unto Himself."[4] At first glance, it might appear as though Irenaeus has done nothing more here than reiterate what has become a common twofold platitude in theological anthropology: (1) humans are made in the image of God and (2) Jesus is the true image of God. However, if we look more closely at how Irenaeus unpacks this affirmation, we will see that the way he understands this claim has far-reaching implications for how we view the relationship between anthropology and Christology and the extent to which our knowledge of what it means to be human can and should be grounded in the person and work of Jesus Christ. Specifically, we will see that Irenaeus's approach to the *imago Dei* entails four implications.

Theological Anthropology Must Be Rooted in the Embodied Humanity of the Incarnate Christ

To some, Irenaeus's claim may not come across as terribly startling. After all, theologians have long maintained that the Son, as the second person

---

3. For a more extended argument, see Marc Cortez, *ReSourcing Theological Anthropology: A Constructive Account of Humanity in the Light of Christ* (Grand Rapids: Zondervan, 2018).

4. *Dem.* 22. Translation from Iain M. MacKenzie, *Irenaeus's Demonstration of the Apostolic Preaching: A Theological Commentary and Translation*, trans. J. Armitage Robinson (Aldershot: Ashgate, 2002).

of the Trinity, is the perfect image of the Father, the eternal self-repetition of the divine being. Consequently, to say that the Son is the archetype for human persons being made in the image of God seems to say no more than that they have been created to serve as the creaturely analogues to this divine reality, as images of the image.

For Irenaeus, the Son, in virtue of his embodied humanity, is the true image of God. The very idea of an image requires a material form, according to Irenaeus, since an image is what makes something perceivable and available in the material world.[5] Thus, while Irenaeus would certainly not have rejected the notion that the eternal Son is the perfect reflection of the Father's being, he did not describe that relationship using the language of "image." Instead, to be the image of the invisible God, the Son must have a visible and determinate form. Thus he says, "And through the Word Himself who had been made visible and palpable, was the Father shown forth, although all did not equally believe in Him; but all saw the Father in the Son: for the Father is the invisible of the Son, but the Son the visible of the Father."[6] Irenaeus thus locates his understanding of the *imago Dei* within the broader framework of God's self-revelation in creation, maintaining that it is in the embodied Son that we truly see the Father (cf. John 14:9).

Consequently, Irenaeus emphasizes more clearly than most other early theologians that the body itself is intrinsic to the *imago Dei*. He was aware of and explicitly rejected the idea that the *imago* should be restricted to the soul and its capacities, maintaining instead that the entire human person is made in the image of God: "Man, and not [merely] a part of man, was made in the likeness of God. Now the soul and the spirit are certainly a part of the man, but certainly not the man; for the perfect man consists in the commingling and the union of the soul receiving the spirit of the Father, and the admixture of that fleshly nature which was moulded after the image of God."[7] Against his gnostic opponents who devalued the body and its significance, Irenaeus maintained that the body itself was molded by the two hands of God (the Word and the Spirit) to serve as his image in the world.[8] Indeed, although Irenaeus did not always distinguish between his uses of "image" and "likeness" consistently, he frequently reserved the term "image" for that which denotes this embodied dimension of the *imago Dei*.[9]

---

5. *Haer.* 2.7.6 (*ANF* 1:368). Cf. 2.19.6 (*ANF* 1:386–87).
6. *Haer.* 4.6.6 (*ANF* 1:469). See also *Dem.* 11.
7. *Haer.* 5.6.1 (*ANF* 1:531). See esp. Jacques Fantino, *L'homme, Image de Dieu, Chez Saint Irénée de Lyon* (Paris: Cerf, 1986), 87–89.
8. *Haer.* 4.pref.4 (*ANF* 1:462–63).
9. Denis Minns, *Irenaeus* (Washington, DC: Georgetown University Press, 1994), 72–73.

Here Irenaeus's approach enjoys considerable support from modern views of the *imago Dei*, most of which affirm holistic accounts of the image that involve the entire human person, including the body.[10] Indeed, much of the recent work on the *imago Dei* demonstrates that we should understand the image against the ancient Near Eastern concept of an idol as the material means through which a divine being manifests presence in the world.[11] Such studies clearly reinforce Irenaeus's point that we cannot separate the body from the *imago Dei*. Irenaeus's approach would even seem contrary to a mediating approach like the one offered by Gregory of Nyssa, where the soul is the true image of God, and the body is understood merely as an image of the image, a material echo of that more fundamental, spiritual reality.[12] Instead, for Irenaeus, the body is essential to the very meaning of the *imago Dei*. Without the body, there is no image.

This does not mean, of course, that Irenaeus thought we could reduce the image to the body alone. Instead, he affirms as well that the "likeness" of the *imago Dei* includes both capacities like rationality and free will, which he associated primarily with the human soul, and a teleological dimension of the *imago*, whereby human beings are brought into ever-greater conformity with the Son through the indwelling of the Spirit. Nonetheless, throughout his various discussions, the embodied nature of the human person as an "image" of the divine remains fundamental. Yet this emphasis on the embodied nature of the *imago Dei* virtually requires him to maintain that the Son is the true image of God in virtue of the incarnation and not merely in virtue of his eternal relationship with the Father. As John Behr concludes, "But as God himself is immaterial, and therefore formless, the archetype of the image of God in man must be the incarnate Son of God."[13]

In one passage, though, Irenaeus could be interpreted as suggesting otherwise. As he says, "But man he formed with his own hands, taking from the earth that which was purest and finest, and mingling in measure His own power with the earth. For He traced His own form on the formation, that that which should be seen should be of divine form: for [as] the image of God was man formed and set on the earth."[14] By referring

---

10. See esp. David J. A. Clines, "The Image of God in Man," *Tyndale Bulletin* 19 (1968): 53–103.

11. See esp. Catherine L. McDowell, *The Image of God in the Garden of Eden: The Creation of Humankind in Genesis 2:5–3:24 in Light of the* mīs pî, pīt pî, *and* wpt-r *Rituals of Mesopotamia and Ancient Egypt* (Winona Lake, IN: Eisenbrauns, 2015).

12. Gregory of Nyssa, *On the Making of Humanity*, 4.1; 16.3.

13. John Behr, *Asceticism and Anthropology in Irenaeus and Clement*, Oxford Early Christian Studies (New York: Oxford University Press, 2000), 89.

14. *Dem.* 11.

to "His own form" as the archetype for the creation of human persons in his image, Irenaeus could be understood here as referring to something within the divine being itself. We will return to the relationship between the Son's eternal identity and the historic actualization of the incarnation in a moment, but for now we can simply note that it is unlikely Irenaeus has anything like this in mind. Given that we have already seen that Irenaeus associates "form" with "materiality," it seems highly unlikely that he would have imagined that the divine being could have a determinate form that could serve as the archetype for the human body. Instead, it is far more likely that Irenaeus is saying that the human body has been fashioned after the model provided by the incarnate humanity of Christ.[15] Behr thus concludes that "the fashioning of the human flesh is intimately connected to Christ, the archetype of man, and his revelation of the image of God, the manifestation of both God and man."[16] According to MacKenzie, then, we are faced here with "that which pulls us up short in the thought of Irenaeus— that humanity is created according to the pattern of the humanity which the Word assumes. In other words, the sequence is not that humanity has a form which the Word at His incarnation has to take, but that the Word made flesh, in the dispensation of God who, beyond time and space orders the temporal/spatial character of creation, is the pattern which is traced on humanity, and appears as such."[17]

Although Irenaeus has thus offered some interesting reasons for thinking that Christ is the true *imago Dei* in virtue of his embodied humanity, it remains entirely possible to think that Irenaeus has simply misread the biblical texts at this point. Bavinck speaks for many when he rejects any such christocentric understanding of the *imago Dei*. As he maintains,

> God himself, the entire deity, is the archetype of man. Granted, it has frequently been taught that man has specifically been made in the image of the Son or of the incarnate Christ, but there is nothing in Scripture that supports this notion. Scripture repeatedly tells us that humankind was made in the image of God, not that we have been modeled on Christ, but that he was made [human] in our likeness.[18]

---

15. MacKenzie, *Irenaeus's Demonstration of the Apostolic Preaching*, 107.

16. Behr thus contends that since Irenaeus never refers elsewhere to the preincarnate Son as "the image of God" or the "image of the Father," we should interpret this text accordingly (Behr, *Asceticism and Anthropology*, 90).

17. MacKenzie, *Irenaeus's Demonstration of the Apostolic Preaching*, 107.

18. Herman Bavinck, *Reformed Dogmatics*, vol. 2, *God and Creation*, ed. John Bolt, trans. John Vriend (Grand Rapids: Baker Academic, 2004), 554, citing Rom 8:3; Phil 2:7–8; Heb 2:14.

From this statement, we can see that Bavinck offers three concerns about the kind of christological anthropology Irenaeus represents, concerns that I frequently encounter when talking with people about a christological approach to the image. First, he thinks the image should be understood as Trinitarian rather than christocentric. Second, he maintains that there is no biblical support for the idea that humanity has been created in the image of the incarnate Christ.[19] And third, he thinks this approach is further undermined by the fact that the biblical texts say that Christ was made in our likeness rather than the other way around. Such criticisms, if valid, would render a christological approach like Irenaeus's untenable. I want to deal with the first two of those concerns now, reserving the third for our discussion of the relationship between Adam and Christ a bit later.

Bavinck's first argument is that a christological approach is insufficiently Trinitarian, since presumably that is what Bavinck has in mind with his reference to the "entire deity." However, it is difficult to see why this would be the case. In the first place, Irenaeus would agree wholeheartedly that the *imago Dei* is about the triune God. Remember that Irenaeus thinks the *imago* is primarily about God's self-revelation in creation, preeminently through the Son who is the true image bearer. Consequently, when he claims that other humans have been made in the image of the Son, he means they have been made in the image of one who is himself the means through which the triune God reveals himself in creation. In other words, for Irenaeus, the *imago* is christological not in the sense that the image terminates on the incarnate Christ but in the sense that in him we see the true reality that all human persons are oriented toward the triune God in and through Christ. Irenaeus's christological view of the *imago* is already Trinitarian.

Bavinck's second point primarily relies on the lack of biblical texts that declare unequivocally that Jesus is the archetype in whose image all other humans have been created. However, to declare that there is no biblical support for such a position stretches the point considerably. For instance, we might reflect further on Paul's declaration that the Son is the image of God (Col 1:15), immediately before identifying him also as the source of creation (v. 16) and "the head of the body" that serves as the ultimate expression of God's intentions for his people, the church (v. 18). And Paul often uses the language of "firstborn" in the immediate context of

---

19. It is important to note here that Bavinck is not rejecting the idea that the human body is part of the *imago Dei*. Indeed, Bavinck argues strongly in favor of a holistic and embodied account of the image (see Bavinck, *Reformed Dogmatics*, 2:554–62).

passages dealing with Christ as the image (Rom 8:29; Col 1:15; Heb 1:6). I have argued elsewhere that this term refers to more than mere temporal primacy or even preeminence, denoting instead that as the *prōtotokos* the Son inaugurates a way of being in which he both participates alongside others—his "brothers"—yet is radically unique from them as the eternal paradigm and telos.[20] The clearest text that would require further elaboration in this context would be Paul's statement that God's people have been "predestined to be conformed to the image of his Son" (Rom 8:29), clearly suggesting that the Son's status as the *imago Dei* played a constitutive role in the shaping of humanity from the beginning. We could spend considerable time developing this material further, but it suffices here to establish that there is far more biblical warrant for Irenaeus's claim than this critique suggests.

THEOLOGICAL ANTHROPOLOGY MUST BE ROOTED IN THE ETERNAL IDENTITY OF THE SON

We have now established that Irenaeus thinks that the incarnate Christ is the true image of God, the one in whose image all others are formed, and thus the archetype for what it truly means to be human. Yet this raises a question about the temporal relationship between the incarnation and the creation of humanity. What exactly does it mean for Irenaeus to claim that the human nature asleep on the hay that Christmas morning somehow provides the ground for the humanity God shaped from the dust in the primordial dawn of history? For this to be the case, there must be some sense in which the archetype of humanity exists eternally even if it is not actualized in history until the advent of Christ.

One way of understanding how this might work would be to argue that the real archetype of humanity is a kind of divine idea. Christian doctrines of creation have long emphasized the importance of the divine ideas. They often play a role similar to that of the Platonic forms, eternal patterns that provide the basis for creating every creaturely particular.[21] On this account, then, the divine idea of true humanity is logically and ontologically prior to the creation of *any* human being, including the humanity of the incarnate Christ. However, although this approach would place ontological primacy

---

20. Cortez, *ReSourcing Theological Anthropology*, 136–38.
21. For an excellent discussion of this, see Matthew Levering, *Engaging the Doctrine of Creation: Cosmos, Creatures, and the Wise and Good Creator* (Grand Rapids: Baker Academic, 2017), 29–72.

on the divine idea of humanity, we could still affirm the primacy of Christ's humanity *in history* as the perfect actualization of this eternal ideal.

It is difficult to anticipate how Irenaeus might have responded to such an argument since he does not seem to have made any significant use of the divine ideas in his doctrine of creation, possibly because some gnostic thinkers utilized the notion of divine ideas to emphasize the eternality of creation and the intimate union of all things with the divine. At the very least, however, we should recognize that Irenaeus never posits an eternal *idea* as the archetype of humanity, even though such a view would have been quite well known to him. Instead, for Irenaeus, the archetype of humanity is always the person of Jesus Christ. And this is consistent with the language of the New Testament as well. For the biblical authors, *the Son* is the image of the invisible God.

Friedrich Schleiermacher offers a slightly different option, maintaining that *Jesus* was the blueprint for humanity and that *this* blueprint (i.e., the idea of Jesus) is what existed eternally in the mind of God.[22] In other words, it is not merely that God has an eternal idea of what constitutes true humanity that provides the ground for the humanity of all humans, Jesus included. Instead, Jesus simply is the divine idea that serves as the archetype of humanity.[23] James Dunn offers a similar argument, maintaining that the Son preexists in the eternal plan of God.[24] God creates humanity "through" the Son in the sense that the idea of the Son is the driving purpose behind the act of creation rather than a personal agent directly involved in that work.

However, many of those who opt for this kind of approach end up denying the real preexistence of the Son himself.[25] If the first option errs by emphasizing eternity at the expense of history, this approach focuses so exclusively on the *historical* reality of the incarnation that the significance of the Son's eternal existence is undermined or even lost entirely. Yet this runs contrary to Irenaeus's commitment to the personal preexistence of the Son,[26] not to mention the growing number of contemporary scholars emphasizing the significance of the Son's preexistence in the biblical material.[27] Of

---

22. Friedrich Schleiermacher, *The Christian Faith*, ed. H. R. Mackintosh and J. S. Stewart (Berkeley, CA: Apocryphile, 2011), 89.3.

23. See esp. Friedrich Schleiermacher, "On Colossians 1:15–20 (1832)," trans. Esther D. Reed and Alan Braley, *Neues Athenaeum* 5 (1998): 48–80.

24. James D. G. Dunn, *Christology in the Making: A New Testament Inquiry into the Origins of the Doctrine of the Incarnation* (Philadelphia: Westminster, 1980), 54–56.

25. See, for example, G. B. Caird, "Son by Appointment," in *New Testament Age: Essays in Honor of Bo Reicke*, ed. William C. Weinrich (Macon, GA: Mercer University Press, 1984), 73–81.

26. See Douglas McCready, *He Came Down from Heaven: The Preexistence of Christ and Christian Faith* (Downers Grove, IL; InterVarsity, 2005), 216.

27. Simon J. Gathercole, *The Preexistent Son: Recovering the Christologies of Matthew, Mark, and Luke* (Grand Rapids: Eerdmans, 2006).

course, we could try to address this by emphasizing both the preexistence of the eternal Son *and* the notion that Jesus exists eternally as an idea in the divine mind. But this is simply a variation of the first option. And as Wingren points out, Irenaeus would have rejected any attempt to bifurcate the eternal Son from the incarnate Christ in this way.[28] Like many of the early theologians, Irenaeus saw a fundamental unity between the eternal Son and the incarnate Christ and refused to draw sharp theological distinctions between the two.[29]

Both approaches fail precisely because they pit eternity and history against one another in equally problematic ways. A better approach would follow Wingren's suggestion and maintain the inseparability of the two in the singular identity of the Son. Here it might be appropriate to draw on similar accounts that have been provided in modern theology. Most commonly associated with the theology of Karl Barth, this approach contends that although the Son has a real, personal existence from all eternity, the *identity* of the Son is determined by the concrete particularities of his historic existence.[30] To understand this argument, we need to appreciate the challenges created whenever we try to understand the relationship between time and eternity. On the one hand, the incarnation is a temporal event, something enacted in history. On the other hand, though, the incarnation is something that God determined to do from all eternity. If that is the case, although from a historical perspective we might distinguish between a time when the Son was incarnate (*logos ensarkos*) and a time when he was not (*logos asarkos*), from God's perspective there is no such distinction. The Son's identity has been shaped eternally by the reality of the incarnation.[31] In this way, we can say both that the *imago Dei* is something true of the Son in virtue of the incarnation *and* that it is eternally true of the Son in virtue of God's decree of election because the identity of the eternal Son is shaped by the reality of the incarnation.[32]

---

28. Gustaf Wingren, *Man and the Incarnation: A Study in the Biblical Theology of Irenaeus*, trans. Ross MacKenzie, (Philadelphia: Muhlenberg, 1959).

29. M. C. Steenberg, *Of God and Man: Theology as Anthropology from Irenaeus to Athanasius* (London: T&T Clark, 2009), 3.

30. See esp. Barth's discussion of election in *CD* II/2.

31. None of this requires us to think that this somehow makes creation "necessary" for God's eternal being. Theologians have long maintained that God's decrees are eternally true without drawing the corresponding conclusion that the content of those decrees is now ontologically necessary for God. Similarly, for this argument to be true, we need only hold that the incarnation is eternally true, and thus eternally shaping the identity of the Son, without the corresponding implication that the incarnation (and thus creation itself) is eternally necessary. (Thanks to J. T. Turner for his helpful suggestions on how best to articulate this.)

32. For a more extended discussion of this, see Cortez, *ReSourcing Theological Anthropology,*

Theological Anthropology Must Recognize the Ontological and Epistemological Priority of Christ over Adam

The ontological primacy of Christ flows from what we said above about Christ as the archetype of *all* human persons. Adam himself was "moulded after the image of God" that we see in Jesus Christ.[33] Or as he explains elsewhere, "The Word—the Creator of all—sketched out in advance in Adam the future economy of the humanity of the Son of God: God first gave definition to the first, ensouled, human being (ψυχικός), with a view to its being saved by the spiritual human being (πνευματικός) (cf. 1 Cor. 15.46)."[34] In other words, for Irenaeus, this explains Paul's reference to Adam as a "type" of Christ, "the figure of Him that was to come."[35] As Minns points out, it would be easy to misconstrue Irenaeus's use of typological language here and think that he means no more than that Adam's creation foreshadows or anticipates that which will eventually arrive in the future with the incarnation. As Minns explains, "If we are to understand Irenaeus correctly on this matter we will need to be aware that he understood the word 'type' in this passage of St. Paul in its literal Greek sense: that of 'impression' or 'imprint.' . . . Adam does not simply prefigure Christ, but bears in his own body the lineaments of the incarnate Son of God. Adam was consequent on Christ and not the other way around."[36] Consequently, Adam's humanity has been shaped in a very real sense by the archetype provided by the humanity of Christ.

To understand the Adam/Christ relationship properly, though, we need to recognize that there is at least one sense in which Christ is ontologically dependent upon Adam. In book 3 of *Against Heresies*, Irenaeus rejects the idea that the humanity the Son assumed in the incarnation was a new creation, unrelated to the Adamic humanity that had fallen into a state where it became subject to temptation, suffering, and death.[37] Instead, he argues that for Jesus to be truly and fully human, he had to receive his humanity through Adam in the same way as all other humans. All humans are human insofar as they have received their particular form of being from

---

116–29.

33. *Haer.* 5.6.1 (*ANF* 1:531); cf. 3:23.1 (*ANF* 1:455–56).

34. *Haer.* 3.22.3. This is a textually difficult passage, and here I follow the translation by Minns, *Irenaeus*, 101.

35. *Haer.* 3.22.3.

36. Minns, *Irenaeus*, 100.

37. See esp. *Haer.* 3.22–23 (*ANF* 1:454–58).

Adam. As Irenaeus says, "We are all from him: and as we are from him, therefore have we all inherited his title [image of God]."[38] To affirm that Jesus could have received a different form of humanity, one not directly involved in the humanity that descends from Adam, suggests that "He also appeared putatively as man when He was not man, and that He was made man while taking nothing from man. For if He did not receive the substance of flesh from a human being, He neither was made man nor the Son of man."[39] Without participating in the Adamic lineage, then, Jesus would end up instantiating a new kind of humanity rather than recapitulating and redeeming the people who began with Adam. This suggests that Irenaeus did not view *humanity* or *human nature* primarily as some kind of abstract or a set of properties, both of which might allow the possibility of Jesus participating fully in humanity without receiving that humanity directly from Adam. Instead, Irenaeus views *humanity* primarily in terms of lineage. To be human is to be a part of a particular human community united through a shared relationship with a common "head." For Jesus to qualify as human in this sense, then, he must receive his humanity in the same way, even though this means participating in a humanity that had now become subject to the consequences of the fall.

Nonetheless, even while emphasizing the importance of Christ receiving his humanity from Adam, Irenaeus continues to remind us that Christ is ultimately the one in whose image all other humans are made. He thus presents the ontological relationship between Adam and Christ as somewhat circular, though not viciously so. Both are necessary: Christ as the archetype of what it means to be human and Adam as the historical head from whom all others receive their humanity. As Minns explains, "Although it is in Christ that the image and likeness of God is first revealed, unless here is a real continuity between Christ and Adam, the purposes of God in creating the earth creature in his own image and likeness will not be achieved. Christ's flesh must be Adam's flesh."[40] We can thus affirm that there is a sense in which Christ's humanity is ontologically dependent on Adam's, while still maintaining the ultimate primacy of Christ's humanity.

Understanding the relationship between Adam and Christ in this way can help us address the third concern Bavinck raised: undermining an Irenaean approach to anthropology, the biblical texts affirm that Jesus

---

38. *Haer.* 3.23.2 (*ANF* 1:456).
39. *Haer.* 3.22.1 (*ANF* 1:454).
40. Minns, *Irenaeus*, 103.

became like us but do not identify him as the archetype of our creation. However, as we have seen, Irenaeus's approach actually allows us to affirm *both* that Jesus was the archetype of our creation *and* that he became like us. "He appeared at the end of the times that He might show the image [to be] like unto Himself."[41] In other words, it remains true that the incarnation involves the Son becoming like us, but in doing so he is revealing the fact that humanity had been created in his image from the beginning. Despite Bavinck's concern, there is no necessary tension between these two points.

Having established the ontological primacy of Christ in Irenaeus's anthropology, we can turn our attention to the epistemological question. It is important to realize here that the latter does not follow inevitably on the former. Indeed, in many cases, the order of knowing specifically does not follow the order of being. For example, it seems quite reasonable to maintain that the oak trees surrounding my backyard are ontologically dependent on oak trees that existed hundreds of years ago. Apart from those ancestral oaks, my trees would not exist. Yet, if I wanted to learn about oak trees—maybe seeking to understand the twisted psyche that causes them to wait every year until just *after* leaf collection day to drop their oak droppings all over my yard—I would almost certainly begin by studying the oak trees that currently exist. Indeed, I would likely operate under the presupposition that I can come to know everything I need to know about that which is ontologically primary (the ancestor oaks) by learning about that which is ontologically secondary (the current oaks). In the same way, there does not seem to be anything preventing us from maintaining that despite the ontologically secondary status of Adam's humanity, it might still be the proper epistemological starting point for theological anthropology. Indeed, it remains quite conceivable that one could know almost everything one needs to know about humanity without knowing anything about Jesus, while still maintaining that his humanity is ontologically primary to that of every other human.

However, Irenaeus argues otherwise. According to him, the *imago Dei* requires us to maintain Christ's epistemological primacy as well. Irenaeus famously contended that Adam and Eve were created *good* but not *perfect*. As finite and temporal creatures, they entered existence in a state of relative immaturity with the intention that they would grow toward their ultimate telos of deification through union with the Son in the power of the Spirit.[42] This teleological account of humanity flows directly from

---

41. *Dem.* 22.
42. Wingren, *Man and the Incarnation*, 99–100.

Irenaeus's understanding of the *imago Dei*. Rather than viewing Adam and Eve as already complete in their status as divine image bearers at creation, Irenaeus contends that even before the fall they needed to grow into the likeness of the Son as the archetype of their humanity. This leads Irenaeus to the conclusion that even though humanity was created in the image from the very beginning, we do not see what that truly means until Christ's advent. "For in times long past, it was said that man was created after the image of God, but it was not [actually] shown; for the Word was as yet invisible, after whose image man was created. . . . When, however, the Word of God became flesh, He confirmed both these: for He both showed forth the image truly, since He became Himself what was His image; and He re-established the similitude after a sure manner, by assimilating man to the invisible Father through means of the visible Word."[43] Consequently, as Boersma summarizes, "Adam and Eve give only a dim impression of what it is like to be the image of God."[44] Yet if the *imago Dei* is central to understanding humanity, and if it is only in Christ that we see the true revelation of what the *imago Dei* means, then the epistemological primacy of Christ for theological anthropology follows rather directly.

By this point in the argument, some will be wondering whether this approach does justice to the canonical account of humanity. After all, the Bible does not begin with a statement about the creation of humanity and then tell us that we need to wait for thousands of years before discovering anything about what it means to be human. Instead, the Bible provides a rich description of human existence from the moment of creation, again after the fall, and most intricately through the history of God's redemptive involvement with his people Israel. Thus, when Jesus arrives on the scene, and we have the startling declaration that the divine has become human, we already know what it means to be human. As Steven Long points out, this appears to be not only the logic of the canon but of the creedal tradition as well.[45] The Nicene Creed declares its belief in the one "who for us men, and for our salvation, came down and was incarnate and was made man." According to the logic of both canon and creed, then, "human" is not a mere cipher, an empty concept waiting to be filled with anthropological content once the Messiah arrives on the scene and reveals to us the nature of humanity.

---

43. *Haer.* 5.16.2 (*ANF* 1:544).
44. Hans Boersma, "Accommodation to What?: Univocity of Being, Pure Nature, and the Anthropology of St. Irenaeus," *IJST* 8, no. 3 (2006): 278.
45. Steven A. Long, *Natura Pura: On the Recovery of Nature in the Doctrine of Grace, Moral Philosophy and Moral Theology* (New York: Fordham University Press, 2010), 74.

Here, I think it is important to note that Irenaeus's emphasis on the epistemological primacy of Christ's humanity does not entail the conclusion that we cannot know *anything* about humanity apart from explicit knowledge of Christ. And this for two reasons. First, since the humanity of all other humans was fashioned on the basis of Christ's humanity, there is a very real sense in which studying humanity in general can and should provide insight into Christ's humanity. This is somewhat like saying that I can learn a lot about the Mona Lisa by studying the replica contained in one of my wife's art history books. This move is made more complicated by the fallen state of humanity, which would make it more like trying to learn about the Mona Lisa after one of my daughters has scribbled all over my wife's art history book with a black pen. Nonetheless, the point still holds that the "analogy" between Christ's humanity and our own entails the epistemological availability of humanity even apart from explicit knowledge of Christ.

Second, Irenaeus's developmental account of the *imago Dei* does not denigrate the importance of what we can know about humanity from earlier periods of human development. If anything, his account makes it vital for us to understand humanity at every stage along the way. By describing humanity in terms of development, Irenaeus offers a fundamentally *historical* account of what it means to be human. And although all historical realities are only known fully at the end of their stories, we cannot understand those identities apart from the historical particularities that comprise their respective narratives. Suppose, for example, that someone wanted to know, for completely unfathomable reasons, what it truly means to be Marc Cortez. I would really like to believe that the Marc Cortez who existed as a socially awkward and frequently irrational seventh grader does not reveal the sum of my identity as a person (despite the fact that I am still a socially awkward and frequently irrational human being). Indeed, as Karl Barth has eloquently argued, there is an important sense in which the "meaning" of my personal identity is only realized teleologically. As a historical creature, my identity is fully known only at the end of the story. Nonetheless, it would be equally incorrect to think that seventh-grade-me has nothing to contribute to this rather odd task of seeking to understand who I am. Similarly, Irenaeus's argument that the full reality of humanity arrives only with the coming of Christ does not in any way suggest that we should neglect any part of the story of humanity, especially not the redemptive history contained within the pages of the Old Testament.

THEOLOGICAL ANTHROPOLOGY MUST BE THOROUGHLY PNEUMATOLOGICAL IN A WAY THAT PREVENTS ANY SIMPLE BIFURCATION OF NATURE AND GRACE

Finally, if it is the case that the *imago Dei* is a central truth about humanity and that the image must be rooted in Christology such that Christ's embodied humanity has eternal significance and therefore both ontological and epistemological primacy over Adam's humanity, there are clear implications for construing the common distinction between *nature* and *grace* in our understanding of human persons. According to at least some accounts, we must distinguish between these two aspects of human existence, maintaining that there is either an actual or at least a hypothetical state in which human persons could have existed in a "natural" condition, which involves a state of existence whereby human persons have only natural capacities and the ends that can be achieved through the utilization of those natural capacities.[46] And according to some, this real or hypothetical natural state of humanity provides the basis for affirming that human nature is available for analysis from a variety of perspectives, including nontheological disciplines, thus establishing the possibility of interdisciplinary dialogue on what it means to be human and how we should go about fostering human flourishing in the world today. The fact that God provides the additional gifts of grace that allow humanity to achieve higher (i.e., supernatural) ends like union with Christ and the beatific vision demonstrates that God has gracious purposes for humanity that transcend that which is possible through nature alone. Thus, in addition to understanding humanity through a natural lens, *theological* anthropology has additional resources for reflecting on what it means to be human in the state to which God has graciously called us. A right understanding of the human person thus requires us to recognize and properly distinguish the state of nature from the state of grace.

Some interpretations of Irenaeus lend credence to such a framework. As we noted earlier, Irenaeus does distinguish between aspects of the image that can be understood in terms of such "natural" capacities (i.e., embodiment, rationality, and free will) and those that require the supernatural

---

46. For a good discussion of the historical development of this argument, see Lawrence Feingold, *The Natural Desire to See God According to St. Thomas and His Interpreters*, 2nd ed. (Ave Maria, FL: Sapientia, 2004).

work of the Spirit. We can thus posit at least the hypothetical possibility that humans could have existed in a state of pure nature (i.e., having only the natural capacities of embodiment, rationality, and free will) apart from the additional gift of the Spirit. And in at least some places Irenaeus seems to suggest that this is precisely how he conceives of the state of Adam and Eve before the fall. According to Irenaeus, the gift of the Spirit only comes with the advent of Christ. Thus, although Adam and Eve were created for being indwelt by the Spirit such that they might fully participate in the image of the Son, that supernatural state is only possible after the incarnation and the outpouring of the Spirit. On this interpretation, Irenaeus clearly distinguishes between nature and grace and even imagines that there was an actual time in the history of humanity when human persons existed in a state of pure nature.

Yet Irenaeus's christological anthropology will not allow any such bifurcation of nature and grace, not only because of the way it depicts the relationship between Christology and anthropology, but also because it affirms that a christological anthropology requires a thoroughly pneumatological understanding of the human person. First, and most clearly, such an account typically requires that the natural state of humanity include a natural telos, something that could be achieved through the application of humanity's natural capacities alone. Yet, as we have seen, all humans have been created for the purpose of being conformed to the image of the Son, which can only be accomplished through the power of the Spirit. And Irenaeus's account does not seem to allow even the hypothetical possibility that God *might* have created humanity for some other telos since Jesus himself is the eternal archetype for the creation of all human persons. The most that would seem possible for Irenaeus would be to image a hypothetical reality in which God made some other creature, one that was not designed according to the reality of Jesus Christ. However, even if Irenaeus were to grant the legitimacy of this kind of speculative argument, which is itself unlikely, he would almost certainly contend that such a creature would not qualify as *human* in any meaningful sense of the term.

It also seems unlikely that Irenaeus imagined the creational state of Adam and Eve to be one of pure nature since at least some kind of indwelling by the Spirit seems necessary. Irenaeus clearly affirms that Adam and Eve were created in the image and likeness of God. Although he emphasizes their immaturity with respect to the *imago Dei*, which explains why they fell so quickly, he does not say that they only experienced those aspects of the image that were possible apart from the work of the Spirit. Indeed, given that the latter is far more essential to Irenaeus's understanding of the *imago Dei*, if the Spirit were not at work in them in some way, it would seem far more appropriate for Irenaeus to deny that they were in the image of God at all, reserving that language entirely for the re-creation of human persons in Christ. Yet that is precisely what he does not do, which suggests that he does in fact think that the Spirit was at work in Adam and Eve from the beginning, even if he reserved the language of indwelling for the work of the Spirit in the new creation, further undermining any strong bifurcation of nature and grace in Irenaeus's christological anthropology.

We could strengthen Irenaeus's account further by being clearer about the prelapsarian role of the Spirit in humanity. Although Irenaeus famously affirms the Spirit's work in creation as one of the "two hands" of God,[47] he is reticent to say too much about the Spirit's involvement with humanity lest he undermine Paul's distinction between Jesus as the "life-giving spirit" and Adam as a "living soul" (1 Cor 15:45).[48] However, there may be a much closer link between the "breath of life" and the Spirit than Irenaeus allows.[49] Many have pointed out that the biblical authors frequently depict the Spirit as the "breath" of God by which he creates the universe.[50] And Job explicitly relates this motif to the creation of human persons: "The Spirit of God has made me; the breath of the Almighty gives me life" (Job 33:4 NIV). If this is the case, then we may be able to take the "breath" in Genesis 2:7 as a direct allusion to the Spirit himself, suggesting that Adam and Eve were Spirit-empowered beings from the beginning. Additionally, as mentioned earlier, a number of recent studies have established a link between the *imago Dei* and the ancient Near Eastern conception of an idol as that by which a divine being manifests presence in the world. As I have argued elsewhere, if this is so, then we have to conclude that the *imago Dei* is a thoroughly pneumatological reality since it is only through the Spirit that God manifests his glorious presence in the world.[51] This would also resonate with Irenaeus's contention that the *imago Dei* is primarily about

---

47. E.g., *Haer.* 5.6.1 (*ANF* 1:531–32).

48. Behr, *Asceticism and Anthropology*, 95.

49. For more on this, see Marc Cortez, "'The Giver of Life': The Spirit and Creation," in *The T&T Clark Companion to Pneumatology*, ed. Daniel Castelo and Ken Loyer (New York: Bloomsbury, forthcoming).

50. See, e.g., David T. Williams, "The Spirit in Creation," *Scottish Journal of Theology* 67, no. 1 (2014): 2; Daniel Castelo, *Pneumatology: A Guide for the Perplexed* (London: Bloomsbury, 2015), 66; Frank D. Macchia, "The Spirit of Life: Toward a Creation Pneumatology," in *Third Article Theology: A Pneumatological Dogmatics*, ed. Myk Habets (Minneapolis: Fortress, 2016), 113.

51. Marc Cortez, "Idols, Images, and a Spirit-ed Anthropology: A Pneumatological Account of the *Imago Dei*," in *Third Article Theology: A Pneumatological Dogmatics*, ed. Myk Habets (Minneapolis: Fortress, 2016), 267–82.

God's self-revelation. And none of this requires that we downplay the significance of the outpouring of the Spirit that comes with the arrival of Messiah. We would simply need to acknowledge some important difference between the way humans experience the work of the Spirit in their state of infancy and the fullness that arrives when the true image of God breathes the Spirit into the people of God.

CONCLUSION

Returning to the analogy that began this essay, although Hedgie might be the cutest and most interesting hedgehog ever to waddle upon the earth, and although my daughter might think she is a perfect and unblemished expression of hedgehogianity, it seems reasonable to claim that no particular hedgehog can serve as the ontological and epistemological ground for all other hedgehogs. The same holds true for humanity. If we conducted a thought experiment together and created an image of someone who exists today and is both fully human and a flawless expression of humanity, it would still be quite the stretch to say that we should base theological anthropology on that individual. Any such figure would be *important* for anthropological reflection, but not its fundamental ground. On Irenaeus's view of the *imago Dei*, however, the embodied humanity of Jesus Christ offers something entirely different. Here we have the actualization in history of a reality that has shaped the identity of the Son from all eternity, the archetype for those creatures that God will create to be his image bearers, the ones through whom he will manifest his divine presence and reveal himself in the world. For Irenaeus, that is the only adequate ground upon which to base a properly theological understanding of the human person.

CHAPTER 2

HUMAN SUPERIORITY, DIVINE PROVIDENCE, AND THE ANIMAL GOOD:

A Thomistic Defense of Creaturely Hierarchy

FAITH GLAVEY PAWL

IN ATTEMPTS TO UNDERSTAND Christianity's contribution to contemporary environmental problems, many environmental and animal welfare ethicists locate the blame in a kind of exaggerated Christian anthropocentrism. They target a worldview where humankind occupies the central place in the created order of value, and all other things, living and nonliving, merely set the stage for human salvation history.[1] This kind of anthropocentrism has plenty of critics, historical and contemporary, secular and Christian. Some Christian theologians have turned to the thought of Thomas Aquinas to counter the view that the earth was created merely for the sake of human flourishing, as Aquinas's account of the metaphysics of goodness lays the foundation for a compelling ecological vision where all created things have value.[2] However, the appropriation of Aquinas for this purpose is complicated because the angelic doctor explicitly claims that the final end or purpose

---

1. Lynn White, "The Historical Roots of Our Ecologic Crisis," *Science* 155, no. 3767 (March 1967): 1203–7; Peter Singer, *Animal Liberation: The Definitive Classic of the Animal Movement* (New York: Harper Perennial Modern Classics, 2009).
2. John Berkman, "Towards a Thomistic Theology of Animality," in *Creaturely Theology: On God,*

of the universe is the beatitude of all the saints.[3] In Aquinas's worldview, humans are at the very center of God's creative purposes. Furthermore, he thinks that being is hierarchical, that humans are ontologically superior to all other material creatures and are thus more valuable.

Theologians drawing Aquinas into the ecotheological conversation have rightly stressed those elements of Aquinas's thought that highlight the continuity between humans and all other living creatures. However, there is, among some of Aquinas's apologists, a tendency to *overemphasize* continuity and flatten the topography of value—a move that reveals a marked unease with hierarchy. That unease, I argue, rests on the assumption that the idea of human superiority is itself ethically and theologically problematic. In this chapter I examine that assumption and argue in contrast that Aquinas's view of human superiority does not have the implications that motivate a retreat from hierarchy.

This project then has two aims. The first is primarily defensive, to show that Aquinas's views about nonhuman creation are not problematic in the way some recent ecotheologians have worried. Thomists need not back away from the kind of hierarchy Aquinas sees in the natural world. The second, more interesting, aim is to explore a certain tension that arises when we consider the bigger picture of Aquinas's views about human superiority alongside his views about the value of the natural world. Toward these ends, I begin in the next section by laying out some ethical and theological problems for anthropocentrism in general and then narrow my attention on the specific claims that humans are superior to nonhuman animals and that creation is ordered toward the human good. After that, I outline the elements of Thomistic thought that are most relevant to questions about the respective value of humans and nonhuman animals (henceforward, "animals"). I then turn to Aquinas's *Commentary on the Book of Job* and Eleonore Stump's *Wandering in Darkness* to see how Aquinas's understanding of divine providence can help harmonize the claims that the human good is what matters most and that the animal good is still a divine priority. I conclude with suggestions about how Aquinas's view fares against the anthropocentric problems identified.

What I offer is a constructive account, what I say about animals will not always square with the things Aquinas says elsewhere in his corpus.[4]

Humans and Other Animals, ed. Celia Deane-Drummond and David Clough (London: SCM, 2009), 21–40.

3. *ST* I, Q. 73, A. 1.

4. See, e.g., *ST* II-II, Q. 64, A. 1; *Summa contra gentiles*, 3.112.

I will not offer a direct critique of those areas of disagreement.[5] My hope in any case is that the picture for which I argue is consonant with Aquinas's worldview, as my goal is to offer what I think Aquinas *ought* to have said about animals and humans, given his broader commitments.

WHAT'S WRONG WITH ANTHROPOCENTRISM?

Expressions of the absolute distinctness of humans and exclusive priority of human flourishing can be found throughout the Christian tradition. In a famous passage from *Spiritual Exercises*, Ignatius of Loyola says, "The other things on the face of the earth are created for the human beings, to help them in pursuit of the end for which they are created. From this it follows that we ought to use these things to the extent that they help us toward our end, and free ourselves from them to the extent that they hinder us from it."[6] This attitude toward nonhuman creation, some charge, gives license to any use or abuse of the environment or of animals that humans think could serve their own purposes.

What Ignatius appears to endorse is an extreme form of anthropocentrism —a human-centered view of the created world. The term "anthropocentrism" is itself somewhat problematic, for reasons I will address below. However, it is helpful to get clear on what sort of baggage the term carries. I am not so much concerned with anthropocentrism *per se* but with Aquinas's specific claims that the final end of the created order is the beatitude of the saints and that humans are ontologically superior to animals. Whether the conjunction of these two claims turns out to be anthropocentric depends on how the term is defined.

However, it is necessary to begin by considering what people mean by "anthropocentrism" because one unifying theme of both the environmental and animal rights movements of the past century is the rejection of

---

5. Some differences, though not all, depend on empirical matters about animal intelligence, concerning which we now know much more.

6. George E. Ganss, trans., *Spiritual Exercises of Saint Ignatius: A Translation and Commentary* (Chicago: Loyola Press, 1992), 23. Dennis Hamm, SJ, offers a compelling argument that these oft-quoted lines from the *Exercises*, when understood in context, actually support a deep appreciation for the value of things in nature beyond their instrumental goodness. The point Ignatius was trying to express had to do with healthy detachment from worldly goods and not the lack of intrinsic value in nonhuman creatures. Seen in this light, the suggestion that we should free ourselves from acquiring created goods that hinder our spiritual progress would actually provide an injunction against instrumentalizing creation for our material gain. Dennis Hamm, "The Creation Spirituality of Ignatius of Loyola: Still Pertinent for Life on the Fragile Planet," *Journal of Religion and Society*, Supplement Series 3 (2008): 183–201.

anthropocentric views of the world.[7] This rejection of anthropocentrism is what contemporary ecotheologians are grappling with, so it is helpful to begin with some definitions in order to make explicit what motivates the kind of embarrassment many Christians are tempted to feel about human-centered views of the world. Consider these broad definitions:

STRONG ANTHROPOCENTRISM: Humans are wholly distinct from all other inhabitants of the planet. All other terrestrial living things and natural phenomena have only instrumental value insofar as they serve the human good.

WEAK ANTHROPOCENTRISM: Humans are distinct from all other inhabitants of the planet. No other living terrestrial things or natural phenomena have as much value as humans, and the interests of humans should carry more weight in our practical reasoning than the interests of other living things.

These two ways of viewing the world stake out positions both on how distinct humans are from nonhuman creation and what sort of value humans have relative to the rest of creation. There is a lot of room for variation within *weak anthropocentrism*, depending on just how much more weight human interests are given over the interests of other living things.

Pope Francis, in his 2015 encyclical on the environment, *Laudato Si*, warns against what he calls "tyrannical" or "distorted" versions of anthropocentrism.

> In our time, the Church does not simply state that other creatures are completely subordinated to the good of human beings, as if they have no worth in themselves and can be treated as we wish. The German bishops have taught that, where other creatures are concerned, "we can speak of the priority of being over that of being useful."[8]

By Francis's lights, our current ecological crisis stems from a failure to see the *being* of animals, plants, and ecosystems. That is, we err when we fail to see things for what they are—individuals (and collectives) that are valuable in their own right. We see instead only the utility of things and individuals even though we ought to recognize that the utility of creation is secondary

---

7. Gary Varner, "Environmental Ethics, Hunting, and the Place of Animals," in *The Oxford Handbook of Animal Ethics* (Oxford: Oxford University Press, 2011).

8. Pope Francis, *Laudato Si: On Care for Our Common Home* (Our Sunday Visitor, 2015), 69, quoting the German Bishops' Conference, *Zukunft der Schöpfung—Zukunft der Menschheit: Einklärung der Deutschen Bischofskonferenz zu Fragen der Umwelt und der Energieversorgung* (1980), II.2.

to its noninstrumental value. For Francis, *strong anthropocentrism* is tyrannical, distorted, and gives license to exploitation, and *weak anthropocentrism* might fall under his critique as well, depending on how the value of nonhuman creation is regarded. Francis's concern about overinstrumentalizing nature, we will see, touches at the heart of a potential conflict present in various strains of Aquinas's thought.

Francis's diagnosis mirrors a dominant strand of critique of anthropocentrism offered by secular environmental ethicists and animal welfare ethicists alike. Anthropocentric views fail to account for the actual value of nonhuman things and, as a result, treat the natural world in a way that could justify its abuse. We can call the first two problems with anthropocentrism, especially the strong version, *no constraints* and *wrong reasons*.

1. **NO CONSTRAINTS:** If the human good is given exclusive priority, there are no constraints on what we may do with or to nonhuman creation in the interest of pursuing what is good for humans.

2. **WRONG REASONS:** On anthropocentrism, our reasons for action with regard to nonhuman creation are not the right sorts of reasons. Namely, the reasons offered by anthropocentric worldviews do not reflect the actual value of things, and have only to do with the human good, not the good of nonhuman creation.[9]

What is alleged by these two criticisms is only morally problematic on the assumption that creation has value, as a whole or in its parts, apart from the instrumental value it has for humans.

For secular thinkers untethered to a teleological view of the world, the critique runs even deeper. What reasons could we have in the first place to think humans are so special? For them, anthropocentrism seems unmotivated at best and purely motivated by human selfish interests at worst. Perhaps the most influential contemporary criticism of this sort comes from Peter Singer's *Animal Liberation*. There Singer runs a pessimistic induction, comparing the prioritization of humans over animals to the sexist and racist

---

9. This is roughly the issue with so called "enlightened anthropocentrism" that's called into question by Richard Routley's famous "Last Man" arguments. The enlightened anthropocentrist can insist on most of the same practical principles any other environmentalist would, by arguing that our obligations regarding the environment are all obligations toward future humans. But Routley objects that if a person were to be the last human remaining on earth, it would still be wrong to do something that harms the natural world, even if that action could not harm any future human. Thus, one's reasons for action cannot simply be ones pertaining to the human good, even if the practical choices one makes as a anthropocentrist, in the vast majority of cases, would be identical to, say, some ecological holist's. Richard Routley, "Is There a Need for a New, an Environmental, Ethic?," in *Proceedings of the XVth World Congress of Philosophy* (Sofia Press, 1973), 205–10.

discrimination that has prioritized white males over women and people of color throughout history. Singer calls anthropocentrism of any sort "speciesism" and warns that speciesism is just another form of blind prejudice that we must overcome. Whether speciesism is as morally problematic as Singer argues is debatable, but his call for us to "expand our moral horizons" raises legitimate worries about the grounds of our judgements about moral standing.

In addition to the sorts of ethical worries raised by secular thinkers like Singer, several contemporary theologians have raised concerns about the compatibility of varieties of anthropocentrism with the Christian doctrine of creation. Chief among these is David Clough, whose groundbreaking systematic theology volume, *On Animals*, raises a long series of objections to anthropocentrism.[10] Clough rejects the scholastic metaphysics underpinning Aquinas's worldview, arguing instead for an egalitarian ecology inspired by Karl Barth. But more importantly for present purposes, a number of Thomists have joined in Clough's project and marshalled the support of none other than Aquinas to call human-centered accounts into question.

These Thomists' first worry is that by overemphasizing the centrality of humans in the created order, we run the risk of setting what is created over and above the Creator. The remedy for this vaunted conception of humanity's place in the world is to substitute an anthropocentric view with a theocentric one. As John Berkman explains,

> For Aquinas the entire physical universe . . . is ordered toward "ultimate perfection," which is in turn ordered to God, and by its perfection, gives glory to the goodness of God. Each creature manifests the goodness of God by living according to its own telos. . . . God's plan in creation, while hierarchical, is by no means anthropocentric.[11]

God creates for the sake of God's own glory, and God's glory is manifested by all of creation, not just those humans who bear God's image. Our attempts at classification schemes that differentiate us from other parts of creation, so the worry goes, skew our understanding of God's purposes in creating. Writing elsewhere with Stanley Hauerwas, Berkman says, "It is not clear that Christians have a stake in any classification of ourselves in relation to creatures. . . . Such classifications might underwrite an anthropocentrism antithetical to the Christian conviction that God, not humanity,

---

10. David Clough, *Systematic Theology*, vol. 1, *On Animals* (New York: Bloomsbury, 2012).
11. Berkman, "Towards a Thomistic Theology," 24.

is the end of all creation."[12] Anthropocentrism, they argue, misses the very point of God's creative action in the world.

Second, if we focus exclusively on the place of humans in creation, we neglect what another Thomist, Celia Deane-Drummond, calls the "shared creaturely being" we have in common with other animals.[13] This worry has both an empirical and theological face. From a contemporary empirical standpoint (which as a matter of course is different from the empirical standpoint we find in Aquinas), it is important to acknowledge our continuity with our nonhuman ancestors. Likewise, we must pay heed to the growing body of research suggesting that much of what we thought unique to humans can be found in at least some degree in many other species of animals.

From a theological standpoint, it is necessary to acknowledge the common origin we share with other animals insofar as we are all created by God and bear the imprint of the divine, albeit in very different ways. Humans and animals stand together in relation to God as created things to Creator. This perspective is easily lost if we set humans over and above the rest of creation. Bracketing christological issues, the ontological distance between humans and animals is less than the ontological distance between humans and God.

Finally, Charles Camosy draws on Aquinas in noting one further complication that counts against an anthropocentric view of the world. Citing Psalm 8, he points out that in the Judeo-Christian tradition, humans do not really occupy the highest rung of the chain of created being. Angels do.[14] Thus, a strictly anthropocentric view of the world fails to appreciate the place of at least one kind of nonhuman person, angels, in God's creative work.

The theological issues that Berkman, Deane-Drummond, and Camosy raise attempt in various ways to put humans in their proper place in light of a Christian understanding of God's creative action in the world. They all call out anthropocentrism as sinful and in varying degrees distance themselves from those aspects of Aquinas's worldview that place humans above other animals. Call the theological *and* ethical problem they raise *excessive pride*:

---

12. Stanley Hauerwas and John Berkman, "The Chief End of All Flesh," *Theology Today* 49, no. 2 (1992): 196–208, at 198–99.

13. Celia Deane-Drummond, "In God's Image and Likeness: From Reason to Revelation in Humans and Other Animals," in *Questioning the Human: Toward a Theological Anthropology for the Twenty-First Century*, ed. Lieven Boeve, Yves De Maeseneer, and Ellen Van Stichel (New York: Fordham University Press, 2014), 60–75.

14. Charles C. Camosy, *For Love of Animals: Christian Ethics, Consistent Action* (Cincinnati, OH: Franciscan Media, 2013), 32ff.

3. **EXCESSIVE PRIDE:** Anthropocentric views run the risk of mis-characterizing the reality both of where humans stand before God and where humans stand in relation to other creatures, which manifests the sin of pride.

For the reasons these theologians cite, and for a few more that I will outline in the next section, Aquinas's view cannot be described as a version of *strong anthropocentrism*. Aquinas thinks that the universe is ultimately ordered to God's glory, even if in his view this is achieved through the fulfilment of humankind's greatest good. Furthermore, Aquinas would deny that humans and animals are wholly distinct, given his views about shared creaturely being. And in what follows, it should become clear that Aquinas's account of the metaphysics of goodness rules out the possibility that only humans have noninstrumental value.

Given how fraught the term "anthropocentrism" is, I will avoid the label and focus instead on two specific claims Aquinas makes: that the final end of the created order is the beatitude of the saints and that humans are ontologically superior to animals. The conjunction of these two positions could represent a form of *weak anthropocentrism*, but some of the theologians just mentioned, especially Berkman, would dispute this characterization. For present purposes, what matters is not so much whether Aquinas's worldview fits the definitions of anthropocentrism that I give but whether his specific views about humanity's place in the created order are vulnerable to any of the three problems identified in this section: *no constraints*, *wrong reasons*, and *excessive pride*.

AQUINAS ON THE ONTOLOGICAL SUPERIORITY OF HUMANS

Asking where humans rank in the created order runs the risk of sounding unseemly, like Jesus's disciples squabbling over who gets to sit at the master's right hand (Luke 22:24). If insistence on human superiority manifests excessive pride, the antidote should be a healthy dose of humility. For Aquinas, humility involves having an accurate assessment of one's own value. Discussing whether humility is a virtue, Aquinas says,

> As Isidore observes, "a humble man is so called because he is, as it were, 'humo acclinis'" [Literally, "bent to the ground"], i.e. inclined to the lowest place . . . and this may be done sometimes well, for instance when

a man, considering his own failings, assumes the lowest place according to his mode: thus Abraham said to the Lord (Genesis 18:27), "I will speak to my Lord, whereas I am dust and ashes." On this way humility is a virtue.[15]

The humble person accurately understands his faults and sees himself for who he truly is and no greater. Thus, Abraham is praised for recognizing that in relation to God he is but dust and ashes.

Aquinas immediately goes on to say, though, that in inclining oneself to the lowest place, it is possible to err in excess, "for instance when man, not understanding his honor, compares himself to senseless beasts, and becomes like to them."[16] There is nothing virtuous, according to Aquinas, with equating one's value with that of an animal. To do so is to fail to appreciate the unique dignity one has as a human being.

Why, then, does Aquinas think humans are more valuable than animals? The answer lies in what Aquinas says about the metaphysical ground of goodness. For Aquinas, everything that exists has value simply by virtue of existing.[17] Here he follows the medieval tradition pairing being and goodness as correlatives. As Eleonore Stump explains, on this metaethical account of value, "'being' and 'goodness' are the same in reference but different in sense."[18] One and the same thing will be the truth maker for both the proposition that "an object x is good" and the proposition that "an object x has being." We know one and the same thing under different aspects though: being presents a thing according to what it is, and goodness presents a thing under the aspect of its desirability.[19]

According to Aquinas, God created the world in order to communicate God's goodness to creatures. Everything that has being expresses God's goodness in some way, and the great diversity we see in nature is the result of God's desire to express different aspects of God's unlimited goodness in different, limited creatures.[20] God's goodness could not be adequately expressed by God creating just one kind of thing.

The measure of a creature's goodness lies in the kind of thing it is, which in turn implies the kind of potential it has. To understand the goodness of creatures, we need to study the natures of the various kinds of things we

---

15. *ST* II-II, Q. 161, A. 1, ad 1.
16. *ST* II-II, Q. 161, A. 1, ad 1.
17. Aquinas's discussion of being and goodness can be found, among other places, in *ST* I, Q. 5.
18. Eleonore Stump, *Aquinas* (New York: Routledge, 2005), 62.
19. *De Veritate* Q. 1, A. 1.
20. *ST* I, Q. 47, A. 1.

encounter in the world by considering the types of potential or powers those kinds of creatures have, according to their natures. On this scheme, species of creatures come in various metaphysical sizes, as there is a gradation of kinds of powers from lesser to greater, and a corresponding gradation of goodness. Aquinas says,

> Hence in natural things species seem to be arranged in degrees; as the mixed things are more perfect than the elements, and plants than minerals, and animals than plants, and men than other animals; and in each of these one species is more perfect than others. Therefore, as the divine wisdom is the cause of the distinction of things for the sake of the perfection of the universe, so it is the cause of inequality. For the universe would not be perfect if only one grade of goodness were found in things.[21]

Aquinas claims that within each broad genus there seem to be degrees of perfection, and the world admits of such diversity in order to display God's goodness more comprehensively.

This picture would be implausible if we took Aquinas to mean that there is some tidy hierarchy of species within each genus of living things. How could we rank the relative powers of rhinoceroses and hippos or oaks and maples? A more charitable read suggests that what he envisions are creatures at various rungs of a hierarchy having powers that make possible certain kinds of lives that are qualitatively very different from each other, with some holding more objective value than others.

Such is the hierarchy Aquinas inherits from Aristotle, ordered according to the kinds of souls, or animating principles, that all living things have. The powers that plants, animals, and humans have for reproduction and growth distinguish living creatures from nonliving ones, and thus living things are more valuable than nonliving ones. In addition to having the powers that plants have, animals and humans have perceptual powers that make possible things like phenomenal consciousness. Thus, animals and humans are more valuable than plants. Humans, in turn, fall into the same genus as other animals, but the powers humans have for practical and theoretical rationality distinguish us from all other terrestrial creatures. Thus, we are metaphysically bigger, so to speak, and more valuable than all other kinds of terrestrial creatures.

Now, one implication of Aquinas's view about a hierarchy of value in nature is that though God loves everything that God has made, God loves

---

21. *ST* I, Q. 47, A. 1.

some things more than others. At first blush, this makes God sound like a bad parent. However, in light of Aquinas's concepts of love and of the metaphysical ground of goodness, this worry should dissolve. For Aquinas, to love something is simply to will the good for that thing. He says,

> God loves all existing things. . . . Now it has been shown above that God's will is the cause of all things. It must needs be, therefore, that a thing has existence, or any kind of good, only inasmuch as it is willed by God. To every existing thing, then, God wills some good. Hence, since to love anything is nothing else than to will good to that thing, it is manifest that God loves everything that exists. Yet not as we love. Because since our will is not the cause of the goodness of things, but is moved by it as its object, our love, whereby we will good to anything, is not the cause of its goodness . . . whereas the love of God infuses and creates goodness.[22]

The idea is that God is the cause of all goodness, since God loves everything into existence. God's love "infuses and creates" the goodness correlative of every creature's being. He goes on,

> It must needs be, according to what has been said before, that God loves more the better things. For it has been shown that God's loving one thing more than another is nothing else than His wiling for that thing a greater good: because God's will is the cause of goodness in things; and the reason why some things are better than others, is that God wills for them a greater good.[23]

God loves every thing in the fullest measure that it can be loved, infusing whatever being each thing has in virtue of the nature it possesses. But since humans are metaphysically bigger than animals, God loves humans more.[24]

One natural worry concerning such a hierarchy is that a ranking of powers which assigns greater value to humans might be arbitrary, the invention of human self-interest.[25] Why think the powers we possess and other animals lack make us more valuable, the objects of greater love from

---

22. *ST* I, Q. 20, A. 2.

23. *ST* I, Q. 20, A. 4.

24. It is helpful here to remember that the scale of value applies to different species of things, not members within one species. Simply in virtue of possessing a human nature, any human being is more valuable than things belonging to those species lower in the hierarchy, and thus more loved by God. I'm grateful to Steven Nemes for calling attention to this.

25. See David Clough, "Putting Animals in Their Place: On the Theological Classification of Animals," in *Animals as Religious Subjects* (New York: Bloomsbury, 2013).

God? There are, after all, plenty of powers that animals have which we lack, like flight or echolocation. For Aquinas, the answer is simple. Powers like flight or echolocation do reflect aspects of God's goodness which humans do not manifest. However, the powers we have that distinguish us from other creatures are the ones that uniquely fit us for friendship with God.[26]

Aquinas distinguishes between bearing the likeness of God and bearing the image of God, two different ways a thing can manifest God's goodness by way of similarity. Both "likeness" and "image" are kinds of unity, as they involve some sort of sameness between God's goodness and the goodness God expresses to a thing in creating and sustaining it in existence.[27] Whatever goodness created things have in common with God, they have by way of participation in God's goodness, whereas God's own goodness is simply identical to who God is. Thus, whatever goodness things share in common with God is had in a very imperfect way in created things, whose goodness causally depends on God.[28]

All created things bear the likeness of God insofar as they show some aspect of God's goodness. Humans, however, bear not only the divine likeness, but the divine image as well. For Aquinas, image "means a likeness which, in some degree, however small, attains to a representation of the species."[29] By this he means that one thing can bear the image of another only if what is common between the two is essential to what kinds of things both are. He offers an analogy: Some ordinary object might share accidental properties, like whiteness or height, with the king and thus bear some likeness to the king. However, a coin bears the king's image because the coin shows a picture of who the king actually is. The only created things that can be like unto God in species are ones with natures endowed with intellects and wills. For Aquinas, humans are the only material beings that can represent God as bearers of the divine image.

Because humans bear the divine image, we have God as our final end in a unique way. We are able to know God and to choose to love God,

---

26. "Reasonable creatures, however, have in some special and higher manner God as their end, since they can attain to Him by their own operations, by knowing and loving Him. Thus it is plain that the Divine goodness is the end of all corporeal things" (*ST* I, Q. 65, A. 2).

27. *ST* I, Q. 93, A. 9.

28. It is necessary to proceed with caution when discussing what Aquinas says about what created things share in common with their Creator. These caveats concerning the way the goodness of divine image and likeness are possessed by created things is explained very nicely in Jennifer Ashworth's helpful discussion on Aquinas in "Medieval Theories of Analogy," *The Stanford Encyclopedia of Philosophy* (Fall 2017), ed. Edward N. Zalta, https://plato.stanford.edu/archives/fall2017/entries/analogy-medieval/.

29. *ST* I, Q. 93, A. 8.

with the assistance of divine grace. And since we have intellects and wills, we share a special role in creation because we have a say in how the world turns out. In laying out the foundation of his theory of natural law, Aquinas says, "Now among all others, the rational creature is subject to Divine Providence in the most excellent way, in so far as it partakes of a share of providence, by being provident both for itself and for others."[30] Providence is just that part of prudence that directs all things toward their end, and humans are able to exercise a kind of providence over the rest of creation, cooperating with God in ordering the created world toward its ultimate good.

At this point we can return to the question, what is the ultimate good or purpose of the created world? Is it simply the good of humankind? As Berkman is right to draw out in his criticism of anthropocentrism, Aquinas takes the final end of the created world to be the glory of God, which is achieved by each part of creation striving toward its telos, contributing to the perfection of the whole. Humans are not the only important characters in the drama. But nevertheless, in explaining the order of creation in the work of six days, Aquinas explicitly claims that while the first perfection of the world is the "completeness of the universe at its first founding," the final perfection of the whole universe consists in "the perfect beatitude of the Saints at the consummation of the world." The ultimate realization of God's purpose in creation lies in the elect of human- and angel-kind achieving their supernatural end of beholding the beatific vision.

While the vision of the world that Aquinas argues for is theocentric, humans matter more than all other terrestrial beings. At the same time, Aquinas's emphasis on human superiority is embedded in and dependent on a worldview where all things have intrinsic value and a distinct way of manifesting God's goodness and where all things are loved by God, even if to varying degrees. So to reframe the issue in the language of Francis's *Laudato Si*, can Aquinas hold onto the superiority of rational creatures and the primacy of their good, while still respecting the priority of *being* over *being useful* in the rest of the created order? And if these two strands can be held together in tension, does the resulting picture face the three problems with anthropocentrism identified above: *no constraints, wrong reasons,* or *excessive pride?*

---

30. *ST* I-II, Q. 91, A. 2.

PROVIDENCE AND THE ANIMAL GOOD: GOD'S DISCOURSES WITH JOB

In my view, the most compelling articulation of Aquinas's vision for humanity's place in the created world comes in his commentary on God's discourses with Job concerning animals. For Aquinas, the book of Job is not aimed at addressing questions about the problem of suffering so much as exploring the mysterious operations of divine providence. Aquinas's Job commentary provides an interesting model for how to think about humankind's relationship to animals and the rest of the created order, since in Job 38 and 39 God speaks at length about the marvels of the earth, sea, air, and animal kingdom in order to communicate the goodness of God's providence. In Aquinas's commentary on those chapters, the emerging themes paint a picture of how insistence on the superiority of humans can be reconciled with a robust appreciation for the goodness of the rest of the created order and in doing so resolve some of the tension highlighted by Francis's concerns about overinstrumentalizing nature.

First, Aquinas reiterates throughout his *Commentary on the Book of Job* that the created order serves humankind. Even so, the natural world's use is not primarily for human comfort or material gain but for guiding humans toward their ultimate, supernatural end. In one telling example he says, "Everything which happens in the corporeal creature redounds to the usefulness of man. Earthquakes and other such terrible things are useful in that man, being terrified, may desist from their sins."[31] If the usefulness of *earthquakes* is what Aquinas has in mind in saying the world exists for the sake of humans, it should be clear that the notion of *use* in play is rather broad and that the end toward which the created world is most useful cannot be just material or temporal goods. Indeed, this reflects one of the broader themes of Aquinas's Job commentary: God cares for the good of human beings, but the ultimate good for human beings is not in this life.[32]

Second, Aquinas describes God's relations to all of creation, living and nonliving, as the relationship between a father and his children. Discussing verses about the weather, Aquinas says, "Next he discusses the rains without the wind when he says, 'Who is the father?' that is, the efficient cause 'of the rain' not from necessity, but from the order of providence which befits

31. Aquinas, *Commentary on the Book of Job*, trans. Brian Mulladay, ch. 38, lesson 2, http://dhspriory.org/thomas/english/SSJob.htm.

32. Eleonore Stump, "Aquinas on the Suffering of Job," in *Reasoned Faith: Essays in Philosophical Theology in Honor of Norman Kretzmann* (Ithaca, NY: Cornell University Press, 1993), 334.

a father."[33] God does not direct natural phenomena by way of impersonal mechanistic causation but with the kind of care a father expresses for his children in directing them to their final ends. God's fatherly care extends well past the boundaries of the human. If God acts as a *father* to the wind and to the crow, we are mistaken to think they exist only for our good.

Third, Aquinas sees in the divine discourses a clear message that God's action in the created world aims at many goods that are completely independent of human concerns. By calling Job's attention to all that is beyond his ken in the created world, God communicates to Job that God's care extends much farther than Job, given his limited perspective, can even fathom. Discussing goats who give birth while hiding in the rocks, Aquinas explains, "For when women give birth they need the assistance of midwives, but in the animals, whose giving birth is hidden from men, God comes to their aid by his providence with what is necessary for them to give birth, in as much as he gives them a natural aptitude to know what they should know in such things."[34] God has endowed goats with all they need to flourish and safely reproduce, even if these acts themselves are hidden from human sight. What is good for goats matters, even if it has nothing to do with our story.

According to Aquinas, God's care for some creatures has nothing to do with us, and the wild ass is his most telling example. He says,

> Certain animals, when they are domesticated, cannot sustain themselves without the care of man. Yet there are some pertaining to the same species which are wild and govern themselves without the providence of men. This is especially remarkable in the ass who when he is domesticated seems totally given to human service. But asses which are called wild asses are free from this service, and so he says, "Who has let the wild asses (undomesticated) go free," from human service?[35]

The wild ass is biologically the same as the domesticated ass, but for the sake of its own good, God has freed it from the chains of human service. Aquinas goes on in a lengthy digression to marvel at the wild ass's freedom, to wonder at the fact that it can flourish in the most remote habitats without any help from humans. This strikes Aquinas as remarkable, because the wild version is basically the same as its domesticated cousin, which would not survive without human help.

---

33. Aquinas, *Commentary on the Book of Job*, ch. 38, lesson 2.
34. Aquinas, *Commentary on the Book of Job*, ch. 39.
35. Aquinas, *Commentary on the Book of Job*, ch. 39.

The implication seems to be that it is good that God has given some animals to be under our care, and we ought to exercise a parental providence over them. That involves the careful use of prudence to interact with animals in ways conducive to their flourishing. At the same time, it is also part of God's wisdom that some creatures belong in the wild, free as far as possible from the influence of humankind. Wild animals do not belong to us, even if they are useful for humankind in the broad sense of *use* suggested above.

These three themes help show how Aquinas's insistence on human superiority does not necessarily violate Francis's injunction against over-instrumentalizing the created world. However, Aquinas's vision becomes even more attractive with help from a metaphor Eleonore Stump employs in her commentary on Job. In *Wandering in Darkness*, Stump examines Job's narrative, which, while distinct from Aquinas's commentary in important ways, is deeply under its influence. She follows Aquinas in reading the divine discourses as primarily demonstrating God's fatherly providential care over all of creation. Stump argues that the narrative of Job is best understood as a nested series of stories of God's providence. The first tells of God's care for Satan, the second of God's care for Job, and the last of God's care for the rest of creation—and how by the mysterious workings of providence those can be harmonized.

Stump describes the relationship between the parts of the story as representing a fractal, a geometric figure where each part resembles the shape of the whole. The details of each character in the story reflect the details of the story overall. On Stump's reading, God wants Job to know he was never outside the reach of God's loving providence, even while God allowed Job to be used as a means by Satan. She explains, "The book of Job is an illustration of the ways in which God's relations with creatures is to be understood. God is able to use those creatures whom he treats as ends in themselves within their stories also as means to ends for others of his creatures, who are ends in themselves in their own stories."[36] Satan was granted a kind of providence over humankind, which God permitted for Satan's own good. But in the mysteries of divine providence, this was all consistent with God's providing for Job in Job's story.

According to Stump, something similar can be said about animals, whose story is subordinated to Job's. She says,

---

36. Eleonore Stump, *Wandering in Darkness: Narrative and the Problem of Suffering* (New York: Oxford University Press, 2010), 221.

In the content of the divine speeches to Job, there is the quasi-story of God's relations with the animals and inanimate parts of God's creation. In each part of that quasi-story, the focus of the story is the animal or thing in question. God finds food for the baby birds because they are hungry. God does not treat them as just incidentals in some other, bigger story. Nevertheless, the story of God's as-it-were personal relations with the beasts and the sea and all the rest of God's creatures is set within the story of God's personal relations with Job, which is itself set within the story of God's personal relations with Satan.[37]

The story of each individual animal is subordinated to the human story, but at the same time, God cares for individual animals themselves and expects humans to exercise a kind of providential care over them too.

Stump's view of the value of animals is much stronger than Aquinas's. She uses the language of "ends in themselves" for animals, where Aquinas would not be comfortable with the implications of such an attribution. It is clear in many places in his corpus that he does not think animals bear anything like what contemporary deontologists would call animal rights.[38] But as we have already seen, Aquinas does think animals have their own value and are loved by God according to their own being. Fr. Stephen Brock makes this point well in a reflection on the very passage where Aquinas denies animals have natures fit to make them objects of love like humans are. As Brock notes, Aquinas says that in loving animals in the way most fitting to their kind, God desires that animals be "conserved in their being."[39] Brock's point is that the fact that God desires to conserve animals in their being suggests that it is their existence itself that is the object of God's desire.[40]

RESPONSE TO OBJECTIONS

Applying Stump's fractal metaphor to the view of the created world we see in Aquinas's Job commentary, I can now begin to make the case that Aquinas's view does not have the problematic implications associated with anthropocentrism outlined above. First, take *no constraints* and *wrong reasons*.

---

37. Stump, *Wandering in Darkness*, 220.
38. See, e.g., *ST* II-II, Q. 25, A. 3; and *Summa contra gentiles* 3.112.
39. *ST* II-II, Q. 25, A. 3.
40. Stephen C. Brock, "Aquinas the Conservationist" (lecture, Philosophy colloquium, University of St. Thomas, St. Paul, MN, September 19, 2017).

Although humans matter more than animals, and the created world serves the human good, the fact that animals have their own value and are loved by God places constraints on what we may do with or to them in the interest of serving human needs. And contrary to what is charged by *wrong reasons*, those constraints depend on reasons having to do with the value of animals themselves, not just humans.

This is first because the human need, toward which animals (and the whole created world) are *primarily* ordered, is humanity's achievement of beatitude—animals are designed to serve the human good because they point to the glory of God and help us on our path to loving God into the afterlife. When Ignatius or Aquinas say that "the created order redounds to the usefulness of man," it is necessary to bear in mind that, ultimately, only one thing is needful for humankind—a proper relation to God so as to enjoy God in the next life. Just because animals are useful, it does not follow that they are at our disposal for just any purpose. The problem with human use of the environment is not that we see the good of the rest of creation as subordinate to the good of humans but that we continually misunderstand what the human good consists in. Attachment to temporal goods leads us to squander the goodness of creation and use animals in ways unsuited to their natural ends, *and ours*. Doing whatever we see fit with animals is actually contrary to the purpose for which they were placed under us.

From Aquinas's point of view, in addition to the goodness animals have just in virtue of their existence, they are useful in other ways besides their witness to the Creator. We use them all the time for food, clothing, labor, and experimentation—and Aquinas makes it clear that these kinds of use can be licit.[41] We must ask though, what dictates why and in what manner it is acceptable to use them for such purposes, given the value animals have? This draws us into difficult questions in applied ethics, many beyond the scope of this chapter. However, philosopher Andrew Tardiff has a tremendously helpful discussion about killing animals for food that illustrates how Aquinas's natural law reasoning can lead to stringent demands for treating animals.[42]

In a sophisticated argument that I can only give in brief here, Tardiff traces out the proportionality reasoning operative in the doctrine of double

---

41. See, e.g., *ST* II-II, Q. 64, A. 1.
42. Andrew Tardiff, "A Catholic Case for Vegetarianism," *Faith and Philosophy* 15, no. 2 (1998): 210–22.

effect and its application to our food choices. One constraint on action in the natural law tradition says that when a choice brings about both positive and negative consequences, the choice is only permissible if the positive consequence outweighs the negative, *and* if there is not some better means to attain the positive consequence that does not incur the negative one. Tardiff argues that though the good of human sustenance of life through eating meat outweighs the negative consequence of the death of animals, there is indeed a way to have the good of human sustenance of life without killing animals, by eating a plant-based diet. All things being equal, it is better to sustain ourselves at the cost of plant life, which, though valuable, is less valuable than animal life.

There are plenty of objections one could raise to this argument, but I present it to illustrate that in a natural law context, where our choices should be attuned to the value of the people and things we interact with, there are definite constraints on what we can do with or to animals, given their value and God's love for them. And those constraints depend on reasons having to do with the goodness of animals themselves. This is all consistent with prioritizing the good of humans over that of animals.

Lastly, Aquinas's view itself does not lead into the problem of *excessive pride* either, though we do a good enough job straying into that territory on our own. For Aquinas, humility requires an accurate assessment of one's value and thus requires appreciation of both the high dignity we have in virtue of our human nature, and the fact that we ourselves are not the final end of the universe. Here Aquinas's discussion of the operations of divine providence in Job is helpful.

God has placed us a little lower than the angels, whom he allows to exercise a kind of providence over us. We, in turn, are above animals, over whom we exercise providence. We have a kind of authority and power over animals, an unhealthy attachment to which could lead us into pride. But the model we should strive after in exercising the providence God has given us over creation is none other than the kind of care God shows animal-kind, illustrated in God's discourses with Job. It is true that all animals are useful to us insofar as they point us to God, but we may only use them to suit our other needs if we keep their well-being at the forefront of our practical deliberation.

That is because, for Aquinas, we are to imitate God, who is at pains to show Job how much God's providential care extends to all creatures. Some of those creatures are under our immediate care, and so we are responsible for treating them in ways that direct them to their natural ends.

Many other creatures, like the wild ass, do not belong to us—their stories are at a remove from ours. That this is so reflects God's providential care for those wild things, and we ought to help them stay wild, to flourish as the kind of creatures they are.

In short, Aquinas instructs that by holding fast to a proper understanding of what the human good consists in, we can and should exercise the dominion we have been given over creation with an eye toward harmonizing what is good for us with what is good for the world under our care.[43]

43. I am grateful to Tim Pawl for insightful comments on a draft of this paper and to Fr. Stephen Brock for helpful conversation concerning Aquinas's views about ecological conservation.

CHAPTER 3

THE RELEVANCE OF BIBLICAL ESCHATOLOGY FOR PHILOSOPHICAL ANTHROPOLOGY

RICHARD J. MOUW

HOW SHOULD THE CLAIMS of Christian eschatology guide our explorations of topics in philosophical anthropology? More specifically, what bearing do our biblically based beliefs about the postmortem survival of human individuals have on our understanding of the metaphysical composition of the human person?

The relationship between our philosophical accounts of human composition and our beliefs about the afterlife have been getting considerable attention these days, both by philosophers and theologians. One reason for this attention is the groundbreaking work done in recent decades in the scientific study of the brain and its relationship to what we ordinarily classify as states of consciousness. What is the relationship between a thought I am having about a slice of pepperoni pizza and the neural processes occurring in my brain when I am having that thought? Does the brain event *accompany* the mental event? Or is the mental event in some important sense *identical with* the brain event? Is our ordinary talk about brain and mind actually referring to two separate things or is it really only about one thing—so that we are using two modes of discourse, consciousness talk and brain talk, to refer to what is in fact one metaphysical "stuff"?

Those are big and complex metaphysical topics, and I do not intend to address them adequately here. But I do want to offer some observations about how we should think about the link between what we take to be the relevant biblical data and our compositional affirmations. Nor can we solve anything simply by citing this or that passage from the Bible. The biblical data themselves need some careful sorting out. The Dutch theologian G. C. Berkouwer rightly observed that any attempt, for example, to single out specific biblical terms for human "parts" ("spirit," "flesh," "body," "heart") in exploring compositional issues will inevitably run into much messiness. The biblical writers, he says, use such terms "in very concrete and extremely varied ways." But while the Bible does not offer us a theoretical account of human composition, it does, Berkouwer observes, "incidentally" point to certain compositional realities along the way.[1]

We can pose the proper question, then, in this way: What kind of metaphysical entity must a human person *be* in order to be capable of the kinds of things the Bible says about us? Given that we cannot get a lot of metaphysical mileage from the Bible's unsystematic references to "spirit" or "heart" or "soul," we can at least discern what kinds of beings we must be, in metaphysical terms, in order for the Bible to say what it means to say about us when it is using these terms.

The eschatological topic that is especially poignant in this regard is the question of "the intermediate state," the segment of time between an individual person's death and the final resurrection of the dead. When the apostle Paul celebrates that when he is "absent from the body," he is "present with the Lord" (2 Cor 5:8 KJV), or when he affirms that being "with Christ" after dying is better than "living in the body" (Phil 1:22–23 NIV), what compositional account of human nature best explains the metaphysical way of understanding his confident claims?

We do need to keep in mind that while the present-day compositional explorations have special significance because of current neuroscientific research, the question of a continuing state of consciousness between one's death and the resurrection has long been disputed within Christian theology. It was a point of difference, for example, during the time of the Reformation. John Calvin issued a strong rebuttal against those who denied a continuing consciousness, dividing his opponents into two groups. There are some, he says, who admit to the reality of a nonphysical human soul but "imagine that it sleeps in *a state of insensibility* from death to the judgment-day, when it will awake from its sleep." But there are others,

---

1. G. C. Berkouwer, *Man: The Image of God* (Grand Rapids: Eerdmans, 1962), 203.

he observes, who "will sooner admit anything than [the soul's] real existence, maintaining that it is merely a vital power which is derived from
arterial spirit on the action of the lungs, and being *unable to exist* without
body, perishes along with the body, and vanishes away and becomes eva-
nescent till the period when the whole man shall be raised again." Against
these denials, Calvin insists "both that [the soul] is a substance, and [that]
after the death of the body [it] truly lives, being endued both with *sense
and understanding.*"[2]

Calvin was opposed in this view by none other than Luther himself,
who proclaimed in a sermon that "we shall suddenly rise on the last day,
without knowing how we have come into death and through death. We
shall sleep, until He comes and knocks on the little grave and says, 'Doctor
Martin, get up!' Then I shall rise in a moment, and be with him forever."[3]

The "soul sleep" option has continued to be defended in Protestantism
since the sixteenth century, most prominently in the Adventist tradition
that was birthed in the nineteenth century. In recent years, however, the
issues have been explored with a more explicit attention to philosophical
categories and concerns.

The recent theological debates over issues relating to composition have
been stimulated in good part by the "biblical theology" movement that
emerged shortly after World War II, which featured a strong reaction against
the "Platonistic" metaphysics that was seen as having long held sway in
systematic theology. Much damage had been done, it was argued, by the
"Greek dualism" wherein a human being was seen to be a composite of
two different kinds of substances: a rational-spiritual soul and a physical
body, with the nonphysical component of our shared human nature being
"higher"—closer to God—than the corporeal aspects of our nature. At
its worst, Christian theology had borrowed heavily from the Platonistic
notion that "the body is the prison house of the soul" and that death is a
release of human souls from their present state of bondage.

While those contentions loomed large among the post–World War II
biblical theologians, the philosophical references were often unnuanced,
with broad-stroke contrasts between "Greek dualism" and what was identified as the Bible's "Hebraic view." The lack of nuance was clearly on display,
for example, in a brief summary of biblical anthropology given by Robert

---

2. John Calvin, *Psychopannychia*, in *Tracts and Treatises in Defense of the Reformed Faith*, tr. Henry
Beveridge (Grand Rapids: Eerdmans,1958), 3:419–20.
3. Quoted by T. A. Kantonen, *The Christian Hope* (Philadelphia: United Lutheran Church in
America, 1954), 37.

McAfee Brown in a 1958 theological handbook. The title of the entry is "Body (Soul)," and Brown simply treats the terms "body" and "soul" as two different ways of referring to the whole person, without any mention of eschatological implications of such a view.[4] And when the relevance of the intermediate state was in fact acknowledged, as in Berkouwer's efforts to incorporate biblical theological themes into a systematic theological framework, there was often a heavy reliance on the word "mystery."[5]

Well, how do we gain the proper nuance? Nicholas Wolterstorff offers a helpful way of framing our efforts in his 1976 book, *Reason within the Bounds of Religion*, where he argues that the essential beliefs associated with "authentic Christian commitment" should serve as "control beliefs" in guiding Christian scholars in the "devising and weighing of theories" that bear on the topics they are considering.[6] The requisite control beliefs, Wolterstorff notes, do not simply "contain" the theories, "just waiting to be extracted." Rather, "a Christian scholar has to obtain his [or her] theories by using the same capacities of imagination that scholars in general use."[7]

What this suggests, then, is that the Pauline verses I have quoted about being "with" Christ immediately after bodily death are not in themselves theoretical claims. Rather, it is our task to assess the relevant metaphysical theories to decide which of them—and this is Wolterstorff's felicitous term—"comports" best with our sense or our understanding of authentic Christian belief.

Full disclosure: I subscribe to a compositional dualism. But I am convinced that serious debates about these matters are necessary and healthy. My disagreements with those of my friends who hold to a Christian version of a "nonreductive physicalism"[8] take place within a larger context of strong shared agreement on key issues in eschatology. Of special importance here is our shared affirmation of the final resurrection. And in their affirmation of the doctrine of the resurrection of the body, they are highlighting one of the key gains of the anti-"Platonist" emphases of the biblical theology movement. Plato's version of compositional dualism was intimately linked to a "higher-lower" dualism. The soul, in Platonism, is intrinsically immortal,

---

4. Robert McAfee Brown, "Soul (Body)," in *A Handbook of Christian Theology*, ed. Arthur Cohen and Marvin Halverson (New York: Meridian, 1958), 354.

5. Cf. Berkouwer, *Man: The Image of God*, 269–78.

6. Nicholas Wolterstorff, *Reason within the Bounds of Religion*, 2nd ed. (Grand Rapids: Eerdmans, 1976, 1984), 76.

7. Wolterstorff, *Reason within the Bounds of Religion*, 77–78.

8. Cf. Nancey Murphy, *Bodies and Souls, or Spirited Bodies?*, Current Issues in Theology (Cambridge: Cambridge University Press, 2006).

belonging to the unchanging realm of noncorporeal Forms, while the body is of a lower reality, working to inhibit the soul's focus on the eternal.

The post–World War II biblical theology movement rightly insisted that the New Testament's distinction between "spirit" and "flesh" should not be understood in terms of two different substances but as pointing to the basic patterns with which we direct our lives. To put it in blunt terms, marital physical intimacy can be for believing couples "spiritual," whereas a prideful attachment to a philosophical theory can be "fleshly."

Nor do those who deny a disembodied postmortem consciousness mean to be denying the *truth* of those biblical claims that seem to affirm a continued intermediate state consciousness; rather, they interpret those claims—such as "absent from the body, present with the Lord"—in alternative ways. Luther's homily points to this kind of interpretation. God has not forgotten Martin Luther, even though he is not presently a continuing consciousness. Luther is "with" Christ as one who continues to be loved by him. The Lord remembers the reformer's name and will call him back into consciousness on Resurrection Day. This way of viewing the situation is often supplemented by observations about our experience of time. On the experiential level, Luther will be immediately resurrected after his death. There is no experienced temporal gap between his dying and his being raised up.

It is tempting to proclaim a theological truce and simply leave the discussion there. Each of the views—the denial and the affirmation of a continuing state of disembodied consciousness—satisfy the Wolterstorffian "comportability" criterion. We can proceed, then, with the more philosophical stages of the exploration, without having to worry about any real disagreements regarding authentic Christian belief.

I am not ready to give in to that temptation, however, because of another requirement set forth in what I quoted above from Wolterstorff: that in weighing theories Christian scholars should employ "the same capacities of imagination that scholars in general use." This still leaves us, then, with the question of which of the compositional perspectives that bear on our understanding of the intermediate state—dualism or monism—is the most "imaginative." And my own sense is that the monistic conception falls short in the exercise of theological imagination.

One way to free up our metaphysical imaginations is by refusing simply to accept the broad-strokes compositional claims by those theologians who move quickly from a condemnation of "Platonist dualism" to physical monist claims about life after death. It is good, I suggest, to linger a bit on the exegetical level, giving our attention to those biblical commentators who offer accounts of these matters with a willingness to deal with some compositional subtleties.

Oscar Cullmann's treatment of the key New Testament passages is an excellent case in point. In an insightful essay published in the 1950s, entitled "Immortality of the Soul or Resurrection of the Dead: The Witness of the New Testament," Cullmann, while celebrating the doctrine of the resurrection of the body as the central teaching with regard to postmortem survival, also gives careful attention to the nature of the intermediate state. He observes that in 2 Corinthians 5:1–10 the apostle Paul expresses anxiety over the "nakedness" of an interim condition when he is no longer in the body but not yet resurrected, while also voicing much confidence that he will experience "Christ's proximity, *even in this interim state*." For Paul, says Cullmann, the inner person is not abandoned by the Holy Spirit when the outer person disappears.[9] And Cullmann is willing to live with the metaphysical implications of this. Those who are "dead in Christ," he says, do experience some sort of state of consciousness prior to the resurrection. They "are still in time; they, too, are waiting. 'How long, oh Lord?' cry the martyrs who are sleeping under the altar in John's Apocalypse ([Rev] 6:11)."[10]

Having acknowledged this, Cullmann asks "whether in this fashion we have not been led again, in the last analysis, to the Greek doctrine of immortality." And the fact is, he continues, that "there is a sense in which a kind of *approximation* to the Greek teaching does actually take place, to the extent that the inner man, who has already been transformed by the Spirit (Romans 6:3ff) and consequently made alive, continues to live with Christ in this transformed state, in the condition of sleep. . . . Here we observe at least a certain analogy to the 'immortality of the soul,' but the distinction remains nonetheless radical."[11] For Cullmann, a residual consciousness for the human person after dying is not due to "the natural essence of the soul." Rather, he says, the interim state is for the believer one of "waiting for the resurrection."[12]

It is important to note that all Cullmann says on this subject applies exclusively to the Christian believer. He tells us nothing about the postmortem prospects of human beings in general. More recently, N. T. Wright

---

9. Oscar Cullmann, "Immortality of the Soul or Resurrection of the Dead: The Witness of the New Testament," in *Immortality*, ed. Terence Penelhum (Belmont, CA: Wadsworth, 1973), 81.

10. Cullmann, "Immortality of the Soul or Resurrection of the Dead," 79.

11. Cullmann, "Immortality of the Soul or Resurrection of the Dead," 83.

12. Cullmann, "Immortality of the Soul or Resurrection of the Dead," 83.

does address the postmortem condition of both believer and unbeliever in his own nuanced discussion of these same issues. Wright is well known for his theological campaign against Hellenistic philosophical influences, with Plato playing a villain role of sorts in his theological narrative. Past theologians have too often taught, says Wright, that we can look forward to a "*disembodied* immortality," a perspective heavily influenced by the Platonistic insistence that "all human beings have an immortal element within them, normally referred to as 'soul.'"[13]

Like Cullmann, however, Wright does not deny a conscious state of "being with Christ" between a person's death and the final resurrection. This state is, he says, one "in which the dead are held firmly within the conscious love of God and the conscious presence of Jesus Christ while they await that day."[14] What Wright wants us to be clear about in all of this, however, "is that heaven and hell are not, so to speak, what the whole game is about. . . . The major, central, framing question is that of God's purpose of rescue and recreation for the whole world, the entire cosmos. The destiny of the individual human beings must be understood within that context."[15]

Having given some attention to the condition of those who, having died, enter into a conscious state of "being with the Lord," Wright directly addresses the state of the unredeemed after their individual deaths and prior to the general resurrection. Wright is no universalist. He refuses to accept the view that "there will be no ultimate condemnation, no final loss, no human beings to whom, as C. S. Lewis put it, God will eventually say, '*Thy* will be done.'" Those who have openly rejected God's redeeming purposes will have, Wright says, so dehumanized themselves so as to have fatally damaged the image of God in which they were created. Thus, "with the death of the body in which they inhabited God's good world, in which the flickering flame of goodness had not been completely snuffed out, they pass simultaneously not only beyond hope but also beyond pity," as they "still exist in an ex-human state, no longer reflecting their maker in any meaningful sense."[16]

So, what do these nuanced thoughts about the intermediate state suggest for exercising our eschatological imagination? Wright's views about the afterlife have been particularly influential in recent years, and in spite of his insistence—as we have just seen—on the reality of a conscious intermediate

---

13. N. T. Wright, *Surprised by Hope: Rethinking Heaven, the Resurrection, and the Mission of the Church* (New York: HarperOne, 2008), 160.

14. Wright, *Surprised by Hope*, 172.

15. Wright, *Surprised by Hope*, 184.

16. Wright, *Surprised by Hope*, 182–83.

state, his overall emphasis has been on what he sees as the long-standing portrayal of the afterlife as a condition of disembodied existence. I want to raise the question here, though, whether not only making some room for a temporary state of disembodied consciousness but actually *emphasizing* that reality in our teaching and preaching might have some theological—and pastoral—merit.

In a helpful comparative study of diverse religious conceptions of the afterlife, Colleen McDannell and Bernhard Lang have distinguished between "anthropocentric" and "theocentric" perspectives on postmortem survival. In theocentric accounts, they observe, the souls of the dead in heaven experience a beatific union with God, even to the point, in some accounts, that their memories of previous experiences are lost. In anthropocentric conceptions, on the other hand, the sense of personal identity is an extension of the individual's previous earthly existence, and the preoccupations of heaven are not unlike those that occupy us in our present lives.[17]

Those anthropocentric perspectives, then, that focus on intrahuman relations and activities—reunion with loved ones, life in "the Peaceable Kingdom," the perfect actualization of justice for the oppressed, and so on—stand in contrast to those that theocentrically focus exclusively on, say, "being with Jesus" or the beatific vision.

Obviously, we do not have to see these two conceptions in either-or terms. As Carol Zaleski has helpfully insisted, rather than having to choose one or the other, "a more adequate perspective would be theocentric and anthropocentric at once." To illustrate this, she cites an account of heaven she found in a story from tenth-century Ireland, where the visionary "discovers that the saints who encircle the throne have acquired the power to face in all directions at once"—"a scene that captures the sociability of the beatific vision."[18]

John Calvin certainly did not see the need to choose between the theocentric and the anthropocentric. He observes that while it is a blessed hope to know that in the resurrected state "the Kingdom of God will be fulfilled with splendor, joy, happiness, and glory" for the redeemed, it is even more blessed to know that when "that day comes . . . [Christ] will reveal to us his glory, that we may behold it face to face."[19]

---

17. Colleen McDannell and Bernhard Lang, *Heaven: A History* (New Haven, CT: Yale University Press, 1988), 48–68.

18. Carol Zaleski, "Fear of Heaven," *Christian Century*, March 14, 2001, at https://www.christiancentury.org/article//fear-heaven.

19. *Inst.* 3.25.10 (1004–5).

The gains brought about by the antidualist emphases of recent decades in Christian thought have been significant. It is a good thing to understand our eternal destinies as believers in the terms that N. T. Wright has set forth so eloquently: that the glorification of the individual has to be seen in the larger context of "God's purpose of rescue and recreation for the whole world, the entire cosmos."

However, there remains a need for healthy employment of the theological imagination on these matters. For one thing, we should not simply view past teachings regarding eternal destinies through the lenses of the biblical theology movement's antidualist themes. It is important to recognize that the long-held popular conception of a disembodied individual existence has not been the only popular picture of the afterlife in the Christian community. There has also been much anthropocentric talk of extensive family reunions, of expressions of hope that there will be perfectly designed golf courses within the walls of the New Jerusalem, of anticipations of heavenly banquet tables filled with one's favorite cuisine. One need only read the hymns collected in the "afterlife" and "heaven" sections of old evangelical hymnbooks to see how much of a role images of embodiment played: meetings with loved ones "on that beautiful shore," "walking the golden streets," "swimming over Jordan," and so on.

Furthermore, our theological imaginations must be closely conversant with those exercising pastoral imaginations. Whatever metaphysical accounts we set forth about individual personhood, the *imago Dei*, and human composition, we need to wrestle with the challenges posed by concrete questions about dementia, disabilities, and pastoral care for the dying and the grieving.

We must use our theological imaginations to discern where positive spiritual yearnings at work in the realities of the human condition, looking for expressions of a legitimate longing for a participation in a new creation in which the best of the old creation is radically transformed. The danger here, though, is that the coming kingdom can be portrayed as a mere upgrade of our present "horizontal" life. And even more dangerous is the failure to acknowledge that the "vertical" dimension of our eternal future is intimately connected to the biblical promise of the *visio Christi*. Whatever our understanding of the metaphysics of the human "soul," our hope for the future is grounded firmly in the gracious promise that while we are already sons and daughters of the living God, it "doth not yet appear what we shall be," but that when the Savior appears "we shall be like him; for we shall see him as he is" (1 John 3:2 KJV).

CHAPTER 4

FROM SIN TO THE SOUL
A Dogmatic Argument for Dualism

HANS MADUEME

> One widespread tradition has it that we human beings are responsible
> agents, captains of our fate, *because* what we really are are *souls*, immaterial
> and immortal clumps of Godstuff that inhabit and control our material
> bodies rather like spectral puppeteers. . . . But this idea of immaterial
> souls, capable of defying the laws of physics, has outlived its credibility
> thanks to the advance of the natural sciences.[1]

This opening quote from Daniel Dennett, one of the Four Horsemen of
New Atheism, challenges the idea that human persons are embodied souls.
He thinks dualism is a lost cause; human beings are material organisms,
plain and simple. Immaterial substances may be interesting research for
historians of antiquity but hardly the sober truth about human ontology.
Since Dennett and fellow atheists do not believe in God, angels, or any
other supernatural entities, none of this is surprising. Most antidualists
opt for physicalism, though atheists do not have a monopoly on physicalist
anthropologies.[2] They are joined by many believing philosophers, theologians, and biblical scholars who urge dualism to die so that a Christian
materialism can rise from the ashes.

---

1. Daniel Dennett, *Freedom Evolves* (New York: Viking, 2003), 1.
2. In this chapter, I will use the term "physicalism" generically for any anthropology in which
human beings are essentially physical-biological beings whose souls—if there are any—are necessarily dependent on their bodies. For my purposes, then, materialism, emergentism, nonreductive
physicalism, and dual-aspect monism would all count as physicalist anthropologies.

The Catholic theologian John Haught warns that dualism is "evasive, artificial, and theologically shallow."[3] The physicist-theologian John Polkinghorne remarks that "for many people [dualism] has become an extremely problematic way of conceiving human nature."[4] Philip Hefner, then systematic theologian at the Lutheran School of Theology in Chicago and the founder of the Zygon Center for Religion and Science, claimed that "dualism is foreign to the authentic Christian tradition."[5] He gave that opinion in the 1960s; today, in some circles, he voices a truism (the sky is blue; theologians are beautiful; Nigeria will win the World Cup).

Dualism has indeed fallen on hard times. On the standard account, early Christian dualism was forged in dialogue with Platonic and Aristotelian philosophies, the "sciences" of their day.[6] Many find dualism implausible given current science and the physical understanding of the world. In a post-Darwinian age that sees continuity between human beings and all other living organisms, the claim that Homo sapiens is ensouled seems like special pleading. Physicalism makes the most sense in light of neuroscience and the intimate connection between the mind and brain. In the words of Malcolm Jeeves, "Our mental processes are not free-floating somewhere out in space but are firmly embodied in our physical makeup."[7] Human spirituality is completely embodied.

A growing consensus in biblical studies argues that the Old and New Testaments are most consistent with a physicalistic anthropology (to clarify, in this chapter I use "physicalism" and "materialism" interchangeably).[8] Older dualistic exegesis was, allegedly, misled by a Hellenistic picture. Dualism has also been challenged by philosophers, though it still has significant defenders.[9] In theological writing, relational anthropologies and

---

3. John Haught, *Making Sense of Evolution: Darwin, God, and the Drama of Life* (Louisville: Westminster John Knox, 2010), 46.

4. John Polkinghorne, *The God of Hope and the End of the World* (New Haven, CT: Yale University Press, 2002), 104.

5. Philip Hefner, introduction to *Changing Man: The Threat and the Promise*, ed. Kyle Haselden and Philip Hefner (Garden City, NY: Doubleday, 1968), 12.

6. On these developments, see LeRon Shults, *Reforming Theological Anthropology: After the Relational Turn* (Grand Rapids: Eerdmans, 2003), 163–88.

7. Malcolm Jeeves, "Brains, Minds, Souls, and People: A Scientific Perspective on Complex Human Personhood," in *The Depth of the Human Person: A Multidisciplinary Approach*, ed. Michael Welker (Grand Rapids: Eerdmans, 2014), 102.

8. E.g., see Joel Green, "'Bodies—That Is, Human Lives': A Re-examination of Human Nature in the Bible," in *Whatever Happened to the Soul? Scientific and Theological Portraits of Human Nature*, ed. Warren Brown, Nancey Murphy, and H. Newton Malony (Minneapolis: Fortress, 1998), 149–73. For a notable exception, see John Cooper, *Body, Soul and Life Everlasting: Biblical Anthropology and the Monism-Dualism Debate*, 2nd ed. (Grand Rapids: Eerdmans, 2001).

9. See the arguments by Howard Robinson, J. P. Moreland, Stewart Goetz, Charles Taliaferro, Keith Yandell, and others. Other more exotic, nonphysicalist species are also gaining attention—e.g.,

more functional approaches have outstripped substantivalist ways of thinking about personhood. On these views, the image of God inheres in our capacity to relate with others or to enact the cultural mandate.

Nonetheless, these shifts away from dualism are mistaken. Some form of soul-body dualism was overwhelmingly the consensus of the church—Roman Catholic, Orthodox, and Protestant—either as substance dualism which casts soul and body as distinct substances (with the soul permeating every part of the body) or as hylomorphism which holds the soul as the form of the body (the soul organizes matter to be a living body). As one Christian materialist concedes, "Most, if not all, orthodox Christian theologians of the early church were anthropological dualists."[10] In line with that tradition, the central thesis of this chapter is that anthropological dualism makes the best sense of the human experience of sin. First, I critically examine three Christian physicalist approaches that have tried, and failed, to offer compelling accounts of moral responsibility. I then argue that the biblical presentation of sin assumes that human persons are embodied souls, which suggests that dualism offers a more plausible ontological basis for moral responsibility and culpable sin. In the final section, I clarify lingering questions about causal and theological determinism.

CHRISTIAN PHYSICALISM AND THE DOCTRINE OF SIN

Reflecting on the mystery of conscious experience, the late philosopher of mind Jerry Fodor confessed: "Nobody has the slightest idea how anything material could be conscious. Nobody even knows what it would be like to have the slightest idea about how anything material could be conscious. So much for the philosophy of consciousness."[11] David Chalmers dubbed this conundrum the "hard" problem of consciousness.[12] I think there is a corresponding *hard problem of sin*—namely, can Christian physicalism fully account for the reality of sin? If it cannot, the stock value of dualism rises.[13] The biblical story casts all people as *sinners* in need of divine grace.

Joshua Farris and S. Mark Hamilton, eds., *Idealism and Christian Theology* (New York: Bloomsbury, 2017); William Seager, ed., *The Routledge Handbook of Panpsychism* (New York: Routledge, 2018).

10. Kevin Corcoran, *Rethinking Human Nature: A Christian Materialist Alternative to the Soul* (Grand Rapids: Baker Academic, 2006), 121.

11. Jerry Fodor, "The Big Idea: Can There Be a Science of Mind?" *Times Literary Supplement* (July 3, 1992): 5.

12. David Chalmers, "Facing Up to the Problem of Consciousness," *Journal of Consciousness Studies* 2, no. 3 (1995): 200–219.

13. Dualism is not the only nonmaterialist option; for example, panpsychism and idealism are other contenders. But since I'm making a hamartiological case for dualism, I largely ignore them in the present essay.

In the words of the liturgy, "Most merciful God, we confess that we have sinned against you in thought, word, and deed, by what we have done and by what we have left undone." Christianity collapses without a viable notion of moral responsibility; this is the hard problem of sin.[14] Christian materialists have offered various lines of response; I will review three of them in the writings of Joel Green, Nancey Murphy, and Philip Clayton.[15]

JOEL GREEN AND THE BIBLICAL WITNESS

In *Body, Soul, and Human Life*, Green devotes one chapter to this question: "If, as cognitive science urges, thought and intent are embodied, most of our thought occurs at a subconscious level, and our behavior is generated preconsciously, do the findings of the cognitive sciences not stand in tension with traditional views of freedom and sin?"[16] He answers no and provides justification by drawing neurobiology into dialogue with the New Testament, specifically 1 Peter, James, and Romans.[17]

The epistle of 1 Peter captures how human lives are enmeshed in sin. Christians used to live in a "former time of ignorance" (1:14), not realizing "the emptiness of [our] inherited way of life" (1:18). We were caught up in a "flood of unrestrained immorality" (4:4), living lives full of "acts of unrestraint, lust, drunkenness, . . . and unseemly idolatry" (4:3).[18] Sin pervades our lives and patterns of thought. Green highlights these features and insists that for Peter the pervasiveness of sin never excuses individual sin. As Green says, "Genuine choice can come only in the context of authentic options, and this highlights both the profundity of Peter's diagnosis of sin-as-power and the importance for him of the work of the Spirit in hearing the good news."[19] We are at God's mercy.

Green is signaling points of convergence between neurobiology and biblical theology. According to 1 Peter, human freedom is very constrained, precisely what neurobiology is telling us. Green thus finds it ironic that human freedom is often seen as *the* point of tension between hamartiology

---

14. By "moral responsibility," I am not taking sides on the various responsibility theories; I simply mean that our ascriptions of praise and blame are appropriate and deserved.

15. Derk Pereboom defends Christianity *without* moral responsibility "in the basic desert sense"—I find his position impossible to square with Scripture and catholic tradition (not least the doctrine of hell). Cf. Derk Pereboom, "Libertarianism and Theological Determinism," in *Free Will and Theism: Connections, Contingencies, and Concerns*, ed. Kevin Timpe and Daniel Speak (New York: Oxford University Press, 2016), 112–31.

16. Joel Green, *Body, Soul, and Human Life: The Nature of Humanity in the Bible* (Grand Rapids: Baker Academic, 2008), 87.

17. My summary of Green's exegesis comes from *Body, Soul, and Human Life*, 72–105.

18. For the sake of argument, I am using Green's versions of the cited passages in this section.

19. Green, *Body, Soul, and Human Life*, 90.

and neurobiology. The misunderstanding, he suspects, lies in the fact that many Christians harbor naïve notions of moral responsibility and "self-conscious agency." Drawing on Peter, Green argues instead that our freedom is always constrained by innate sinfulness and the sinful structures of society.

In James, human desire—not God—is the source of sinful temptation. Because sin comes from within, the gospel must be internalized, for it is the power of God for salvation. Once again, Green is shining the light on connections between neurobiology and biblical theology. The scientific evidence suggests that character and behavior are deeply shaped neuro-biologically; similarly, the biblical evidence suggests that character and behavior are deeply shaped by sin. Green's analysis of Romans follows the same script. He concludes that there is no conflict between scientific and biblical pictures of freedom.

Green's implicit critique of libertarian assumptions makes him an unlikely ally with Augustinian, Lutheran, and Reformed traditions. However, he assumes without warrant that the neuroscientific evidence entails physicalism; he imposes that philosophical assumption on the exegetical data. But, more significantly, there is an unresolved ambiguity in his bridge-building between neurobiology and Scripture. At face value, he seems to be defending a neurobiological determinism, which is no hamartiology at all. If neurobiological determinism is true, then sin is biologically inevitable, and sinfulness seems to be *constitutive* of humanity. Given an evolutionary creationism without a historical fall,[20] God has then created us sinners and is thus responsible for our depraved natures. Green dodges this unhappy inference by insisting we are neurobiologically *inclined*—not determined—to sin. He justifies this move largely by appealing to top-down causation (on which, more below),[21] but it is hard to make sense of top-down causation and whether it is even coherent within a physicalist paradigm. Since Green doesn't defend this concept, he merely begs the question. Moral responsibility appears out of nowhere.

NANCEY MURPHY AND NONREDUCTIVE PHYSICALISM
Nancey Murphy provides the missing theoretical pieces in her account of moral responsibility under the auspices of nonreductive physicalism. She describes reality as a hierarchy of levels with no new metaphysical entities

---

20. Cf. Joel Green, "'Adam, What Have You Done?' New Testament Voices on the Origins of Sin," in *Evolution and the Fall*, ed. William Cavanaugh and James K. A. Smith (Grand Rapids: Eerdmans, 2017), 98–116.

21. Green, *Body, Soul, and Human Life*, 104.

added as we move from the lower- to the higher-level processes. There are only physical substances (hence *physicalism*). But Murphy also accepts the reality of genuine mental properties that have intrinsic causal powers; the direction of causation does not run only bottom-up (hence *nonreductive*). The laws described in the higher-level sciences are not reducible to the laws of physics. But how does this work exactly?

Murphy, in her early work, appealed to the concept of *supervenience*. On this view, while it is true that the physical is all there is, rationality and free will cannot be causally reduced to physical properties. The mental is dependent on the physical but not reducible to it. Critics of the supervenience relation, however, worry that it tries to have its cake and eat it too. In several influential essays, Jaegwon Kim leveled precisely that criticism: "If a relation is weak enough to be nonreductive, it tends to be too weak to serve as a dependence relation; conversely, when a relation is strong enough to give us dependence, it tends to be too strong—strong enough to imply reducibility."[22] The "physicalism" in nonreductive physicalism is doing all the work; the "nonreductive" part is impotent.[23]

Murphy concedes that a viable nonreductive physicalism needs more than supervenience.[24] So she recruits the concept of "downward" or "whole-part" causation. Downward causation implies that higher level entities can have genuine causal powers without breaking causal closure at the micro level. Physical substances still have a complete monopoly on reality, but the causal powers of the higher-level entities are not reducible to the properties of the constituent parts. Lower-level entities exist in larger systems, which can then exert specific constraints on their constituent parts. Those broader systems set boundary conditions that constrain the parts without abrogating the laws of physics.

In Murphy's anthropology, human persons are not substances but complex, dynamic, nonlinear information processing systems. Washing her hands of any reductive notions of mechanisms and aggregates, she relocates the level of description from the atom to the organism; the properties

---

22. Jaegwon Kim, *Supervenience and Mind: Selected Philosophical Essays* (New York: Cambridge University Press, 1993), 276.

23. Nancey Murphy has challenged Kim's critique of nonreductive physicalism in Murphy and Warren Brown, *Did My Neurons Make Me Do It? Philosophical and Neurobiological Perspectives on Moral Responsibility and Free Will* (Oxford: Oxford University Press, 2007), 233–36.

24. She concedes this point in an exchange with Lindsay Cullen who argued that Murphy's application of the supervenience relation is too idiosyncratic, "eccentric," and "unhelpful." Cf. Lindsay Cullen, "Nancey Murphy, Supervenience and Causality," *Science and Christian Belief* 13 (2001): 39–50, at 39. Murphy's rejoinder is in "Response to Cullen," *Science and Christian Belief* 13 (2001): 161–63.

of the constituents are precisely dependent on their place in the larger system. Human beings just are relations and processes that are subject to causal feedback loops. Organic systems grow in complexity as we move from prokaryotic to eukaryotic cells, and by the time we arrive at Homo sapiens, the level of information processing and self-recognition has become so complex that we are compelled to invoke theories of language, self-transcendence, and full-blown moral responsibility.[25]

Despite her rich conceptual apparatus, Murphy's account fails. I agree with Jaegwon Kim that supervenience cannot secure genuine mental causation. Her additional category of whole-part causation is only plausible if one redefines human beings as a hierarchy of levels or systems, but "levels" or "systems" are inadequate to yield real causal *powers*. Granted, Murphy reinterprets humans as "relations" and "processes," but such ideas do not capture a robust enough notion of moral agency—they are *impersonal* levels of organization, not concrete subjects or persons. Causal reductionism remains a clear and present danger.[26] In the end, Murphy's nonreductive physicalism yields a reductive, deterministic account of the mind. She is yet to find a credible alchemy that can transmute neurobiology into the gold of moral agency.

PHILIP CLAYTON AND EMERGENTISM

Hunting for the same holy grail, Philip Clayton seeks a middle position between reductive physicalism and supernatural dualism. The operative category is *emergence*: "Although physical structures and causes may determine the initial emergence of the mental, they do not fully or solely determine the outcome of the mental life subsequent to its emergence."[27] According to Clayton, a viable notion of moral responsibility requires *strong* emergence, that is, the appearance of actual new entities. By "emergence," Clayton means more than whole-part causation; the emergent level should have distinct laws and causal activities, which in turn have real influence on the lower levels.

Clayton points to multiple cases of new and unpredictable phenomena that have emerged *naturally* during evolution as a result of increasing

---

25. For detailed defense, see Murphy and Brown, *Did My Neurons Make Me Do It?*

26. Cf. William Hasker, "On Behalf of Emergent Dualism," in *In Search of the Soul: Four Views*, ed. Joel Green and Stuart Palmer (Downers Grove, IL: InterVarsity, 2005), 89: "If the higher-level organization is to make a difference, it can only do this by *affecting the interactions of the constituents at the base level*—but this it is forbidden to do by the thesis of microdeterminism. Causal reduction has in no way been avoided."

27. Philip Clayton, "Neuroscience, the Human Person, and God," in *Bridging Science and Religion*, ed. Ted Peters and Gaymon Bennett (Minneapolis: Fortress, 2003), 108.

complexity in the biosphere. The natural world, he says, is full of new emergent levels of reality, such as eddies at the base of a waterfall, the formation of snow crystals and snowflakes, or the evolution of new organisms—we could not have predicted any of these phenomena from their constituent particles. Clayton chronicles countless examples of new emergent levels across a range of disciplines like physics, chemistry, and biology.[28] Admittedly not all of them are genuine instances of the *strong* emergence that Clayton thinks we need for moral agency.

But human consciousness is a clear exception. Clayton showcases the mind as strong emergence *par excellence*. This theory of emergence is not emergent *dualism* by another name; rather, it is a thesis about *natural* history. Dualism implies that the world contains only physical and mental causes, but Clayton's notion of emergence—what he calls "ontological pluralism"— posits that there are many different levels of reality and many different kinds of causes. The human mind is only one of many emergent properties in the universe. Natural emergentism replaces supernatural dualism. As Clayton puts it, "Really distinct levels occur within the one natural world and . . . objects on various levels can be ontologically primitive . . . rather than being understood merely as aggregates of lower-level, foundational particles."[29] This is not your old-fashioned dualistic kingdom; Clayton's proposal is a modern, democratic, pluralistic ontology.

That's all well and good, but Clayton is looking for the possibility of genuine freedom, an ontological level of reality that is not bounded by finite causal structures. We only seem to have an ontological horizon of *finite* causes, Clayton argues, of which we humans are a part; that horizon cannot give us enduring spirit. How do we know that our capacity for moral agency is not merely an evolutionary epiphenomenon? Clayton offers a transcendental argument—he posits an *infinite* ontological ground which renders real moral agency possible in the world. By positing God's existence, we can justify the existence of other morally free agents in the world. God who possesses freedom preeminently *must* exist if we are to be truly free.

This transcendental argument overpromises. It is true we all live *as if* we are free, but it does not follow that the "infinite horizon" of theism is the right one. Perhaps we are self-deceived—maybe it *is* atoms and quarks all the way down. The transcendental argument merely begs the question;

---

28. Cf. Philip Clayton, *Mind and Emergence: From Quantum to Chaos* (Oxford: Oxford University Press, 2004).

29. Clayton, *Mind and Emergence*, 62.

it assumes moral responsibility without offering any grounds for doing so. As one commentator writes, "That is why such arguments rarely, if ever, convince anyone; despite their usefulness as a 'rumor of angels,' transcendental arguments always leave one with the nagging doubt that the infinite horizon toward which we strain may, in the end, be more illusion than reality."[30] In Clayton's transcendental argument for moral agency, God does all the real metaphysical work. What is missing is an account of human sinfulness that has an ontological frame of reference in human beings themselves, not in opposition to, or in competition with God's transcendence and immanence, but precisely as a metaphysically subordinate, dependent, and yet genuine creaturely reality.

These three accounts of Christian materialism are representative of recent proposals at the interface of science and theology, yet none of them ultimately delivers. As we review supervenience, top-down causation, and emergence, none of these moves can avoid causal reduction within a complex feedback system. The hard problem of sin remains. In light of these heroic efforts to keep spiritual entities out of the explanation of human persons, one wonders what is the end game? If their aim is to show that biblical faith can hang with world-class secular science, such Christians must still acknowledge a *spiritual Creator* who allegedly sets up the conditions for natural emergence. But then a spiritual creator is offensive to secular scientists whose approval motivated emergence theory in the first place. If we accept embarrassment at *that* level, why not accept it at the level of spiritual human persons as well?

SIN AND DUALISM IN THE BIBLICAL TRADITION

These efforts to save moral responsibility within the bounds of physicalism reflect a much broader discussion. Is free will possible in a physical world? Does quantum indeterminacy imply that our actions are undetermined? Am I responsible for actions that are determined by subconscious neurological events? Building on a free will debate that stretches back to antiquity, the current philosophical debates tend to focus on whether free will is compatible with causal determinism (the view that every event is necessitated by prior events together with the laws of nature). Compatibilists reply yes; incompatibilists say no. Contemporary philosophers have addressed

---

30. Larry Chapp, review of *Is Nature Enough*, by John Haught, *Modern Theology* 23 (2007): 643.

these questions with a wide range of ingenious solutions, the various proposals swelling in erudition and complexity.[31]

However, this philosophical literature is usually abstracted from the biblical material or any distinctive theological tradition. Furthermore, the scientific picture still sets the agenda for the debate. Christian theology should engage their proposals with gratitude, but critically, in ad hoc fashion (that is, philosophy should play a ministerial not magisterial role). It is also noteworthy that most philosophers of mind reject dualism, with their Christian counterparts following not far behind.[32] In the present milieu, the doctrine of sin can offer a needed dogmatic corrective to common philosophical intuitions—or so I shall argue.

FREEDOM AND ORIGINAL SIN

Our very existence as fallen creatures is conditioned by sin, antecedent to any actual sinful desires or deeds (cf. Rom 5:12–21; 1 Cor 15:21–22). In his riposte to Erasmus, Martin Luther maintained that human wills are bound to sin and need transformation by divine grace.[33] Beyond Luther, the magisterial Reformers agreed that our wills are fallen and conditioned by original sin. This broadly Augustinian picture was enshrined as sober truth in Protestant confessional statements. For example,

> It is taught among us that since the fall of Adam, all human beings who are born in the natural way are conceived and born in sin. This means that from birth they are full of evil lust and inclination and cannot by nature possess true fear of God and true faith in God. Moreover, this same innate disease and original sin is truly sin and condemns to God's eternal wrath all who are not in turn born anew through baptism and the Holy Spirit.[34]

> The condition of man after the fall of Adam is such, that he cannot turn and prepare himself, by his own natural strength and good works, to faith,

---

31. E.g., see Michael McKenna and Derk Pereboom, *Free Will: A Contemporary Introduction* (New York: Routledge, 2016); Robert Kane, ed., *The Oxford Handbook of Free Will*, 2nd ed. (New York: Oxford University Press, 2011). For a lucid primer, see Aku Visala, "Free Will, Moral Responsibility and the Sciences: A Brief Overview," *ESSAT News & Reviews* 26, no. 3 (2016): 5–19.

32. For the dominance of physicalism among philosophers, see David Bourget and David Chalmers, "What Do Philosophers Believe?" *Philosophical Studies* 170, no. 3 (2014): 465–500, at 476 and 496.

33. Cf. E. Gordon Rupp, ed., *Luther and Erasmus: Free Will and Salvation* (Louisville: Westminster John Knox, 2006).

34. The Augsburg Confession (1531) in *The Book of Concord: The Confessions of the Evangelical Lutheran Church*, ed. Robert Kolb and Timothy Wengert (Minneapolis: Fortress, 2000), 37–38.

and calling upon God: Wherefore we have no power to do good works pleasant and acceptable to God, without the grace of God by Christ preventing us that we may have a good will, and working with us when we have that good will.[35]

From this original corruption [of our first parents], whereby we are utterly indisposed, disabled, and made opposite to all good, and wholly inclined to all evil, do proceed all actual transgressions. . . . This corruption of nature, during this life, doth remain in those that are regenerated; and although it be, through Christ, pardoned and mortified, yet both itself and all the motions thereof are truly and properly sin.[36]

The doctrine of original sin reconfigures the contemporary free will debate.[37] On the one hand, God condemns high-handed sins like adultery, murder, theft, bearing false witness, and the like (e.g., Deut 5:6–21). One might think that people have the capacity to avoid overt, deliberate rebellion against God, that they can make a conscious choice for good. On the other hand, the voluntarist dimension to sin is only one side of the coin. In the biblical picture, sin is also portrayed as a deeper, more sinister reality. Sin is a slave master, and we are its captives; rather than controlling sin, it controls us. In the Pauline self-diagnosis, "I am unspiritual, sold as a slave to sin. I do not understand what I do. For what I want to do I do not do, but what I hate I do" (Rom 7:14–15 NIV). Sin is inevitable, despite the best will to change.[38]

Many have rejected the traditional Augustinian picture because it is allegedly paradoxical—"that sin is *both* unavoidable *and* culpable is logically incoherent."[39] This inference is wide of the mark for two reasons. In the first place, each of us is born in a state of original guilt and corruption because all humanity was implicated in Adam's fall; that we all thereby invariably sin is not incoherent or unfair.[40] In any case, sin's inevitability *in general* is

---

35. The Thirty-Nine Articles of the Church of England (1571), in *Creeds and Confessions of Faith in the Christian Tradition*, vol. 2, ed. Jaroslav Pelikan and Valerie Hotchkiss (New Haven: Yale University Press, 2003), 531.

36. The Westminster Confession of Faith (1647), in *Creeds and Confessions of Faith*, 614.

37. I accept a broadly Augustinian hamartiology, but I can only assume it here without argument. For my defense of a traditional doctrine of original sin, see Madueme, "An Augustinian-Reformed Perspective," in *Five Views on the Fall and Original Sin*, ed. Chad Meister and James Stump (Downers Grove, IL: InterVarsity, forthcoming).

38. I am drawing on Edward Welch, *Addictions: A Banquet in the Grave* (Phillipsburg: P&R, 2001), 33.

39. Ian McFarland, "The Fall and Sin," in *The Oxford Handbook of Systematic Theology*, ed. John Webster, Kathryn Tanner, and Iain Torrance (New York: Oxford University Press, 2007), 145. McFarland himself does not think the Augustinian view is incoherent.

40. I recognize these are contested claims—especially original *guilt*—but space prevents me from defending this position. See Madueme, "An Augustinian-Reformed Perspective."

consistent with my ability to avoid sinning *on any specific occasion*. In the second place, Scripture never endorses an autonomous free will but instead depicts us as slaves to sin *and also* fully responsible. The biblical story falls apart without this latter notion of accountability.[41]

Sin is therefore better understood in Scripture as a compatibilist, not libertarian, phenomenon.[42] As Jesse Couenhoven notes, "Emphasizing [libertarian] control has distracted us from noticing that we have very little control . . . over a wide range of beliefs, cares, desires, inattentions, and even volitions that we commonly consider persons responsible for."[43] Moral agency, seen through the biblical lens, is more "self-disclosure" than "self-making."[44] Jesus said that evil thoughts, murder, adultery, and other such sins flow "out of the heart" (Matt 15:19). Our sins arise from "the overflow of the heart" (Matt 12:34)—the "heart" is what most fully discloses *me* (e.g., Gen 6:5; Pss 14; 58:3; Mark 7:21; Rom 3:9–20). Human persons are therefore culpable before God for internal desires or external actions that truly disclose their hearts. The individual in the presence of God is the proximate explanation for why anyone sins—"Against you, you only, have *I* sinned" (Ps 51:4). I call this canonical picture of moral agency *compatibilist agent-causation*.[45]

Attempts to secure agent-causation within a physicalist framework are not robust enough to capture the sense of ownership implicit in Scripture.[46] A *dualistic* anthropology makes better sense of compatibilist agent-causation for several reasons. First, since physicalism implies a causal

---

41. Scripture irrevocably ties the sobering reality of moral responsibility to the costly gift of redemption (e.g., Eph 2:3–10; Col 2:13–14). Cf. Bonnie Howe, "Accountability," in *Dictionary of Scripture and Ethics*, ed. Joel Green (Grand Rapids: Baker Academic, 2011), 37–39.

42. Biblical or theological compatibilism, as I define these terms, rejects the idea that God's providence over human choices is achieved by divine manipulation of natural causality. As I clarify below, God determines all events much like an author narrates the characters and events in a story; I thus depart from natural deterministic compatibilist accounts that are common in the philosophical literature.

43. Jesse Couenhoven, *Stricken by Sin, Cured by Christ: Agency, Necessity, and Culpability in Augustinian Theology* (New York: Oxford University Press, 2013), 127.

44. Jesse Couenhoven, "What Sin Is: A Differential Analysis," *Modern Theology* 25, no. 4 (2009): 577.

45. Among philosophers, agent-causation typically accompanies *indeterminism*, but agent-causation is actually motivated by anti-reductionism and is therefore separable from the incompatibilism vs. compatibilism debate. Cf. Ned Markosian, "A Compatibilist Version of the Theory of Agent Causation," *Pacific Philosophical Quarterly* 80 (1999): 257–77; Dana Nelkin, *Making Sense of Freedom and Responsibility* (New York: Oxford University Press, 2011); and, strikingly, Christopher Franklin, "If Anyone Should Be an Agent-Causalist, then Everyone Should Be an Agent-Causalist," *Mind* 125 (2016): 1101–31. However, my *theological* compatibilism eschews physical causal determinism.

46. For examples of this strategy, see Markosian, "A Compatibilist Version," 260; Randolph Clarke, *Libertarian Accounts of Free Will* (Oxford: Oxford University Press, 2003), 210; Helen Steward, *A Metaphysics for Freedom* (Oxford: Oxford University Press, 2012), 16n37, and *passim*.

chain of deterministic microphysical events, my desires and/or actions are not up to me in the morally relevant sense. Second, the more robust sense of moral agency afforded by dualism allows for human sinning that is "by *my* fault, by *my* own fault, by *my* own most grievous fault"—as the Lutheran liturgy avows.[47] That means humans are the proximate source of our own iniquities, and *God* is not directly responsible for our wayward desires and actions.[48] And third, even if for the sake of argument physicalism can offer a plausible account of agent-causation, dualism coheres better with other dogmatic commitments (I will return to this question of dogmatic fit).

ON SCRIPTURE'S DUALISTIC ASSUMPTIONS

Scripture presents a holistic picture of human persons. God made us embodied creatures. The wide range of anthropological terms in the Bible (e.g., *nephesh, ruach, psuche, nous, pneuma*) do not refer to isolated parts of the human constitution. As John Cooper admits, "Modern scholars largely agree [that these anthropological terms] pick out distinct but overlapping and interdependent aspects, powers, and functions that constitute an integral existential unity."[49] Anthropological holism is true, but that does not entail physicalism. Robert Gundry remarked, "It is not so much that the Bible teaches dualistic anthropology as it is that what it teaches on other matters often depends on the dualistic anthropology it presupposes."[50] Just so, the biblical depiction of sin takes dualism for granted.[51]

I will defend this claim by briefly examining four biblical texts: Matthew 5:27–30; Mark 7:19–23; Romans 2:28–29; and Ezekiel 36:26–27. They represent a range of texts throughout the Bible that contrast the inner and outer man, the material and the immaterial (e.g., 2 Cor 4:16). While the biblical authors reject any gnostic ideas that demonize the physical body, they do present the inner person as the ultimate source of volition, will, and moral responsibility. A dualistic anthropology fits hand in glove.

47. *Lutheran Book of Worship* (Minneapolis: Augsburg, 1978), 42, my emphasis.
48. For a helpful essay that complements my claims about agent-causation, see Meghan Griffith, "Agent Causation and Theism," in *Free Will and Theism: Connections, Contingencies, and Concerns*, ed. Kevin Timpe and Daniel Speak (New York: Oxford University Press, 2016), 172–94, esp. 190–93. To clarify, Griffith only argues for agent causation, *not* dualism.
49. John Cooper, "Scripture and Philosophy on the Unity of the Body and Soul: An Integrative Method for Theological Anthropology," in *The Ashgate Research Companion to Theological Anthropology*, ed. Joshua Farris and Charles Taliaferro (Abingdon: Ashgate, 2015), 31.
50. Robert Gundry, *The Old Is Better: New Testament Essays in Support of Traditional Interpretations* (Tübingen: Mohr Siebeck, 2005), 192.
51. Even if Scripture does not explicitly teach a dualistic anthropology, dualism may still be one of its philosophical implications. See Cooper, *Body, Soul and Life Everlasting*, 100–102.

The Sermon on the Mount warns that if you look at a woman lustfully you have already committed adultery with her in your heart (Matt 5:28). Jesus explains that the inner thought, not the external act, is the ultimate origin of sin. There is a distinction made between adultery of the heart (cause) and physical adultery (effect). Coveting someone's possession is the root sin, stealing it a manifestation. As one commentator puts it, "The culprit lies elsewhere, in the heart, the inner person."[52] The source of sin lies beyond the physical body and its outward actions.

A similar dynamic appears in Mark 7:19–23 (par. Matt 15:17–19). The Pharisees thought that sin could be transmitted physically, by unclean hands contaminating the food which would then contaminate the person. Jesus argues instead that sin is not fundamentally a problem of ritual uncleanness but a *spiritual* problem. Sin does not contaminate from the outside, for whatever enters the mouth passes through the stomach and is discharged from the body. Moral depravity arises from the nonphysical. "For from within, out of men's hearts, come evil thoughts, sexual immorality, theft, murder, adultery, greed, malice, deceit, lewdness, envy, slander, arrogance and folly" (Mark 7:21). As Calvin put it, "Man's heart is the seat of all evils."[53]

Consider Romans 2:28–29. The apostle Paul insists that being outwardly Jewish is inadequate; spiritual circumcision is not merely outward and physical (*en sarki*). "No," Paul writes, "a man is a Jew if he is one *inwardly*; and circumcision is circumcision *of the heart*, by the Spirit, not by the written code" (v. 29, emphasis added). This contrast between the "inner" and "outer" parts of the person is not just a perspective on a larger monistic whole; it is best understood by a deeper immaterial versus material reality. True circumcision, H. C. G. Moule commented, is "a work *on the soul*, wrought by God's Spirit, not . . . a legal claim supposed to rest upon a routine of prescribed observances."[54] Certainly regeneration and human sinfulness apply to the *whole* person. Nonetheless, Paul's claims about the seat of sin and the object of regeneration presuppose an inner person who is not exhausted by material, physical reality.

---

52. Donald Hagner, *Matthew 1–13*, WBC 33A (Dallas: Word, 1993), 121. As Robert Gundry remarks: "Against 'heart' stand 'eye', 'hand', 'members', and 'body' in verses 29–30" (Gundry, *Sōma in Biblical Theology, with Emphasis on Pauline Anthropology* [Cambridge: Cambridge University Press, 1976], 111).

53. John Calvin, *A Harmony of the Gospels: Matthew, Mark and Luke*, trans. A. W. Morrison (Grand Rapids: Eerdmans, 1972), 165, on Matt 15:19.

54. H. C. G. Moule, *The Epistle to the Romans* (Fort Washington: Christian Literature Crusade, 1975), 73, my emphasis.

Jesus and the apostles did not engage in metaphysical speculation. Nowhere does their teaching lay out an explicit philosophical anthropology. But the biblical language has an *implicit* anthropology. It is not enough to say, as some Christian physicalists do, that the "inner" and "outer" terms are only aspects of an indivisible, physical whole; nor does it suffice to say that the "inner"/"heart" terms are merely references to our corrupted desires. Physicalism does not adequately explain the emphatic contrasts in the biblical texts ("not . . . but")—for example, "*not* heart . . . *but* stomach" (Mark 7:19); "*not* outward and physical/flesh . . . *but* inward" (Rom 2:28–29). This contrast is found in other texts too (e.g., Matt 10:28—"body *but not* soul"; perhaps also Rom 7:21–24). Yet it is difficult to feel the force of the warning in Matthew 10:28 if body and soul are not separable. The most plausible significance of the biblical language is that the volitional, moral core of humanity is not exhausted by the physical.

The ontological distinction between body and heart is also previewed, famously, in Ezekiel 36:26–27 (cf. Jer 31:31–34). The heart stands in metaphorically for the inner person, the seat of the mind and thought, decision and will.[55] Ezekiel promises that Yahweh will give his people a new heart and a new spirit, replacing the heart of stone with a heart of flesh (Ezek 36:26; cf. 11:19). These rich metaphors do not refer to physical realities, "for what could circumcision of the foreskin of the heart possibly mean unless the term 'heart' has lost its physical connotation?"[56] On the physicalist view, these divine promises have no metaphysical implications and merely refer to new spiritual desires and habits; while true as far is it goes, it falls short of the radical transformation implied in these texts. Ezekiel is an anticipation of the same inner–outer contrast in Mark 7:19–23 and Matthew 15:17–19. Human sinfulness is a problem that tracks deeper than our physical bodies. This problem inheres in our very souls.[57]

Our experience of sin is usually conditioned by embodiment. Scripture assumes a tight connection between the frailty of our bodies and our sinful

---

55. Walther Eichrodt, *Ezekiel: A Commentary*, trans. Cosslett Quin (London: SCM, 1970), 499; Christopher J. H. Wright, *The Message of Ezekiel: A New Heart and a New Spirit* (Downers Grove, IL: InterVarsity, 2001), 296.

56. Gundry, *Sōma in Biblical Theology*, 126.

57. Regarding the implicit dualism of Scripture, a physicalist might respond that the biblical authors were reflecting their own limited (ancient) scientific knowledge; we now know far more scientifically about the human constitution. This objection opens up difficult questions about divine accommodation that would take us too far afield; minimally, however, it risks placing undue confidence in current scientific, extrabiblical knowledge. E.g., see Vern Poythress, "Rethinking Accommodation in Revelation," *Westminster Theological Journal* 76 (2014): 143–56; and for historical background, see Glenn Sunshine, "Accommodation Historically Considered," in *The Enduring Authority of the Christian Scriptures*, ed. D. A. Carson (Grand Rapids: Eerdmans, 2016), 238–65.

condition.[58] Sin reigns in our mortal bodies (Rom 6:12), typically exerting its power over us *through* our bodies; it uses the body as an instrument of wickedness (Rom 6:13). Humans are embodied souls, higher than animals but a little lower than angels (Ps 8:4–6). Embodiment gives our sins a "bodily" character. As Herman Bavinck clarifies, "While the sensual nature of humans is not itself sin, nor the source or principle of sin, *it is its dwelling place.*"[59] Sin is not physical, but it operates in and through the physical body (Rom 7:23)—"corporeal flesh is weak because of its physical needs and desires, and therefore easy prey for sin."[60] We serve our bodily appetites instead of the Lord Jesus (Rom 16:18); our minds are distracted by earthly things and our stomach becomes our god (Phil 3:19). Creaturely desires are a divine gift, but they are also expressed by "misdeeds of the body" (Rom 8:13).

Dualism makes better sense of human sinning than physicalism. It is difficult to understand how moral responsibility can emerge from a material base. How would it be possible, given material determinism, for a physical thing to sin? But Christian physicalists have responded with a "parity thesis"—namely, it is hard to understand how moral responsibility can emerge from an *immaterial* base. How would it be possible, given immaterial determinism, for an immaterial thing to sin? *Tu quoque*, what's good for the goose is good for the gander.[61] However, I reject the parity thesis because fallen angels—demons—are immaterial creatures *and* quintessential sinners.[62] Ergo, there is nothing mysterious about immaterial creatures who have the capacity to sin.

The crux of the matter is this. The kind of moral agency presupposed throughout Scripture, I have argued, is most consistent with agent-causation in the context of divine determinism. When human desires, choices, and actions truly disclose who I am, they cannot be reduced to part of a causal chain of physical events. Immateriality as such does not automatically resolve this problem, as there are deterministic accounts of dualism in which every

---

58. Herman Bavinck, *Reformed Dogmatics*, vol. 3, *Sin and Salvation in Christ*, ed. John Bolt, trans. John Vriend (Grand Rapids: Baker Academic, 2006), 55.

59. Bavinck, *Reformed Dogmatics*, 3:55, emphasis added.

60. Gundry, *Sōma in Biblical Theology*, 137.

61. Cf. Clifford Williams, "Christian Materialism and the Parity Thesis," *International Journal for Philosophy of Religion* 39 (1996): 1–14, which triggered a protracted exchange with J. P. Moreland. The parity thesis is deployed in Peter van Inwagen, *Metaphysics*, 4th ed. (New York: Westview, 2015), 234–37; Corcoran, *Rethinking Human Nature*, 61–63.

62. On the medieval dispute over the immateriality of angels and demons, see John Wippel, "Metaphysical Composition of Angels in Bonaventure, Aquinas, and Godfrey of Fontaines," in *A Companion to Angels in Medieval Philosophy*, ed. Tobias Hoffmann (Leiden: Brill, 2012), 45–78.

mental state is caused by prior mental states. However, my claim is that in the biblical perspective, the soul *grounds* ownership and responsibility; the soul is the metaphysical basis on which I transcend and act upon chains of causal determinism, whether that determinism be physical, biological, psychological, or socio-cultural. Therefore, the threat of "immaterial determinism" is largely a red herring because the soul, as designed by God, is not an entity that is caused by, or dependent on, more basic, deterministic mental states. Quite the opposite: mental states and actions are metaphysically dependent, subsidiary *effects* of the ontologically primitive soul.

A CODA ON SIN AND DETERMINISM

Christian hamartiology, I claim, is dualistic, agent-causal, *and* compatibilist. But my argument assumes that causal determinism rules out moral responsibility and, by implication, the reality of sin. I also hail from the Reformed tradition and accept a form of theological determinism.[63] One might object that theological determinism rather obviously *entails* causal determinism. Presumably God exercises his sovereignty by determining all events by means of prior events in conjunction with the laws of nature; and if so, causal determinism holds true after all, moral responsibility thereby vanishes, and—*voilà!*—my thesis collapses.

At this point I happily concede an irreducible level of mystery; some aspects of God's sovereignty are beyond our ken. In what follows, then, I offer *a* possible way of holding theological determinism consistently with an agent causal, dualistic anthropology. In my view, physical causal determinism offers a reductive understanding of moral agency that contradicts the biblical picture. There are different kinds of determinisms, and they are not all mutually entailing. Specifically, theological determinism (i.e., *divine* causal determinism) as I define it does not entail physical causal determinism. When God decrees sin, his sovereign rule does not operate as one among many other "intramundane" causes (creaturely causes that exist within the nexus of our world). Divine ordination operates on a different level from creaturely, intramundane causation. God's superintendence of human affairs might be considered on the analogy of an author's relationship to the characters and events in a novel. Just like a fiction author,

63. For an alternative take on the Reformed tradition, see Richard Muller, *Divine Will and Human Choice: Freedom, Contingency, and Necessity in Early Modern Reformed Thought* (Grand Rapids: Baker Academic, 2017).

God determines everything that happens in the story. As James Anderson explains, "In a broad sense, the novelist is the first and ultimate sufficient cause of everything that takes place in his creation. Yet at the same time, this authorial causation operates on a very different level than the *intranarrative* causes."[64] So too with God. He is not one more cause in a long sequence of creaturely causes, earlier events necessitating later events. The biblical picture suggests that God is *the Cause*, sustaining and enabling every other creaturely cause. God, of course, does at times act at the horizontal level. As Anderson puts it, "Just as an author can write himself into his own novel, appearing as one character among the others, so God can write himself into the creational storyline."[65]

The objection remains: some think that theological determinism rules out the very idea of sin. According to theological determinism, my sins are the consequences of God's decree in eternity. But, the objection goes, it is not up to me what went on before I was born, and neither is it up to me what God's decrees are. Therefore, *none* of my sins are up to me. So much for moral agency.[66] I have two things to say in reply. First, I reject physical causal determinism because it eviscerates moral agency. My desires and actions are no longer *mine* in a true, meaningful sense, but are traced instead to more fundamental physical forces. Second, theological determinism implies that I lack libertarian or "leeway" freedom, the ability to do otherwise. However, given my commitment to exhaustive divine sovereignty, moral agency does not require *that* kind of freedom anyway; it is sufficient for the agent to be the significant originator or "source" of the action.[67] Accordingly, my main objection to the consequence argument is that it effectively overturns the Creator-creature relationship. I agree that if intramundane causal determinism is true, then we lose moral agency, and God is responsible for human sinning.[68] But the biblical story is clear that God

---

64. James Anderson, "Calvinism and the First Sin," in *Calvinism and the Problem of Evil*, ed. David Alexander and Daniel Johnson (Eugene: Pickwick, 2016), 208–9. This paragraph is indebted to Anderson's essay.

65. Anderson, "Calvinism and the First Sin," 210. Aside from the incarnation, this point applies more generally to special divine action.

66. I'm restating the consequence argument. See Peter van Inwagen, *An Essay on Free Will* (New York: Oxford University Press, 1983), 16.

67. For helpful analysis of "leeway" and "sourcehood" conceptions of freedom, see Kevin Timpe, "Leeway vs. Sourcehood Conceptions of Free Will," in *Routledge Companion to Free Will*, ed. Kevin Timpe, Meghan Griffith, and Neil Levy (London: Routledge, 2017), 213–24.

68. Leigh Vicens's analysis misses this motivation (see her "Free Will and Theological Determinism," in *Routledge Companion to Free Will*, ed. Kevin Timpe, Meghan Griffith, and Neil Levy [London: Routledge, 2017], 515–16). Vicens also interprets Paul Helm as a Calvinist proponent of causal or natural determinism (514), but Helm in context is adopting an *ad hominem* argument,

himself empowers moral agency *within* the intramundane horizon, and he also sovereignly determines everything—including our sinful choices—*apart from* intramundane causation (precisely *how* he does that, I plead agnostic).[69]

CLOSING REFLECTIONS

Most Christian physicalists recognize that science can neither prove physicalism nor falsify dualism. The relation between neural firings and the mind is consistent with *correlation* without causation; the human soul is immaterial and thus inaccessible to empirical science. The debate turns on two principal questions: (1) Does my anthropology resonate with current scientific plausibility structures? (2) Does my anthropology enjoy dogmatic fit with other deliverances of Scripture? Typically, Christian physicalists privilege scientific consonance while Christian dualists favor dogmatic fit. Since our anthropology is *underdetermined* by our current science, the case for dualism is strengthened in making better sense of human sin and in offering greater dogmatic fit with other areas of Christian doctrine.

The doctrine of the intermediate state suggests that we are immaterial souls. "When he opened the fifth seal, I saw under the altar the souls of those who had been slain because of the word of God and the testimony they had maintained. They called out in a loud voice, 'How long, Sovereign Lord, holy and true, until you judge the inhabitants of the earth and avenge our blood?'" (NIV). Revelation 6:9–10 with its disembodied souls of the martyrs is only one of numerous biblical texts that undergird dualism.[70] Such texts press the question of pastoral integrity. Does our anthropological theorizing actually preach? Are we able to minister the consolation of the gospel when someone has died? "She is now with the Lord"—such blessed words are a source of hope and comfort in a time of loss (cf. Phil 1:23–24; 2 Cor 5:6–8).[71] But if the intermediate state doesn't hold, we speak empty

---

which Vicens wrongly glosses as Helm *endorsing* causal determinism. E.g., see Paul Helm, "God, Compatibilism, and the Authorship of Sin," *Religious Studies* 46 (2010): 115–24, at 116–18.

69. I cannot respond here to the "manipulation argument" against divine causal determinism. For recent analysis, see Guillaume Bignon, *Excusing Sinners and Blaming God: A Calvinist Assessment of Determinism, Moral Responsibility, and Divine Involvement in Evil* (Eugene: Pickwick, 2018).

70. Jesus, Peter, and Paul, to name only three, agreed with the Pharisees that dead persons enter a disembodied state before the final resurrection. Cf. N. T. Wright, *The Resurrection of the Son of God* (Minneapolis: Fortress, 2003), 131–34, 190–206, 366–67, 424–26. On Wright's subsequent wobbling on this point, see Stewart Goetz, "Is N. T. Wright Right about Substance Dualism?" *Philosophia Christi* 14, no. 1 (2012): 183–91; Brandon Rickabaugh, "Responding to N. T. Wright's Rejection of the Soul," *Heythrop Journal* 59, no. 2 (2018): 201–20.

71. Cf. Theodore G. Van Raalte, "In Between and Intermediate: My Soul in Heaven's Glory," in *As You See the Day Approaching: Reformed Perspectives on the Last Things*, ed. Theodore G. Van Raalte (Eugene: Pickwick, 2016), 70–111.

platitudes. Christian physicalism seems to lead to pastoral malpractice when followed through consistently.

Dualism is also in harmony with Christology. If it is not true that our lives continue after physical death, then Christ's divine and human natures must have been separated between his death and resurrection. That scenario violates Chalcedon, which insists that the person of Jesus is "to be acknowledged in two natures, inconfusedly, unchangeably, indivisibly, inseparably." Our union with Christ is everlasting and indestructible (see Rom 8:38–39). If Christian physicalism is true, then our lives do *not* continue between death and resurrection, and Christ failed to keep his promise to abide with us always.[72] I put my wager on dogmatic fit over scientific congruence.[73]

In conclusion, let us return to Philip Clayton's emergentism, the strongest account of Christian physicalism I am aware of. He recognizes that modern physics and the scientific method raise difficult questions for special divine action.[74] Clayton discovered that modern thinkers rely on theories about human mental causation in order to understand divine causality.[75] This led him to the following thesis:

> The question of God's relation to the world, and hence the question of how to construe divine action, should be controlled by the best theories we have of the relationship of our minds to our bodies—and then corrected for by the ways in which God's relation to the universe must be different from the relation of our mental properties to our brains and bodies.[76]

The result is Clayton's panentheistic analogy: just as the human mind is to the body, so God is to the world. "God is analogous to the mind which dwells in the body," Clayton writes, "though God is also more than the natural world taken as a whole."[77] Since his emergence thesis implies that human mental causation breaks no natural laws, so too his panentheistic argument reconceives divine action without breaking any natural laws. But notice the method: start with what our best sciences say about human

---

72. I am drawing from Mary Vanden Berg, "The Impact of a Gap in Existence on Christology and Soteriology: A Challenge for Physicalists," *Calvin Theological Journal* 49 (2014): 248–57.

73. For an argument against Christian physicalism, based on its conflict with dogmatic realities like faith, regeneration, original sin, and perseverance of the saints, see Matthew Hart, "Christian Materialism Entails Pelagianism," in *Christian Physicalism? Philosophical Theological Criticisms*, ed. R. Keith Loftin and Joshua Farris (Lanham: Lexington, 2018), 189–211.

74. Cf. Nicholas Saunders, *Divine Action and Modern Science* (Cambridge: Cambridge University Press, 2002).

75. Philip Clayton, *God and Contemporary Science* (Grand Rapids: Eerdmans, 1997).

76. Clayton, *God and Contemporary Science*, 233.

77. Philip Clayton, *Adventures in the Spirit: God, World, Divine Action* (Minneapolis: Fortress, 2008), 128.

persons (i.e., emergentism), and then use that picture to solve the problem of divine action. Call this approach *scientific understanding seeking biblical faith*.

This is theologically backward. Our triune God is existentially and epistemologically fundamental. As immaterial spirit, this God sustains creation naturally and sometimes intervenes in the world supernaturally. Our knowledge of God controls how we understand ourselves—call this approach *biblical faith seeking scientific understanding*. There is, then, nothing mysterious in the claim that the immaterial acts in and through the material world. As creatures fashioned in the image of God who is spirit, it makes perfect sense to ground human moral agency in a dualistic anthropology. Or so it seems to me.[78]

78. My thanks to James Anderson, Robert Erle Barham, Steve Cowan, Bill Davis, Alan Thompson, Ted Van Raalte, John Wingard, and especially John Cooper, Paul Manata, and Aku Visala for helpful comments on an earlier draft. I am also grateful for the valuable feedback I received from those who heard my talk at the LATC18 conference.

CHAPTER 5

HUMAN COGNITION AND THE IMAGE OF GOD

AKU VISALA

MANY CONTEMPORARY THEOLOGIANS seem to think that identifying the image of God in humans with certain psychological or metaphysical structures must be abandoned. Not only is the view that links human cognition and the *imago Dei* biblically unwarranted, but it is also ethically problematic and empirically implausible, or so the argument goes. What I want to suggest is that such criticisms are far from conclusive. Indeed, it is difficult to formulate an account of the image of God without any reference to human cognitive uniqueness. Surprisingly, current cognitive sciences offer some support for this view as well.

In the first part, I will provide an outline of what I mean by the image of God. On this view, the image of God is identified with the potential to develop uniquely human cognitive mechanisms, mainly reason and will. I think that such a view can incorporate the best aspects of its competitors, namely, the relational, functional, and christological accounts. The second part will introduce recent work from the cognitive sciences that offer empirical and theoretical support for the uniqueness of human reason. Far from undermining human cognitive uniqueness, this work suggests that humans have many unique cognitive mechanisms. We have, for instance, unique capacities for representing complex mental states of others, adopting moral norms, and controlling our actions.

STIG: THE STRUCTURAL/SUBSTANTIAL VIEW OF THE IMAGE OF GOD

It is fair to say that the structural/substantial view of the image of God (henceforth, STIG) has been the default position among Christian theologians until the twentieth century. It has not been, by any means, the only approach, but it seems clear that some reference to human cognitive uniqueness has generally been made.[1] According to Augustine, for instance, the image of God in humans ought to be identified with the rational soul. Humans are images of God insofar as the rational capacities of their souls reflect God's rational (albeit perfect and infinite) capacities. So, central to STIG is an analogy between the capacities of God and human beings. This analogy is, of course, far from similarity or identity, but it is nevertheless meaningful to talk about God and humans having capacities that are on the same spectrum. Such capacities are most often identified with reason, intellect, and will. Moreover, this analogy is supposed to be uniquely human: although nonhuman animals might enjoy some measure of reason and will, they nevertheless do not qualify as images of God because there is a relevant difference between reason and will of humans and those of nonhuman animals. The nature of this difference is, of course, the key issue.

The extent to which sin blemishes or distorts the image of God is a controversial issue among defenders of STIG. All agree that sin has corrupted some of the capacities of the soul, usually will and desire, but this does not mean that the *imago Dei* has been completely lost. The operations of human cognition might very well be impaired—because of the disordering of desires, for instance—but at least some core functions still remain operational. For the purposes of my argument, I will leave these debates aside. It is enough for me that the capacities for reason and will are not completely lost in the fall and remain operational in our sinful state as well.

Consider the *Catechism of the Catholic Church*, which makes many of the convictions of STIG explicit. First, it affirms the uniqueness of God-human relationship that STIG entails: "Endowed with 'a spiritual and immortal' soul, the human person is 'the only creature on earth that God has willed for its own sake.' From his conception, he is destined for eternal beatitude."[2] Humans are unique both in the sense of being spiritual

---

1. For an interesting overview of the *imago Dei*, see J. Wentzel van Huyssteen, *Alone in the World? Human Uniqueness in Science and Theology* (Grand Rapids: William B. Eerdmans, 2006), ch. 3.
2. *CCC* 1703.

beings with reason and freedom but also in that they have been created for a special kind of communion with God. Humans, in this sense, are the only animals capable of responding to God's call and can therefore be called *homo religiosus*, religious beings.

Second, the catechism also confirms that the image of God in humans is intimately interrelated to the kinds of cognitive capacities humans have: "By virtue of his soul and his spiritual powers of intellect and will, man is endowed with freedom, an 'outstanding manifestation of the divine image.'"[3] Third, by virtue of possessing a soul that provides the capacities of reason and will, the human being can discern or perceive moral, aesthetic, and religious truths:

> The *human person*: with his openness to truth and beauty, his sense of moral goodness, his freedom and the voice of his conscience, with his longings for the infinite and for happiness, man questions himself about God's existence. In all this he discerns signs of his spiritual soul. The soul, the "seed of eternity we bear in ourselves, irreducible to the merely material", can have its origin only in God.[4]

Finally, the potential to develop reason and will that make humans moral, intellectual, and religious *persons* (instead of just beings or things) confers upon them a special kind of objective dignity and value:

> Being in the image of God the human individual possesses the dignity of a person, who is not just something, but someone. He is capable of self-knowledge, of self-possession and of freely giving himself and entering into communion with other persons. And he is called by grace to a covenant with his Creator, to offer him a response of faith and love that no other creature can give in his stead.[5]

As we can see from these passages, STIG highlights the fact the human cognition has a crucial place in our moral, rational, and spiritual life. Interpersonal relationships characterized by faith, trust, and love require some level of reason and freedom to begin with. This applies both to human–human and God–human relationships. Similarly, human beings can only respond to God's revelation insofar as they have some basic capacities for reason and will: animals, rocks, and plants cannot discern God in nature (beauty, morality) or in revelation.

---

3. *CCC* 1705.
4. *CCC* 33.
5. *CCC* 357.

STIG: CHALLENGES AND MODIFICATIONS

Despite the prevalence of STIG in the theological tradition, most contemporary theologians have moved away from it. Other accounts of the image of God have been developed in its place. The functional account emphasises the mission and task of humans in creation. The relational theory locates the image in interpersonal relationships. The christological account identifies Christ as the only image of God. [6] In this section, I will address some criticisms that have been offered against STIG and suggest STIG can not only respond to these criticisms but also incorporate the best parts of its competitors.

In recent theological anthropology, there has been a strong push to recover the link between the image of God and Christology. It is Christ who is the perfect image of God and humans are images of God only insofar as they have been incorporated into Christ or participate in Christ. John Kilner, Ian McFarland, and Oliver Crisp, just to mention a few, have developed the doctrine of the image of God in a christological context.[7] They maintain that STIG is mistaken in assuming that the image of God can be identified without any reference to Christ. Both Kilner and McFarland maintain that God has chosen to relate to humans through Christ and that all other aspects of humanity, such as their function in creation, their ability to reason, and to form loving relationships, are grounded in Christ.

It has also been argued that STIG has problems with another biblical issue, namely, that in Genesis the image of God is not identified with human cognitive capacities but with the God-given mission of humans in creation. Humans are not images of God by virtue of having certain kinds of minds but because God chose them as stewards and caretakers of creation.[8] STIG's focus on rationality is thought to have arisen more from the Greco-Roman philosophical context rather than the older, Jewish tradition exemplified by Genesis.

Matthew Levering develops a novel version of STIG that takes these worries into account. I am convinced that Levering is on the right track,

---

6. See, e.g., Marc Cortez, *Theological Anthropology: A Guide to the Perplexed* (London: T&T Clark, 2010), 18–21; Oliver Crisp, "A Christological Model of the *Imago Dei*," in *The Ashgate Research Companion to Theological Anthropology*, ed. Joshua R. Farris and Charles Taliaferro (Farnham: Ashgate, 2015).

7. John Kilner, *Dignity and Destiny: Humanity in the Image of God* (Grand Rapids: Eerdmans, 2015); Ian McFarland, *The Divine Image: Envisioning the Invisible God* (Minneapolis: Fortress, 2005).

8. See, e.g., J. Richard Middleton, *The Liberating Image: The* Imago Dei *in Genesis 1* (Grand Rapids: Brazos, 2005).

so let me follow his argument here. Levering takes the criticism seriously. The Scriptures indeed teach, at least in part, that the image of God in humans has to do with certain functions. Similarly, the New Testament as well as the theological tradition link the image of God closely to Christ. Finally, the image of God is intimately intertwined with our ability to form and maintain loving relationships. Granting these points, Levering argues that not only is STIG not undermined by them but also makes sense of them better than the alternative accounts:

> It seems to me that the best way to locate the image of God in each human, while retaining the royal rule emphasized by biblical exegetes and while insisting upon the relationality of the image, is to defend the view that the image of God is in the soul's powers of knowing and loving, and thus fully manifested in Jesus Christ.[9]

Regarding the christological issue, Levering points out that in addition to being the Redeemer, Christ is also *Logos*, the Word of God. Following Athanasius, he develops the idea that the Word, essentially God's reason and wisdom, is present and structures the created world. He writes:

> If the Son is the Word, and humans are the image of the Word, then why should not this human image be associated uniquely with reason/word? As Athanasius points out, this association belongs to the New Testament's canonical testimony to the Word (John 1) as Image of God (Col. 1:15). I agree with Athanasius that if the human image of God is connected uniquely with the Word, then it is connected with reason and freedom, intellect and will.[10]

Levering suggests that christological accounts of the image of God that reject all image-bearing from human individuals without any connection to Christ suffer from a basic problem. How can non–Christians be images of God if participation in Christ comes through only via the church? If humans are images of God only insofar as they participate in Christ, and they explicitly reject Christ, it seems that such people do not reflect God at all. To solve this problem Levering argues that we should see humans bearing the image of God by virtue of having Christlike cognitive capacities, like reason and will, that make love and moral life possible. Levering claims that,

---

9. Matthew Levering, *Engaging the Doctrine of Creation: Cosmos, Creatures, and the Wise and Good Creator* (Grand Rapids: Baker, 2017), 155.

10. Levering, *Engaging the Doctrine of Creation*, 153.

following Aquinas, humans and Christ are both images of God. In Christ, the image is perfectly present in his divine nature and expressed in his human nature. Christ exhibits perfect wisdom and love. He also exhibits the regal/functional role in his compassion and finally ascending to heavens and assuming an authoritative place in the cosmos. Human beings bear the image to a much lesser extent, but they are nevertheless called to participate and imitate Christ. Through this process they may become more Christlike, more like God's image.[11] In this way, STIG can incorporate the christological emphasis of so many contemporary accounts of the image of God without giving up its distinctive emphasis on analogy between God's mind and human mind.

Regarding the *imago Dei* in Genesis, Levering discusses the work of Richard Middleton. According to Middleton, Genesis attempts to democratize the Mesopotamian idea that kings are images of God. The king is the person through whom God's will becomes manifest and is acted out in this world. An individual king is the image of God insofar as the king performs his role, fulfils his function. In addition, this role is partly cultic or priestly in the sense that the king is also a central figure in the worship of the gods. It is the king that represent humanity in the eyes of the gods. Genesis takes on this view of the regal/cultic role of kings but includes every human being in the image. Not only do all humans have this role of manifesting and representing God in creation, but all humans can also be considered priests in the sense that they too have access to God. Thus, all humans are representatives of God in creation and should take on the role of being functional middlemen between God and the rest of creation.[12]

Levering points out that the functional view has a problem if no unique cognitive capacities are posited. If we associate image-bearing with royal rule, then those who rule or have the ability to rule are more in God's image than those who have not. If we want the image of God to have a democratizing effect, we will have to admit that it is not the actual stewardship and rule that constitutes the image of God but the capacity or ability to do so. Communities and individuals can choose not to accept the God-given mission to rule and become evil, or there might be some other reasons, such as illness, that stop these abilities from actualizing. This interpretation, according to Levering, is supported by other parts of Genesis. In the story of Cain and Abel, for instance, Cain himself is neither wise nor loving,

---

11. Levering, *Engaging the Doctrine of Creation*, 176–77.
12. Levering, *Engaging the Doctrine of Creation*, 164–66.

but the text makes clear that he is still an image of God. So, to bear the image of God it is enough to have the capacity to function as a steward of creation, not to actualize it.[13]

Second, the regal/functional view sees human stewardship as mirroring God's wise and loving dominion. God's dominion is wise and loving, not coercing or violent in the sense that it calls its subjects to cooperation. Here we see how the regal/functional view ultimately rests on an analogy between human cognitive capacities and God's capacities, just like STIG has maintained all along. Levering writes that "it is logically necessary that human nature possess intellect and will in order for humans to image God's royal rule."[14] The cognitive capacities for Godlike dominion thus include reason, freedom, and morality, which together make loving and caring stewardship possible.

STIG has also been subjected to moral and ethical criticism. Take, for instance, J. Wentzel van Huyssteen who writes:

> An anthropology that finds the imaging of God only in the mental aspects of the human person inevitably denigrates the physical and directly implies that God, and the image of God, can be related only to theoretical analysis and control. Identifying a specific disembodied capacity like reason or rationality as the image of God by definition implies a negative, detrimental view of the human body—a move that inevitably leads to abstract, remote notions of the *imago Dei*. In this sense substantive definitions of the image of God can rightly be seen as too individualistic, and too static.[15]

Here we have a barrage of moral criticisms. First, there is the suggestion that if the image of God is identified with reason and will, this inevitably denigrates the nonmental aspects of our existence. Second, if the *imago Dei* consists of having the ability to reason, this seems to suggest our primary relationship to the world and others is that of theoretical analysis and control. Finally, van Huyssteen echoes the sentiments of many contemporary theologians in suggesting that when STIG identifies the image of God with individual cognitive capacities, it fails to account for the communal and political nature of humans. In other words, STIG entails an objectionable individualistic and atomistic view of humans.

---

13. Levering, *Engaging the Doctrine of Creation*, 172.
14. Levering, *Engaging the Doctrine of Creation*, 175.
15. Van Huyssteen, *Alone in the World?*, 134.

Defenders of STIG have much to say as a response to such worries. First, there is no reason to think that STIG would somehow denigrate or give less value to our physical existence because of its emphasis on cognitive capacities. Even if we adopt mind-body dualism, there is no reason to deny that the soul is closely associated with our bodily existence. As I have argued elsewhere, various forms of contemporary dualism also converge on this point (as do the cognitive sciences, as we will soon see).[16] Embodied reason, according to Levering, is affirmed by Thomas as well. Reason is not a disembodied capacity in the morally problematic sense. Instead, it is closely tied to the workings of our brain, bodies, environments, and social contexts.

The second moral worry concerning STIG has to do with the claim that associating the image of God with reason makes our primary way of relating to the world a form of abstraction and control. Here again we see how the critics of STIG fail to account for the connection of reason to freedom, morality, and love. Following Aquinas, Levering claims that wisdom and love are not opposite to reason but in fact require it. The capacity to grasp moral truths and principles, to identify and pursue goodness, and guide one's behaviour accordingly (freedom and will) are intertwined with reason.[17] As the following sections claim, we can arrive at this view of reason through empirical means as well. If this view of reason is plausible, it is unwarranted to claim that our primary relationship to the world would be analysis and control. Indeed, even the most basic moral actions and loving relationships require some form of reason and action control.

Contrary to van Huyssteen's critique, STIG does not entail that the image of God in humans is somehow static and unchanging—quite the opposite. Levering maintains that God calls and transforms humans in different ways at different times and places. So not only is the human cognition in a constant process of spiritual and moral development (acquiring virtues, for instance), it also develops biologically and psychologically over an individual's lifetime. Furthermore, the individual herself can and should be active in this God-given development towards reflecting the image of Christ more fully. Free, reasonable, and conscious decisions are required that in turn form virtues and habits, which have effects on behaviour as well as the functioning of the intellect itself. This involvement of both divine and human agency in the process of reflecting God

---

16. Aku Visala, "*Imago Dei*, Dualism and Evolutionary Psychology," *Zygon* 49 (2014): 101–20.
17. See, e.g., Olli-Pekka Vainio, "*Imago Dei* and Human Rationality" *Zygon* 49 (2014): 121–34.

more fully guarantees that the image in humans does not remain "static" but is very dynamic.[18]

Finally, I want to briefly address a worry that van Huyssteen does not explicitly mention but features prominently in many other critiques of STIG. Kilner, for instance, suggests that associating the image of God with certain cognitive capacities is problematic, because such capacities come in degrees. So, if someone has her cognitive functions impaired, she is not to be regarded as God's image like someone whose reason is normally functioning. For this reason, we should not see the image of God as coming in degrees at all, but instead it should be all or nothing.

One way to respond to this is to point out that it is not just a problem for STIG, but it also besets both functional and relational views as well. People with disabilities might be completely unable to function as stewards and caretakers. They might be unable to form the kind of loving and wise relationships that the relational view requires. Such individuals would be much less images of God than those who can actually rule and engage in diverse relationships. In this sense, STIG is no worse off than its main competitors.

However, STIG might have some resources at its disposal to respond to this worry better than its competitors. First, Levering follows Aquinas and argues that even those individuals that suffer from significant bodily and mental disabilities can still be images of God in a very strong sense. This is possible because even though such individuals might be unable to actualize their reason and love in interpersonal relationships, they can still be in loving communion with God. Through God's actions in Holy Spirit, the rational soul (no matter what its conditions) can acquire infused virtues that make it possible to participate in God's rule.[19] Second, the fact that the soul is (at least to some extent) distinct from the body also guarantees that the image of God is present even in individuals that suffer from mental and bodily disabilities. It is not the actualization of reason and will that constitute the image of God in humans but the potential to actualize them. All humans have the same kind of rational soul even if its capacities cannot be actualized because of some defect.

The defender of STIG need not adopt the kind of dualism that Levering inherits from Aquinas. I think it is enough that STIG can maintain a reasonable distinction between actualizing the abilities that reason enables

---

18. Levering, *Engaging the Doctrine of Creation*, 183–84.
19. Levering, *Engaging the Doctrine of Creation*, 174.

and having those abilities potentially without actualization. Here we might seek help from Nicholas Wolterstorff. Wolterstorff suggests that we should locate the image of God not with actualized capacities but with human nature itself. What Wolterstorff means by this is that all humans share in the same design plan or overall design. We could also say that human biological nature gives all humans similar developmental pathways. Some individuals fail, through no fault of their own, to actualize these pathways. However, this does not make them less human; they still have the potential to develop the capacities of reason and will. This potential is why all humans, not just those whose cognition is properly functioning, can be images of God.[20]

In sum, the defenders of STIG will insist that loving interpersonal relationships, stewardship of creation and our relationship to Christ require a certain kind of cognitive machinery. Given what Aquinas (and the cognitive sciences) say about reason, the mistake of the critics of STIG becomes clear: they take reason as a disembodied, abstract, individualistic, and distinct faculty. Contrary to this, the defender of STIG can (and should) maintain that reason is not disembodied (in the morally problematic way), is not directed towards abstract truths only, and is closely linked to the functioning of other faculties. Indeed, reason makes loving relationships, moral actions, and the understanding of moral norms possible in the first place. Without these capacities, humans could not be moral and free, discover truths about the world, or respond to God's call in their conscience and in Christ. Without them, humans would be incapable of performing the royal/functional role that God has given human beings in creation.

PROBLEMS WITH COGNITIVE UNIQUENESS

Many theologians still seem to think that it is scientifically unwarranted to posit human uniqueness or distinctiveness, especially at the mental level. This is one reason for the widespread rejection of STIG: nonhuman animals and hominids preceding our species seem to be much smarter and able than we previously assumed. This seems to cast doubt upon all attempts to find cognitive distinctiveness or uniqueness in Homo sapiens. Psychologists Justin Barrett and Tyler Greenway put the worry like this: "If Homo sapiens are descended from other species that were not *imago*

---

20. Nicholas Wolterstorff, *Justice: Rights and Wrongs* (Princeton: Princeton University Press, 2008), 349–52.

Dei through a series of tiny, incremental steps, then it is reasonable to suppose that the modern human population overlaps importantly with earlier species on any number of dimensions that one may want to identify with the *imago Dei*."[21] So, either the bar for human uniqueness is set so high that at least some modern humans fail to reach it or it is set so low as to include many nonhuman animals or at least a number of (now extinct) hominid species.

For STIG to be plausible, this worry must be addressed. Traditionally, candidates for unique capacities have included at least one or more of the following: reason, intellect, freedom, morality, and language. Levering himself discusses mainly symbolic language and what he calls "rational consciousness." He locates their emergence in the explosion of symbolic cultural variation that occurred around forty or fifty thousand years ago. Apart from some general remarks about consciousness, Levering does not really tell us what reason is and what makes it unique.[22] What I want to do next is introduce some results and theories from the cognitive sciences that support the thesis of human cognitive uniqueness.

Before we go any further, we should examine the notion of "human uniqueness" a bit more carefully. As I have argued elsewhere, it is useful to distinguish at least three different types of uniqueness.[23] First, we can take uniqueness to mean the *uniqueness of abilities or the range of behaviours.* In this sense, we can say that humans are unique insofar as they can do things that no other species can do. This form of uniqueness is rather uncontroversial: humans can dance the tango, speak Klingon, and play chess. As far as we know, no other being engages in such behaviours or is even capable of engaging in them. This form of uniqueness is uncontroversial also in the sense that most nonhuman species have a range of their own unique behaviours. Some can fly, others can live under water, and so on.

The uniqueness of abilities or behaviours, however, is not really what STIG is after. Instead, STIG entails a commitment to *the uniqueness of cognitive mechanisms* that make uniquely human behaviours possible. This form of uniqueness would entail that our abilities and behaviours are

---

21. Justin L. Barrett and Tyler S. Greenway, "*Imago Dei* and Animal Domestication: Cognitive-Evolutionary Perspectives on Human Uniqueness and the *Imago Dei*", in *Human Origins and the Image of God: Essays in Honor of J. Wentzel van Huyssteen*, ed. Christopher Lilley and Daniel J. Pederson (Grand Rapids: Eerdmans, 2017), 65.

22. Levering, *Engaging the Doctrine of Creation*, 155–62.

23. Agustín Fuentes and Aku Visala, "Introduction: The Many Faces of Human Nature," in *Verbs, Bones, and Brains: Interdisciplinary Perspectives on Human Nature*, ed. Agustín Fuentes and Aku Visala (Notre Dame, IN: Notre Dame University Press, 2017), 16–17.

grounded or made possible by cognitive capacities and mechanisms that no other species has. Here the central question is whether humans might have unique cognitive mechanisms even though our cognition has incrementally developed nonhuman cognition. In what follows, I will mainly focus on this kind of uniqueness.

However, I want to mention a third form of uniqueness that has to do with how cognitive mechanisms come about. We could call this *the uniqueness of origin*. One way to secure absolute uniqueness of origin would be to claim that human reason does not come about through biological evolution at all. Traditionally, some theologians have maintained that God specially creates each and every human soul through supernatural means. At conception, God adds souls to biological organisms to make them personal beings.

I do not want to say that such a view would be necessarily in conflict with the cognitive sciences and the archaeological record of our species. Nevertheless, the view I want to develop in this chapter assumes no supernatural, direct interventions in human cognitive evolution or cognitive development. For the purposes of this article, whatever rational souls are, they do not have supernatural origins—they are not in this sense unique. Rather, they emerge and develop in the same way as all our other features develop: through the interaction of our biology and our physical, social, and cultural environment.[24]

It does not follow that uniqueness of origins should now be completely rejected. Quite the opposite: there are some reasons to think that the evolution of our species and the whole homo lineage has been driven by evolutionary forces that have had only a minor or nonexistent role in the evolution of other species. Indeed, a number of contemporary scholars argue that the evolution of our lineage indeed exhibits some unique characteristics that mostly have to do with the extensive interactions between genes and culture as well as the cultural niche-construction. In this sense, human cognitive evolution has taken place in the context of culture and technology: our species responds to pressures not by developing biological adaptations but by cultural and technological innovation.[25]

---

24. I defend the compatibility of this assertion with dualism in Visala, "Will the Structural Theory of the Image of God Survive Evolution?," in *Finding Ourselves after Darwin: Conversations on the Image of God, Original Sin, and the Problem of Evil*, ed. Stanley P. Rosenberg (Grand Rapids: Baker, 2018).

25. For more on this, see Visala "Will the Structural Theory of the Image of God Survive Evolution?" See also, Jonathan Marks, *Tales of the Ex-Apes: How We Think About Human Evolution* (Oakland: University of California Press, 2015).

CULTURE AND RELATIONAL REASON

Levering draws mainly from Aquinas in his account of human reason and its deep connections with other capacities, such as will and emotion. I will not rehash these arguments here. Instead, I will suggest that contemporary cognitive and evolutionary sciences point towards a certain kind of human cognitive uniqueness. This uniqueness has mostly to do with the social and cultural nature of our reasoning mechanisms. It seems that the beneficial effects of ever-increasing group size and social diversity have been the main drivers of human cognitive evolution. Thus, it is no big leap to posit that humans have unique cognitive mechanisms that prepare us for culture, flexible behaviour, and the use of language. These are enormous topics, of course, and I will not be able to say anything sufficiently detailed. Nevertheless, I will provide some examples of the uniqueness of our reason.

Human cognitive evolution has been thoroughly cultural in nature. Levering suggests that culture cannot be part of what it means to be in God's image because primitive hunter-gatherers did not have culture.[26] I think this is a mistake; he raises the bar for culture too high. For Levering, culture comes into existence during the symbolic explosion circa fifty thousand years ago when we begin to see the diversity of cultures and symbols typical of Homo sapiens. Contrary to this, many scholars think that culture goes much deeper in human history. Indeed, humans are the only species for whom hypersociality through culture has become the first and foremost survival strategy. Humans are the species that is characterised by their immense capacity to learn, to transmit the results of that learning, and adjust their beliefs, behaviours, and practices accordingly. This ability to learn and create cultural environments has fed back into our biological evolution itself so that it is appropriate to call humans the *biocultural species*.[27]

Let me give a couple of examples of the ways human reason is social and cultural. First, a very general point. Evolutionary psychologists Dan Sperber and Hugo Mercier have recently argued human reason did not evolve for general-purpose problem-solving but for social and cultural living.[28] According to Sperber and Mercier, even logical inferences and

---

26. Levering, *Engaging the Doctrine of Creation*, 162.
27. Many scholars have emphasized the centrality of culture in human evolution. See, e.g., Michael Tomasello, *A Natural History of Human Thinking* (Cambridge: Harvard University Press, 2014); Kevin N. Laland, *Darwin's Unfinished Symphony: How Culture Made the Human Mind* (Princeton, NJ: Princeton University Press, 2017).
28. Hugo Mercier and Dan Sperber, *The Enigma of Reason* (Cambridge, MA: Harvard University Press, 2017).

other forms of abstract and conscious reasoning mainly take place in a social context. They write, "Reason, we argue, has two main functions: that of producing reasons for justifying oneself, and that of producing arguments to convince others. These two functions rely on the same kind of reasons and are closely related."[29] The first of these functions is to facilitate the complex and varied social coordination and cooperation abilities that are the hallmark of our cultural species. Via the ability to recognise good reasons and provide reasons for one's own action, individuals learn what to expect from one another. This ability of giving and expecting reasons enables our varied practices of moral responsibility, blame, and praise. The second function is that of argumentation. Argumentation and public reasoning are, for Sperber and Mercier, a way to create and foster trust and enhance communication. We have reason so as to convince and gain the benevolence of those who do not yet trust us.

Such a view of reason contrasts heavily with the more traditional view of reason as a general-purpose problem-solving mechanism aimed at finding out the truth in all domains of life. Sperber and Mercier call their alternative model of reason *interactionism* to highlight that human reason is, first and foremost, a form of social competence. Sperber and Mercier provide strong ammunition for defenders of STIG. Human reason is indeed special but not in the morally problematic way. Rather than being geared towards abstraction and control, reason is mainly for forming and maintaining uniquely human relationships. It enables shared ideas, taking responsibility for one's actions, and the development of trust and cooperation.

In a recent article, psychologists Justin Barrett and Matthew Jarvinen offer a promising candidate for a uniquely human cognitive mechanism: the *higher-order theory of mind* (HO-ToM).[30] Barrett and Jarvinen argue that modern humans have a unique cognitive mechanism that enables them to attribute complex mental states to themselves and other persons. This capacity, they maintain, allows humans to engage in uniquely complex social interactions. By enabling humans to understand and take into account the mental states of others, it also undergirds thinking about God's intentions and, thus, enables humans to acknowledge and respond to God's revelation and love. Such a cognitive mechanism, for Barrett and Jarvinen, would be a good candidate for being part of the image of God.

---

29. Mercier and Sperber, *The Enigma of Reason*, 8.
30. Justin L. Barrett and Matthew J. Jarvinen, "Cognitive Evolution, Human Uniqueness, and the *Imago Dei*," in *The Emergence of Personhood: A Quantum Leap?*, ed. Malcolm Jeeves (Grand Rapids: Eerdmans, 2015), 163–83.

The basic idea behind the theory of mind (ToM) system can be outlined as follows: Some nonhuman animals might have a basic first-order ToM, which is the ability to predict and explain the behaviour of others by positing basic internal states, such as intentions, beliefs, and desires. These mental states have specific content that in turn explains the behaviour involved. In this sense, I can understand that Justin is moving towards the other side of the road because he wants to get to the other side. Second-order ToM is the ability to attribute mental states, whose content refers to the content of other mental states, to first-order mental states. In this sense, I can say that Justin crossed the road because he believed there to be seeds on the other side, but Justin was mistaken. It seems that adult humans also have third-order (or perhaps even fourth-order) ToM: I can understand that Justin believes that I falsely (in his mind) believe that there are no seeds on the other side of the road. The cognitive mechanisms that make the formation and processing of second- and third-order mental states are what we call higher-order ToM.[31]

It is unclear to what extent nonhuman animals (and human babies) have first-order ToM. Michael Tomasello has provided some evidence that certain other species, such as chimps and bonobos, might have rudimentary first-order ToM.[32] Nevertheless, there is no evidence that nonhuman animals would have second- or third-order ToM. If this is true, it would explain why only Homo sapiens are able to form the kinds of complex relationships that we do not see in nonhuman animals. Human interpersonal relationships include the identification and recognition of the mental states and emotions of others as well as the complex ways we respond to them.

Not only does HO-ToM allow for loving relationships, but it also enables a wide range of moral and religious abilities. Without HO-ToM, we could not form and understand collective intentions, shared beliefs, and shared attention. Barrett and Jarvinen refer again to the work of Tomasello, who has argued that human cognition exhibits very early on a distinct capacity for shared attention and collective intentionality. These capacities contribute crucially to the development of morality, reasoning, and language.[33] Without such mechanisms, I could not understand that your beliefs might refer to the same object as my beliefs. I could not even direct my attention

---

31. There is much work on ToM in cognitive science and evolutionary psychology. See, e.g., Kristin Andrews, *Do Apes Read Minds: Towards a New Folk Psychology* (Cambridge, MA: MIT Press, 2012).

32. Tomasello, *A Natural History of Human Thinking*, 20–24.

33. E.g., Michael Tomasello, *The Cultural Origins of Human Cognition* (Cambridge: Harvard University Press, 2001).

to the same object as you do: I could not realize that I have a relationship with the same God as you if I am unable to represent the content of your beliefs and share attention with you.

Following recent developments in cognitive science of religion, Barrett and Jarvinen also suggest that without HO-ToM there could not be religion in the way we understand it. Religious life requires the ability to form collective intentions, shared attention, and moral norms. Cognitive and evolutionary study of religion suggests that religion is not only natural for humans but also uniquely human.[34] Finally, as Tomasello has argued, HO-ToM is crucial for morality as well. Without the ability to understand and form collective intentions and shared attention, I cannot evaluate my beliefs and behaviours (as well as those of others) for their moral content. Indeed, Tomasello suggests that complex theory of mind is necessary for the formation and operation of shared moral norms and duties.[35]

REASON AND FREEDOM AS UNIQUE ADAPTATIONS FOR CULTURAL LIFE

The previous section briefly outlined some results and theories that point towards the uniqueness of our reason in its relational and social capacities. It seems that our reasoning mechanisms enable us to form uniquely complex interpersonal relationships and complex sociality. What I want to suggest is that in order for us to have such relationships our reason must be able to flexibly control our behaviour and respond to shared reasons, moral, and legal norms as well as other shared expectations. This kind of *reason-based action control* is a set of mechanisms that enables us to act freely, morally, and responsibly. Without such capacity for practical reasoning, we could not act freely and rationally.

Here I help myself to the work of psychologist Roy Baumeister and his research team.[36] Baumeister is part of a larger trend, outlined above, that locates human uniqueness in human cognitive capacities for complex culture and social life. He begins by pointing out that there is a clear difference between human and animal behaviour:

---

34. See, e.g., Ara Norenzayan, *Big Gods: How Religion Transformed Cooperation and Conflict* (Princeton, NJ: Princeton University Press, 2013); Scott Atran, *In Gods We Trust: The Evolutionary Landscape of Religion* (New York: Oxford University Press, 2012).

35. Michael Tomasello, *A Natural History of Human Morality* (Cambridge: Harvard University Press, 2017).

36. Roy F. Baumeister, *The Cultural Animal: Human Nature, Meaning, and Social Life* (New York: Oxford University Press, 2005).

We assume that something about the way humans choose and act is different from what other animals do. Human's greater flexibility and deliberate contemplation of alternatives make their behaviour arguably freer than the more rigid and short-term decision styles of other animals. This is the reality behind the idea of free will.[37]

This difference is there because humans are cultural animals—culture is our survival strategy. From the differences between human and nonhuman animal behaviours (especially the diversity of behaviours), we can infer that there are differences in the underlying cognitive mechanisms as well.

Life in the cultural niche requires a significantly different and more complex cognition than that of other, noncultural animals, even those capable of complex sociality. Our biocultural way of life is enabled by unique cognitive mechanisms. We are capable of taking into account the social, moral, and legal expectations, norms, and prescriptions that could be applied to our behaviours. We are capable of regulating our behaviour on the basis of such norms and expectations as well as taking responsibility for our actions.

Such abilities are cognitively very demanding. They require at least three kinds of cognitive mechanisms. First, they require a number of capacities that have to do with sharing norms and expectations and with identifying and evaluating reasons for action. Some of the basic cognitive systems outlined in the previous section, HO-ToM and joint attention, for instance, are crucial for this kind of work. But these mechanisms are hardly enough: what one also needs are cognitive mechanisms that allow for the imaginative creation and assessment of alternative future scenarios, that is, counterfactual thinking. Without a highly flexible counterfactual cognition, it would be impossible to create and execute long-term planning, which is crucial for the survival of the individual and the whole group. Finally, and most crucially, the individual must develop an ability to control one's actions and regulate one's desires and emotions.

There is a mass of evidence for the uniqueness of all three kinds of cognitive systems. Regarding counterfactual thinking and alternative futures, Baumeister and some others have recently argued that our whole cognition is future oriented.[38] Cognitive scientists and psychologists have too often

---

37. Roy F. Baumeister, Cory Clark, and Jamie Luguri, "Free Will: Belief and Reality," in *Surrounding Free Will: Philosophy, Psychology, Neuroscience*, ed. Alfred R. Mele (Oxford: Oxford University Press, 2015), 49–50.

38. Martin E. P. Seligman, Peter Railton, Roy F. Baumeister, and Chandra Sripada, *Homo Prospectus* (Oxford: Oxford University Press, 2016).

looked at cognitive processing from the point of view of the past. Emotion, memory, and perception, for instance, are often seen as driven by past experiences. Contrary to this, argues Baumeister, perception is more about anticipating possible future events than receiving present signals. Memory is more about the construction of future possibilities than just storing representations of past events. Similarly, emotion is more about guiding future actions than reacting to extant conditions determined by past experiences.

One central cognitive mechanism in anticipating the future is consciousness. According to Baumeister, conscious processes are crucial for both long-term planning and the formation of distal intentions. These abilities are needed, for example, when individuals must choose between alternative courses of actions. Consciousness seems to make this kind of cognitive operation possible by enabling the running of offline, complex mental simulations. Such simulations also bring a certain amount of coherence to other mental functioning by stimulating, gathering, and integrating information from different subsystems of the brain.[39]

Finally, let me make some points about the last set of cognitive systems required for life in culture, namely, reason-based action control. I do this because not only do such systems seem uniquely human but they also highlight the connection between reason and will, rationality, and freedom.

Baumeister argues explicitly that humans have free will: they have a unique capacity for reason-based action control or executive control. Human actions do not simply follow automatically from internal mental states, like beliefs and desires. Instead, there is a form of executive control that regulates what mental states are accepted as reasons for actions and how actions are executed. Although we have good evidence that our cognitive systems function more automatically than previously thought, we do *not* have good reasons to think that executive control of the conscious kind is a complete illusion.[40] Baumeister agrees: "Free will in the sense of self-control and rational, intelligent choice comprises an important set of psychological phenomena and is plausible in terms of the evolution and construction of the human psyche. Quite likely human conscious processing emerged as a way to facilitate this new form of action control."[41] On Baumeister's view,

---

39. Baumeister, Clark, and Luguri, "Free Will: Belief and Reality," 59–61.
40. See, e.g., Alfred R. Mele, *Effective Intentions: The Power of Conscious Will* (Oxford: Oxford University Press, 2009). For the case for the illusion of executive control, see Daniel M. Wegner, *The Illusion of Conscious Will* (Cambridge, MA: MIT Press, 2002).
41. Roy F. Baumeister, "Free Will, Consciousness and Cultural Animals," in *Are We Free? Psychology and Free Will*, ed. John Baer, James C. Kaufman, and Roy F. Baumeister (Oxford: Oxford University Press, 2008), 82–83.

conscious, executive control is like a supervisor of a large collection of sub-systems, not wholly unlike a chief engineer, who supervises, perhaps, a large engine room of a ship. This executive control oftentimes does not initiate actions directly, but it can, in the long run, shape and rework the subsystems and how they react to different circumstances.[42]

One of Baumeister's main findings has been that this executive control is somewhat limited and that its functioning is related to other, unconnected cognitive systems. The main idea behind this *ego depletion effect* is that exerting conscious action control draws upon a limited resource.[43] The lack of that resource will in turn impair several different cognitive processes, including logical reasoning, self-control, creativity, conformity, and less effective decision-making strategies. Executive action control is, therefore, possible but costly.

CONCLUSION

I have now given some reasons why STIG is still a viable option in the theological debate about the image of God. I happily acknowledge that I am still far from showing that STIG is in fact true. I merely wanted to point out that STIG cannot be completely brushed aside; it is still a contender. I think Levering has managed to develop a form of STIG that can withstand criticism and embrace the central strengths of its competitors, the functional, relational, and christological accounts. To support this, I also provided some examples of recent work in the cognitive-evolutionary sciences that not only support the idea that human reason is unique but also suggest that human reason is inherently cultural and relational. It seems that our moral, religious, and intellectual life indeed requires special cognitive mechanisms. Without reason, we would not be able to act freely and rationally, engage in loving and meaningful interpersonal relationships, perform our God-given stewardship in creation, and finally, be formed increasingly like Christ, who is the perfect reason and wisdom of God.

---

42. Roy F. Baumeister, E. J. Masicampo, Kathleen D. Voss, "Does Consciousness Cause Behavior?" *Annual Review of Psychology* 62 (2011): 331–61.

43. Baumeister, Clark, and Luguri, "Free Will: Belief and Reality," provides a short introduction to these studies.

CHAPTER 6

"VULNERABLE, YET DIVINE"

Retrieving Gregory Nazianzen's Account of the *Imago Dei*

GABRIELLE R. THOMAS

DISCUSSIONS CONCERNING the Christian doctrine of humanity have come to the fore in recent years with particular reference to the *imago Dei*. Some scholars have argued that the *imago Dei* must be understood in Trinitarian and relational terms (Nonna Verna Harrison and Stanley Grenz), whilst others have oriented towards a christological interpretation (Mark Cortez, John Behr, and Kathryn Tanner) or else have argued that we should continue to search for the *imago Dei* (Alistair McFadyen). Despite excellent work on the *imago Dei*, scholars have rarely attended to the experience of being an *imago Dei*, since much of the focus is upon, "What is the *imago Dei*?" Incorporating both experience and nature, this chapter presents a retrieval of Gregory Nazianzen's multifaceted approach to the doctrine of humanity. By depicting the *imago Dei*'s relationship to God and to the cosmos, Gregory demonstrates how it is both "vulnerable, yet divine." The *imago Dei* is vulnerable to God, having been created with the purpose of becoming "divine," but at the same time vulnerable to "the world, the flesh, and the devil." This results in a dynamic and holistic interpretation, which warrants serious consideration from contemporary theologians who are engaging with the Christian doctrine of humanity.

For centuries, the *imago Dei* has preoccupied scholars of biblical studies and systematic theology alike. The interpretations vary extensively, such as situating the *imago Dei* substantively,[1] relationally,[2] or functionally.[3] Theologians have also argued, quite rightly, that we must speak of the *imago Dei* in light of Christ[4] and therefore also in light of the Holy Spirit.[5] Despite the richness and depth of these discussions, the conversation frequently revolves around the question, "*What* is the *imago Dei*?" The implications remain for further exploration regarding what it might mean for a human being to *be* an *imago Dei*. Therefore, in this chapter I ask, "What might we say about the experience of *being* an *imago Dei*?" To inform my response, I turn to the wisdom and insight offered by an early church father, namely, Gregory of Nazianzus, who espouses a unique, sophisticated narrative concerning the experience of the image of God vis à vis the *imago Dei*.[6]

Often cited alongside his fellow Cappadocians, Gregory of Nyssa and Basil of Caesarea, Saint Gregory of Nazianzus (c. AD 329) is a hugely influential church father. Known as "the Theologian," Gregory writes innovatively about God and the Christian life in virtually every Greek literary form. One example of this is his neologism *theosis*, which continues to be the chief term used to describe deification. Regarding his writing both on God and the Christian life, Gregory searches frequently for meaning in human existence. In his poem *On Human Nature* Gregory asks, "Who was I at first? And who am I now? And who shall I become?" He replies, "I don't know clearly," which could be translated as, "I really don't know."[7] Gregory's response confesses the complexities of being an "image," which is Gregory's shorthand for speaking about the human being.[8] I shall follow his shorthand throughout this essay and refer to the image of God as the whole human being rather than that which resides within the human being.

---

1. Alister E. McGrath, *Scientific Theology*, vol. 1, *Nature* (Edinburgh: T&T Clark, 2002), 198–200.

2. Alistair I. McFadyen, *The Call to Personhood: A Christian Theory of the Individual in Social Relationships* (Cambridge: Cambridge University Press, 1990).

3. J. Richard Middleton, "The Liberating Image? Interpreting the Imago Dei in Context," *Christian Scholars Review* 24, no. 1 (1994): 8–25, 12.

4. David Kelsey, *Eccentric Existence: A Theological Anthropology* (Louisville: Westminster John Knox, 2009), 8–9; John Behr, *The Mystery of Christ: Life in Death* (Crestwood, NY: St. Vladimir's Seminary Press, 2006); Kathryn Tanner, *Christ the Key*, Current Issues in Theology (Cambridge: Cambridge University Press, 2010).

5. Marc Cortez, "Idols, Images and a Spirit-ed Anthropology: A Pneumatological Account of the *Imago Dei*," *Third Article Theology: A Pneumatological Dogmatics*, ed. Myk Habets (Minneapolis: Fortress, 2016), 267–82.

6. I have chosen to follow the convention in contemporary theological anthropology with regard to the application of the phrase *imago Dei*. However, note that Gregory writes in Greek (*imago Dei* is interchangeable with *eikōn theou*).

7. Gregory of Nazianzus, "On Human Nature," *Carm.* 1.2.14, PG 37, 755–67, 757, 17. The translations throughout the essay are my own in order to highlight nuances in the texts.

8. Following one of Gregory's conventions, when I refer to "the image," I speak of the whole human being rather than an aspect of the human being.

To address these complexities Gregory adopts a multifaceted approach in which he writes about both the nature and the experience of the image of God; unlike many interpretations, Gregory's approach defies reduction to a single category of analysis. He does not understand the image of God for example, solely in terms of substance or function.

My broader research argues that Gregory begins by situating the human being as an image of God within the contexts of Christology and pneumatology. Drawing his inspiration from Scripture in dialogue with contemporary beliefs about pagan images and idols, Gregory weaves together themes pertaining to relationality, ontology, function, ethics, sacraments, and experience. Since space does not allow us here to discuss the breadth of Gregory's narrative, I shall focus upon one particular thread relating to the experience of being an image of God: Gregory narrates the story of the image in relation both to God and to the whole cosmos. Amongst other inhabitants, the image shares the cosmos with spiritual beings, namely angels and demons. Through dramatic scenes encompassing a cosmological battle with the spiritual powers of darkness, Gregory's depiction of the experience of the image emerges as "vulnerable, yet divine."[9] The image is vulnerable to "the world, the flesh, and the devil" precisely because the image is created to become divine. Since myriad interpretations and usages abound regarding "vulnerability" in theology, I shall clarify briefly my application of "vulnerability" throughout this essay. I do not intend to suggest that God wounds the image, but rather I apply "vulnerable" to imply an "openness" and "porosity" to God and also to other spirits and moral forces. The Catholic philosopher Charles Taylor applies vulnerability in this manner; I turn next to discuss how his work informs my reading of Gregory's presentation of the image.

Taylor identifies that the ancient and medieval philosophical life meant befriending the highest things to the extent that there was little differentiation between internal and external forces. Said another way, the premodern self was characterised by porous or vulnerable boundaries between the self and external forces, rather than being surrounded by boundaries which are demarcated firmly. Taylor summarises this premodern world as one of "enchantment."[10] By applying this term, like Taylor, I do not intend to invoke

---

9. Note that Gregory does not envisage the cosmos following the dualism evident in Manichaeism. He argues against this consistently by applying the doctrine *creatio ex nihilo*. See *Or.* 28.6, SC 250, 110; *Carm.* 1.1.4, PG 37, 415–23.

10. "Enchantment is an antonym to Weber's application of 'disenchantment' as a means of describing our modern condition": Charles Taylor, *A Secular Age* (Cambridge, MA: Harvard University Press, 2007), 446.

images of fairies and elves but "the world of spirits, demons, [and] moral forces."[11] In the enchanted world the human being is "open and porous and vulnerable to a world of spirits and powers."[12] Regarding Gregory's approach to the battle between the image of God and the spiritual powers of darkness, the image is vulnerable precisely because the image inhabits a cosmos in which there is no option of disengaging with spiritual forces. Through modernity and the rise of humanism, the "vulnerable self" was displaced by a "disenchanted" view of the world and by the "buffered self."[13] Taylor explains that the "buffered self feels invulnerable before the world of spirits and magic forces."[14] The buffered self represents a radically different "existential condition" since for the "modern, buffered self the possibility exists of taking a distance from, disengaging from everything outside the mind."[15]

I believe that Taylor's vision of the premodern, vulnerable world versus the modern, buffered world explicates the landscape in contemporary theological anthropology, particularly pertaining to discussions about the image of God. Often the image is depicted as though it were almost some kind of buffered concept which may be discussed only in relation to itself, or at best in relation to God. Or when scholars situate the image in relation to the cosmos, they commonly do so according to the function of stewarding and governing all that inhabits the earth, with little thought to how the image might relate to the wider cosmos. Gregory's narrative, on the other hand, in which the image inhabits the world alongside spiritual beings, allows us to situate the image within the wider cosmos. Said another way, Gregory's vision of the image's experience creates the space for the reenchantment of the *imago Dei*. Added to this, Gregory's preoccupation with the image alongside the spiritual powers of darkness explores the complexities and challenges of imaging God. With this in mind, let us turn to Gregory's depiction of the spiritual powers of darkness, establishing the prevalence of the devil and demons in the texts.

THE DEVIL

Throughout his corpus, Gregory refers to the human being as an image of God on over 150 occasions. Nearly half involve a reference to a battle with the spiritual powers of darkness; in spite of this, only a few published

---

11. Taylor, *A Secular Age*, 29.
12. Taylor, *A Secular Age*, 27.
13. Taylor, *A Secular Age*, 27.
14. Taylor, *A Secular Age*, 548.
15. Taylor, *A Secular Age*, 38.

works identify the significance of the devil in Gregory's thought.[16] The dearth of research directed towards the devil, not only in reference to Gregory's work but also more widely in contemporary theology, relates to the effect of the Enlightenment on Western culture. Through modernity, scepticism grew towards transcendent beings, such as angels and demons. Consequently, on the rare occasions when early Christian scholars attend, in some way, to the concept of demons, it is often to demythologise themes concerning powers of darkness.[17] I do not support this approach since I contend that we should not confuse the worldview of the premoderns with that which was largely adopted through modernity.[18] Recall Charles Taylor's thesis, which is key to grasping Gregory's narrative of the image in light of the battle with the devil and demons. Moving through a process of disenchantment has meant that the contemporary worldview is radically different from Gregory's, for it is the enchanted world which Gregory inhabits and within which he situates the image of God as vulnerable to the spiritual powers of darkness.

Gregory's presentation of the devil follows the patristic reading of Isaiah 14:12, which interprets Lucifer, the morning star, to be speaking of both Satan who appears in Job and the serpent in Genesis 3.[19] Ezekiel 28 also contributes to this tradition, having been read as linking a cosmic rebel and an earthly king.[20] In the New Testament, Revelation 12:9 draws together the serpent and the devil, which Gregory applies prolifically. Gregory weaves together in a passage in which he speaks about Christ's victory on the cross, the narratives of Lucifer's banishment from heaven, Satan in the book of Job, and the serpent in the garden of Eden. He describes Christ as, "crushing Satan quickly under our feet, whether falling like lightning from

---

16. Notable exceptions are Dayna S. Kalleres, "Demons and Divine Illumination: A Consideration of Eight Prayers by Gregory of Nazianzus," *Vigiliae Christianae* 61, no. 2 (2007): 157–88; Morwenna Ludlow, "Demons, Evil and Liminality in Cappadocian Theology," *Journal of Early Christian Studies* 20, no. 2 (2012): 179–211; Francesco Trisoglio, "Il demonio in Gregorio di Nazianzo," in *L'autunno del diavolo. "Diabolos, Dialogos, Daimon" convegno di Torino 17/21 ottobre 1988, volume primo*, ed. Eugenio Corsini (Milano: Bompiani, 1990), 249–65.

17. Hans Boersma, *Violence, Hospitality, and the Cross: Reappropriating the Atonement Tradition* (Grand Rapids: Baker Academic, 2004), 194. Rudolf Bultmann was a key figure in this trend. See Bultmann, "New Testament and Mythology," in *Kerygma and Myth: A Theological Debate*, ed. Hans Werner Bartsch (London: SPCK, 1964), 1–44.

18. Phillip Wiebe reviews the Enlightenment reluctance to accept the reality of spirits. See Wiebe, *God and Other Spirits: Intimations of Transcendence in Christian Experience* (Oxford: Oxford University Press, 2004), 1–6.

19. Justin Martyr was the Christian forerunner in equating Satan with the Serpent (*Dialogue with Trypho* 45). See also Origen, *On First Principles* 2.9.2.

20. Neil Forsyth, *The Old Enemy: Satan and the Combat Myth* (Princeton, NJ: Princeton University Press, 1989), 139–44.

heaven on account of his former splendour, or fleeing like a serpent due to his later crookedness and his metamorphosis into that which crawls on the ground."[21] Gregory explains that it is Lucifer's rebellion against God that results in God casting out Lucifer from heaven. Gregory generally follows the tradition occurring in 2 Enoch and Origen, where Lucifer's fall from heaven is attributed to his longing for God's glory.[22] Gregory does not attempt to answer the question of how Lucifer came to be proud and hanker after a glory that was not his own, nor does he grapple with the problem of the angels following Lucifer in his evil work on earth. Gregory's only offering towards this is to comment that whilst it is hard to move angels away from good, they are able to turn to evil should they choose.[23]

Throughout his corpus, Gregory refers to the devil by several different titles, most of which derive from Scripture. In making this move, Gregory continues the lively sense of the reality of the devil handed down from the Jewish Apocalyptic tradition.[24] Many of the names that Gregory attributes to the devil exist as a list in the poem entitled *Aversion of the Evil One and Invocation of Christ*: Thief, Serpent, Fire, Belial, Vice, Death, Dragon, Beast, Night, Ambusher, Rage, Chaos, Slanderer, and Murderer.[25] The myriad titles that Gregory bestows upon the devil point to the different ways the devil aims to destroy the image of God and tempt the image into sin. Elsewhere, Gregory refers to "Satan,"[26] the Evil One,[27] "the Devil,"[28] "the Adversary,"[29] "the Tempter,"[30] and "the Enemy."[31] Gregory gives the devil over twenty different epithets, all of which denote the extent of the trouble the devil attempts to cause the image of God. Unfortunately for the image, the devil does not work alone but manages to gather up an army of rebel angels, which Gregory refers to as demons.[32] These are as problematic as the devil himself for the image of God. In one of many evocative passages, Gregory describes demons thus:

---

21. *Or.* 23.14, SC 270, 310; *Carm.* 1.2.1, PG 27, 531, 120; see Luke 10:18.

22. Origen, *Against Celsus* 6.43.

23. *Or.* 38.9, SC 358, 120.

24. Frances M. Young, *The Making of the Creeds* (London: SCM, 1991), 88; Everett Ferguson, *Demonology of the Early Christian World* (New York: Mellen, 1984), 133.

25. *Carm.* 2.1.55, PG 37, 1399–1401.

26. *Or.* 23.14, SC 270, 310.

27. *Or.* 2.88, SC 247, 202; 6.10, SC 405, 146; 28.15, SC 250, 132; 30.6, SC 250, 236–38; 37.10, SC 318, 292; 37.12, SC 318, 296; 38.14, SC 358, 134; 40.10, SC 358, 216, et al.

28. *Or.* 2.62, SC 247, 174; 35.3, SC 318, 232; 38.12, SC 358, 128.

29. *Or.* 26.3, SC 284, 230; 22.13, SC 270, 248; 40.16, SC 358, 230.

30. *Or.* 30.6, SC 250, 236; cf. Matt 4:3.

31. *Carm.* 2.1.70, PG 37, 1418, 4; 2.1.88, PG 37, 1441, 168; cf. Luke 10:19.

32. *Carm.* 1.1.7, PG 37, 444, 74.

attendants of the murderous king of evil, phantoms of the night, liars, wantons, teachers of sin, those who mislead others, drunks, lovers of sensuous laughter, stirrers of revelry, diviners, practitioners of ambiguity, argumentative ones, murderous wretches, inhabitants of darkness, hidden ones, shameless beings, sorcerers. They call on approaching; they hate, whilst dragging away. They appear as night and light either without disguise or in ambush. While this is the way of the army, so it is the way of their chief.[33]

The multiple titles and descriptions of both the devil and demons demonstrate their prevalence in Gregory's thought. I point to one further title that is especially relevant to my argument. Gregory composed a collection of no less than thirteen consecutive poems in which he depicts the devil's assault upon the human being using vivid language. Six of the thirteen poems are entitled "Against the Evil One," which offers an indication of Gregory's preoccupation. These poems are prayers in which Gregory cries out to God for help and protection from the devil. Within one of these poems, Gregory refers to the devil as the "destroyer of the image," thus betraying his belief that the devil is interested in bringing down the image of God specifically. Gregory is an orator who crafted his orations with great care and won a reputation for being a superb rhetor; thus we should assume his intentionality in connecting the devil to the image of God. Fervently, Gregory prays, "If the destroyer of the image trips me up, who might become my guardian, save you, Lord?"[34] Gregory offers several means through which the "destroyer of the image" works to trip up the image, to which we shall turn next.

"THE WORLD, THE FLESH, AND THE DEVIL"

Recall the prayer found in the Litany of the 1662 *Book of Common Prayer*, "From fornication and all other deadly sin; and from all the deceits of the world, the flesh, and the devil, *Good Lord, deliver us*." Whilst Gregory lived in a radically different context from the one in which this prayer was written, the prayer gathers together the pervasiveness of the devil in Gregory's thought, since the devil and his minions infiltrate the world and the flesh in order to attempt to destroy the image of God. First, I shall analyse how

---

33. *Carm.* 1.1.7, PG 37, 444–45, 73–82.
34. *Carm.* 2.1.65, PG 37, 1407, 6–7.

Gregory explores the devil working through the world; following this, I shall discuss how Gregory envisages the devil and the flesh working together. This is not to say that Gregory saw the world in primarily negative terms. On the contrary, when Gregory reflects on God's creation of the world, he describes it positively, observing the order and harmony in which the world was created.[35] Conversely, here I focus on the occasions when Gregory refers to the fallen world negatively, standing in a long line of church fathers who use the concept of "the world" as being in direct contrast with that which is good.[36] In doing this, they follow Saint Paul when he makes such comments as, "Do not be conformed to this world, but be transformed by the renewing of your minds, so that you may discern what is the will of God—what is good and acceptable and perfect" (Rom 12:2).[37] I argue that for Gregory, this negative experience of the world relates to the devil, which becomes evident through the number of occasions on which Gregory refers to the devil directly as "the world-ruler."[38]

For example, in the following passage Gregory posits the devil as the world-ruler who should not be obeyed: "Honour the unity, stand in awe of the archetype, live with God, not the world-ruler. . . . He was a murderer from the beginning. He overpowered the first human being through disobedience, and he brought in the life of labour, and he laid down law to punish and be punished, on account of sin."[39] The devil is evidently the world-ruler to which Gregory refers in the passage, since Gregory's description of the world-ruler as a "murderer from the beginning" is a direct citation from John 8:44, where Jesus is talking to the Jews unambiguously about the devil.[40] Further, when Gregory speaks of the world-ruler as overpowering the first human being through disobedience, he refers specifically to the events which led to the banishment of Adam and Eve from the garden of Eden, equating once more the devil with the serpent. Gregory's belief that the devil is ruling the world occupies a significant amount of his writing on the Christian life, providing the rationale for poems such as *On*

35. *Or.* 38.10, SC 358, 122–24.

36. Elizabeth A. Clark, *Reading Renunciation: Asceticism and Scripture in Early Christianity* (Princeton, NJ: Princeton University Press, 1999), 41.

37. All biblical citations in this chapter are taken from NRSV.

38. For Gregory using "world-ruler" as an epithet for the devil, see *Or.* 1.4, SC 247, 77; 8.12, SC 405, 272; 11.4, SC 405, 338; 14.21, PG 35, 884C; 17.9, PG 35, 976C; 19.6, PG 35, 1049C. For identification of the "world-ruler" with the devil in John 12:31; 14:30, see George R. Beasley-Murray, *John*, WBC (Nashville: Nelson, 2000), 263.

39. *Or.* 17.9, PG 35, 976B-D.

40. Contra Martha Pollard Vinson, *St. Gregory of Nazianzus: Select Orations* (Washington, DC: Catholic University of America Press, 2003), 91.

Dying to the World.[41] Gregory connects the devil as the world-ruler to the image of God by positing the image in opposition to the devil. Observe in the following passage how Christians should flee the world-ruler (i.e., the devil) in order to honour the image: "Let us flee worldly desires, let us flee the world which leads us astray and the world-ruler, let us be cleansed by the Creator, let us honour the image, let us stand in awe of the call."[42]

The world provides one avenue through which the devil may lead the image of God astray, but as I have already commented, the devil also aims, through the flesh, to entrap the image. When Gregory refers to flesh alongside the image of God in terms of wrestling or combat, he does not envisage flesh as coterminous with the body; rather, Gregory applies "flesh" metaphorically to denote the human struggle with sinful nature.[43] In speaking of flesh in this way, Gregory echoes Paul once more who, in his letter to the Romans writes, "For I know that nothing good dwells within me, that is, in my flesh."[44] Indeed, Gregory follows Paul so closely that what has been written concerning Paul's use of "flesh" could also be said of Gregory's application of the concept: "All parts of the body constitute a totality known as flesh, which is dominated to such a degree that wherever flesh is, all forms of sin are present."[45] Whilst Gregory does not provide a systematic treatment of how fallen flesh and the demonic powers are enmeshed, he presents consistently fallen flesh and the devil intertwined with one another. This is apparent, for example, in the poem "Against the Flesh," where Gregory draws together flesh and Belial, which is another name for the devil. It is worth quoting at length since the poem offers an indication of how the devil uses fallen flesh to attempt to incur the destruction of the image of God:

> Deadly flesh, black sea of ill-minded Belial,
>
> Deadly flesh, root of branching sufferings,
>
> Deadly flesh, a companion of the cosmos which flows below,
>
> Deadly flesh, adversary of the heavenly life,

41. *Carm.* 1.2.48, PG 37, 1384, 1–3.

42. *Or.* 19.6, PG 35, 1049B–C.

43. Geoffrey W. H. Lampe, *Patristic Greek Lexicon* (Oxford: Clarendon, 1961), 1224.

44. Rom 7:18; see also Rom 6:19; 2 Cor 10:2; Gal 5:16; Col 2:18. See Dale B. Martin, *The Corinthian Body* (New Haven, CT: Yale University Press, 1999), 173; Eduard Schweizer, "σάρξ" in *Theological Dictionary of the New Testament*, vol. 7, ed. Gerhard Kittel and Gerhard Freidrich (Grand Rapids: Eerdmans, 1971), 125–30; Bruce L. Martin, *Christ and the Law in Paul* (Eugene, OR: Wipf & Stock, 2001), 105.

45. Frederick W. Danker and Walter Bauer, *A Greek-English Lexicon of the New Testament and Other Early Christian Literature*, 3rd ed. (Chicago: University of Chicago Press, 2000), 915.

Flesh, hated and desired, sweet battle, mistrustful good,
Always tasting of the human-slaying tree,
Slimy filth, muddy fetters, heavy leaden weight,
Unconquerable beast born from wrangling matter,
Evil boiling, both tombstone and fetter of your mistress
Of the heavenly image, which we have assigned to us from God,
Will you not stop your shameless evil?[46]

Using evocative language, Gregory presents the devil working in collaboration with the fallen flesh, aiming to target the image of God. This provides the basis for why the image must war against the flesh. Note that the image cannot win the battle alone but requires help from God, which is why Gregory prays, "Warring against the flesh you bring aid to the image."[47]

By adding Gregory's treatment of the flesh to his narrative of the devil working through the world, we build a picture of the challenges of being an image of God, since the devil and his cohort work through both the world and the flesh to damage the image. Observe below that Gregory describes the devil "shaking" the image of God when the devil works through the world and the flesh. When warfare between the image and the devil is at its most challenging, Gregory addresses the devil directly as he engages in the battle to resist the devil's schemes: "You have come to me again, Weaver of Wiles, as you are known, nourishing yourself within the depths of my heart, and through much strong shaking of this life, desiring to bring the holy image to bended knee."[48] In these lines, Gregory depicts the devil attempting to bring the image to bended knee, which is another way of expressing that the devil wants the image to kneel in worship. The image of God already worships God by virtue of being an image; for example, by imaging God, the human being displays the glory of God to the world. However, to receive worship for himself, the devil must first prevent the image from worshiping God, or said another way, the devil must damage the image to the extent that the image cannot image God fully. This provides further explanation regarding why Gregory names the devil "destroyer of the image," which we explored earlier.

Gregory's consistent presentation of the devil attempting to destroy the image, whether through the world, the flesh, or any other means, prompts

---

46. *Carm.* 2.1.46, PG 37, 1378, 1–11.
47. *Carm.* 1.2.3, PG 37, 634, 13–15.
48. *Carm.* 1.2.50, PG 37, 1385, 1–4. Passages such as this have led Dayna Kalleres and Morwenna Ludlow to argue that Gregory envisages a real spiritual enemy.

a question: Precisely what kind of damage does Gregory envisage the devil inflicting upon the image of God? Whilst Gregory does not offer an explicit explanation of the envisaged result, we may discern his ideas through a sequence of prayers titled *Lament*. Gregory sets up the scene for the impact of the devil's attempted destruction of the image by referring to the way the serpent tempted Eve in the garden of Eden. Gregory observes that he is being tempted likewise and that the devil wishes to kill him.[49] Near the conclusion of one of the poems he states, "I perceive the battle" and the following poem clarifies that the battle, like so many others, is over the image of God. Gregory writes,

> The image is emptying out: what word will offer help?
> The image is emptying out: gift of excellent God.
> The image is violated . . . [50]

Above, Gregory describes intensely the effect of the devil's attack on the image of God by applying "*kenoō*." The concept of *kenosis* derives from this verb, which is known due to its occurrence in Philippians 2:7, where it describes the manner in which Christ Jesus took on the form of a slave. Christ's kenosis has received great attention in contemporary biblical studies and systematic theology, but I do not intend to enter current debates here since Gregory's use of kenosis in relation to the image of God and the effects of the devil is the focus of our concern. Whilst Gregory writes elsewhere explicitly about Christ's kenosis, I do not believe that Gregory has in mind Christ's kenosis here because there is a significant difference between Christ's kenosis and Gregory's writing on the image of God: Christ chooses his kenosis, whereas in Gregory's poem the image is being emptied out against its will. I suggest that in order to understand what Gregory intends concerning the emptying out of the image, we must look back to the previous poem in which Gregory states that the devil longs to kill him. In light of this, I argue that Gregory envisages the emptying of the image as equal to the destruction of the image so that the image can no longer glorify God; in turn the devil receives the glory himself.

If we looked no further, we might conclude that Gregory offers a bleak outlook on what it means to be an image of God. Whilst Gregory narrates a challenging account of life as an image of God, it is not without hope. The battle is serious and the image is vulnerable to the devil's schemes; yet the

49. *Carm.* 2.1.60, PG 37, 1403.
50. *Carm.* 2.1.61, PG 37, 1404, 1–3.

devil's desire to destroy the image is ultimately unsuccessful because Christ has defeated the devil and provided the means for the image to continue to image God. Our final passage demonstrates that Gregory anticipates a hopeful outcome for the image through incorporation into Christ and the deification by the Holy Spirit which occurs at baptism. Through this passage we see that the authority over the devil that comes from being an image of God means that the image has the resources to resist the devil fervently.

"Worship Me"

In his oration *On Baptism*, shortly after introducing the subject of baptism, Gregory describes Christ's temptation by the devil as it occurs in the Gospels.[51] According to Gregory's logic, the Gospels locate Christ's temptation by the devil in the desert occurring immediately after his baptism; thus Gregory argues that the same pattern ensues with Christ's followers.[52] Gregory proceeds to depict the ways Christ was tempted by the devil. First, Gregory observes that the devil attempted to persuade Christ to turn stones into bread when Christ was hungry. Gregory informs those who are baptised that if the devil tries the same trick on them, they should "resist him with the saving Word."[53] After this, the devil tries to tempt Christ into throwing himself off the temple in order to prove his divinity (Matt 4:5–7, Luke 4:9–12). Gregory responds, "If he should plot against you through empty glory . . . do not be brought down through exaltation."[54] Having explained that the devil is well acquainted with Scripture and therefore particularly wily, Gregory concludes his discussion by describing how the devil shows Christ all the kingdoms of the world and offers to give them to Christ if he agrees to worship the devil. During this final piece of advice, Gregory addresses the question of how those who are baptised should respond when the devil tries to tempt them to bow down and worship him. First, Gregory notes Christ's response:

> Jesus said to him, "Away with you, Satan! for it is written,
> 'Worship the Lord your God,
> and serve only him.'" (Matt 4:10)

Gregory suggests those who are being tempted should respond as follows:

---

51. Matt 4:8–10 and Luke 4:5–6.
52. *Or.* 40.10, SC 358, 216.
53. *Or.* 40.10, SC 358, 216.
54. *Or.* 40.10, SC 358, 216.

Say, confident in the seal,[55] "I, myself, am also an image of God, I have not yet been thrown down through pride from the glory above, like you. I am clothed in Christ; I have been remodelled Christ by baptism, you ought to worship me!" He will depart, I know well, yielding and being shamed by these words, as he was by Christ the first light, thus will he depart from those who are enlightened by that same Christ.[56]

Gregory weaves three threads into his explanation regarding why the devil should worship the newly baptised, the first of which relates to human identity as an image of God. Note that Gregory does not simply say, "I am an image of God," rather he says, "I, myself, am also an image of God." The use of "and also" implies that there is another image. In the context of the oration, this other image can only refer to the devil or Christ. We reject the former, on the basis that Gregory does not actually refer to angels, fallen or otherwise, as images of God anywhere in his orations or poetry. Hence, when Gregory says, "I, myself, am also an image of God," he intends his readers to understand that the human being is the image of God like Christ. Observe the impact of this through Gregory's description of the newly baptised as having been "remodelled Christ."[57] Gregory does not state that the image is remodelled "like" Christ or "as" Christ but simply "remodelled Christ." Here we see that being an image bears serious implications. Not only is the image expected to follow Christ's example in dealing with the devil, but as far as Gregory is concerned, the image should receive worship as a divine image. Through close association with Christ, the Image of God, and through the deification of the Holy Spirit at baptism, the image is offered hope in this narrative of wrestling with evil. However, Gregory brings us full circle to where we began, since the deification of the image by the Holy Spirit at baptism incites envy from the devil and the battle begins again: "After baptism, if the pursuer and tempter of light makes an assault upon you—and he will make an assault upon you, mark my words, for he even made an assault upon the Logos, my God . . . you have a means of conquering."[58] Although he warns that life as an image of God after baptism continues to be challenging, Gregory encourages his readers with the affirmation that they have a "means of conquering," thus the image is vulnerable but need not be beaten by the devil.

---

55. "The seal" is a way of describing baptism amongst the early church fathers.
56. *Or.* 40.10, SC 358, 218.
57. Gregory applies the verb *metapepoioō* to describe this action, which could also be translated as "change the quality of." See Lampe, *Patristic Greek Lexicon*, 860.
58. *Or.* 40.10, SC 358, 216.

CONCLUSION

So, what of our tour de force through Gregory's description of the image's battle with the devil and demons? As I noted at the beginning, this is only one thread of many which Gregory weaves into his overall narrative of the image of God. It warrants attention because it explores the experience and implications of being an image rather than solely asking, "What is the *imago Dei*?" Whilst contemporary theological anthropology does not refer to the devil frequently, for Gregory the devil is key to both theological anthropology and, moreover, the image of God. Both the wrestling with and the suffering that stems from these spiritual powers of darkness describes an important aspect of the experience of being an image of God. Through these struggles with the devil and his minions, Gregory suggests that the human being made as the image of God should not expect life to be without pain and struggle, whilst at no point suggesting that this is an eschatological reality, rather it is an aspect of life whilst the image grapples with living in the "now and not yet." Ultimately, Gregory's vision of the image is one of hope and deification, but whilst living on earth, life as a "vulnerable, yet divine" image comprises a challenging journey.

Gregory locates the image in perpetual battle with the spiritual powers of darkness, which reminds us that the image of God does not exist in a vacuum. The image exists as porous and vulnerable to God, the cosmos, and all the spiritual beings that reside therein. Thus, Gregory's vision of life as an image of God provides an unusual insight into the implications of the human experience of imaging God. It offers us a heuristic interpretation of some of the challenging aspects of being an image, whilst, at the same time, creating the space for the reenchantment of the *imago Dei*.

CHAPTER 7

CREATED AND CONSTRUCTED IDENTITIES IN THEOLOGICAL ANTHROPOLOGY

Ryan S. Peterson

QUESTIONS ABOUT THE NATURE of constructed identities (e.g., racial, ethnic, national, religious, gender, and sexual) and their relation to biblical-theological identities (e.g., creaturely, covenantal, redeemed, and eschatological) are critical to contemporary theological anthropology. Many of today's pressing ecclesial and ethical issues turn on assumptions about the nature and status of personal and social identities. Yet while the language of "identity" has received wide acceptance in theological discourse, (1) the meanings of "identity" have not been clearly articulated, and (2) identity-language has not been related to the traditional categories of theological anthropology, namely, nature, ends, faculties, and habits.[1] In this chapter, I argue that the use of identity-language in theological anthropology must be disciplined by the doctrines of God and creation and that two forms of "identity"—created identity and constructed identity—need to

---

1. Moreover, there is no traditional theological precedent for analyzing human existence in terms of "identity"—its use in theological anthropology is relatively new. The implementation of identity-language without adequate theological moorings often leads to equivocation on the term "identity" in preaching, such as in the claim that a person "used to find her identity in work but now finds her identity in Christ." Discovering that one's identity is determined by God in Christ is not the same kind of thing as affiliating too strongly with one's job.

be distinguished from one another. When these are distinguished properly, they can be situated with respect to nature, ends, faculties, and habits in a way that illuminates human existence and experience.

PERSONAL AND SOCIAL IDENTITIES

In popular discourse the impetus for using identity-language to interpret the human person arises from the social sciences. The use of "identity" in the social sciences has been unruly, however. So much so, in fact, that in 2000, Rogers Brubaker and Frederick Cooper published a lengthy critique of the ambiguity created by the term. They note that identity-language is used both to "highlight fundamental sameness" and to "reject notions of fundamental or abiding sameness."[2] Through the use of identity-language alone, it is unclear whether an author is highlighting stability or malleability. This ambiguity makes scientific usage of the term unhelpful.

Nevertheless, since 2000 the use of the term "identity" in both the social sciences and general public discourse has increased significantly. The ways it is used remain diverse, and ambiguities persist.[3] But the public use of the term has led to some consensus. The use of identity-language in recent discussions of sexuality and gender, especially, have established a tighter association between identity and malleability. For example, in an article in the *Handbook of Self and Identity*, identities are defined as "the traits and characteristics, social relations, roles, and social group memberships that define who one is."[4] In this definition, human malleability is emphasized by placing characteristics, roles, and social group memberships at the center of a person's identity. These change over time, both through personal development and involvement in varying social contexts. Therefore, one's identities change over time. One could perhaps argue that at least some traits and characteristics remain the same across time, providing a context for describing stable personal and social identities. However, the authors cut such stability off at the pass, concluding that one's

> feeling that one knows oneself is based in part on an assumption of
> stability that is central to both everyday (lay) theories about the self and

---

2. Rogers Brubaker and Frederick Cooper, "Beyond 'Identity'," *Theory and Society* 29 (2000): 1–47, at 8 (emphasis removed).

3. Daphna Oyserman, Kristen Elmore, and George Smith, "Self, Self-Concept, and Identity" in *Handbook of Self and Identity*, 2nd ed., ed. Mark R. Leary and June Price Tangney (New York: Guilford, 2012), 70.

4. Oyserman, Elmore, and Smith, "Self, Self-Concept, and Identity," 69.

more formal (social science) theories about the self. Yet . . . the assumption of stability is belied by the malleability, context sensitivity, and dynamic construction of the self as a mental construct. Identities are not the fixed markers people assume them to be but are instead dynamically constructed in the moment.[5]

The claim that human identities are intrinsically fluid and malleable is made even stronger in another *Handbook* article, which argues as follows:

When a human being first emerges in the world, it has no identity; that is, the neonate is not yet defined in terms of institutional affiliations, self-representations, and social roles by which others recognize it. . . . Plainly put, individuals *acquire* identities over time, identities whose origins and meanings derive from their interactions with the social groups and organizations that surround them. In turn, these identities, once adopted, play a significant role in the organization and regulation of people's everyday lives.[6]

On these accounts of identity-formation, an individual's identities are constructed through the development of social relations, roles, values, and group memberships. Self-identification with one's family, race, ethnicity, nationality, sex, gender, religion, or political perspective becomes self-defining. The apparent stability in one's identity over time, or lack thereof, is due to consistency or inconsistency in one's social contexts and/or in one's orientation to the world.

Note that these psychological accounts of identity-formation are entirely secular in the sense that they assume that no one outside of the individual or social group determines the identity of that person or group. The human context is the definitive one. Such an assumption begs for theological evaluation.

From the perspective of classical Christian anthropology, the contemporary emphasis upon open-ended identity formation grounded in human malleability is intrinsically problematic due to various features of the doctrines of creation, sin, Christology, and eschatology. God is Creator and Lord, and the effort to arrive at self-definition apart from God is understood

---

5. Oyserman, Elmore, and Smith, "Self, Self-Concept, and Identity," 69–70.
6. Richard M. Ryan and Edward L. Deci, "Multiple Identities within a Single Self: A Self-Determination Theory Perspective on Internalization within Contexts and Cultures" in *Handbook of Self and Identity*, 2nd ed., ed. Mark R. Leary and June Price Tangney (New York: Guilford, 2012), 225, emphasis original.

as sinful. Moreover, since Jesus Christ fulfills human nature, humans must take cues about human identity from Jesus. Eschatologically, human destiny for the redeemed is conformation to Jesus and thereby also to God. Far from being unguided or open-ended, then, Christian anthropology looks to these doctrines to establish a stable account of human identity, nature, and ends.

Yet Christian anthropology has also emphasized the reality of human mutability for at least two reasons. First, humans are imperfect creatures, and imperfect creatures are necessarily mutable.[7] This is a good thing since change is required for an imperfect creature to arrive at perfection.[8] Second, humans after the fall are sinful, and sin fragments human experience, exacerbating human malleability. Sin perverts human loves, and these misplaced loves conform sinners to the various objects of those loves.

Initially, then, there are doctrinal reasons to suspect that there is a place within a theological account of human identity for stability as well as mutability. Many have worried that Christians speak of stability only because of a commitment to an "essentialist" metaphysics that seeks to establish stability through reference to an unchanging human nature. Doctrinally, this is not the case. Stability is grounded in God and God's creative determination, not in an immutable human essence. Essentialism is not ruled out by these theological moorings, of course, but neither is it required by them. The doctrines of the Trinity, Christology, creation, and eschatology provide a distinctively theological context for identity claims. Turning our attention to these doctrinal loci will prove illuminating.

TAKING ANTHROPOLOGICAL CUES FROM GOD, CHRISTOLOGY, CREATION, AND ESCHATOLOGY

Recently, Ian McFarland and Sarah Coakley have assessed the malleability and stability of human identity in light of the doctrine of the Trinity. In the following two sections, I evaluate their arguments. Then, I trace Augustine's account, as it has been interpreted by Matthew Drever, and compare it to the accounts offered by McFarland and Coakley. Following this comparison, I offer an account of created and constructed identities,

---

7. I prefer to use the term "mutable" to describe the intrinsic changeability of human creatures (which can be good or bad) and the term "malleable" to describe the tendency for human creatures to be deformed, or to be changed negatively. These terms do not have to be used this way, but I find it to be a useful distinction.

8. See Kathryn Tanner, *Christ the Key*, Current Issues in Theology (New York: Cambridge University Press, 2010), 39–41.

relating them to the traditional categories of nature, ends, relations, and vocations. Finally, I describe the differences between divinely created identities and humanly constructed identities.

DIFFERENCE AS THE KEY TO PERSONHOOD?

Ian McFarland, in *Difference and Identity*, provides a theological analysis of personhood on the basis of the doctrine of the Trinity.

> We may begin by pointing out that if "person" is predicated most properly of the Father, Son, and Holy Spirit, then it cannot be defined in terms of the possession of certain shared qualities or characteristics. After all, that which the divine persons have in common is precisely their divine nature (with its attendant qualities of omnipotence, omniscience, omnipresence, etc.), and it is not this shared nature that distinguishes them as persons. Quite the contrary, their personhood refers precisely to what they do not share.[9]

From this theological observation, McFarland infers two reasons for apophaticism about the nature of personhood, divine or human. First, the three divine persons cannot be isolated and analyzed discreetly. By speaking of one of the divine persons, one is already implicitly depending upon reference to the others. Speaking of the Son, for example, depends for its integrity upon reference to the Father and the Spirit.[10] Second, Jesus's personhood is that of the Son, and one cannot look to Jesus to establish a "general *definition* of the personal."[11] On the basis of the divine persons, then, we are unable to name a common set of criteria that determine personhood.

For McFarland, neither can we do so on the basis of the life of Jesus. When the life of Jesus is considered, the reasons to avoid offering a definition of personhood are deepened. First, Scripture does not provide a clear outline of Jesus's human nature by which we can then judge other performances of human nature. The biblical account of Jesus's humanity is underdetermined.

> As the one who is himself the content of the gospel, he is also the original in whose image all those to whom the gospel is addressed have been created. But the features of this original are such that when we seek to

---

9. Ian A. McFarland, *Difference and Identity: A Theological Anthropology* (Cleveland: Pilgrim, 2001), 34–35.
10. McFarland, *Difference and Identity*, 34.
11. McFarland, *Difference and Identity*, 35.

describe what he is like, we are not permitted to treat him as an ideal against whom others are to be measured and to whom they may be judged to conform more or less closely. Instead, we find that he places our efforts at such categorization under judgment.[12]

Second, we do not know all those included in Jesus. Jesus is risen from the dead and ascended, and by the work of the Holy Spirit the church has become the body of Christ in the world. While we may have good reason to suppose that we can identify parts of Christ's body, there are other parts that are unknown to us. If these others are the body of Christ such that Christ's life is exercised through them, yet they remain unknown to us, then this lack of knowledge regarding the full membership of the body of Christ keeps us from discerning definitively the shape of Christ's life.[13]

Finally, the nature of human personhood cannot be drawn from human experience since there are biblical passages that suggest that the true identity of human persons will only be known in the eschaton. Colossians 3:2–4 suggests that full knowledge of human life depends upon further revelation of life with Christ in glory: "Set your minds on things that are above, not on things that are on earth, for you have died, and your life is hidden with Christ in God. When Christ who is your life is revealed, then you also will be revealed with him in glory."[14] Likewise, 1 John 3:2 suggests that both the full vision of Christ and human likeness to Christ are future realities: "Beloved, we are God's children now; what we will be has not yet been revealed. What we do know is this: when he is revealed, we will be like him, for we will see him as he is." McFarland argues that these passages provide evidence of our inability to delimit human personhood and human identity.

McFarland draws several conclusions from this apparent inability to define human identity. First, if difference is at the heart of personhood, then we should expect that human identities are not meant to be collapsed into Jesus's identity. Rather, each person in Christ is valuable to the body of Christ precisely because of her difference from the others. Second, epistemologically, we should reject hegemonic or totalizing claims that one way of being human is right and all others are wrong. If the body of Christ in its full realization is still unknown, then we cannot know definitively

---

12. McFarland, *Difference and Identity*, 27.
13. See McFarland, *Difference and Identity*, 83–102.
14. Unless otherwise indicated, all Scripture quotations in this chapter come from the NRSV.

which way(s) of being human are in concert with the fulfillment of Christ's body and which are not. Third, humans cannot secure their own identities. Only God in his sovereignty knows the identities of all his chosen ones.[15]

Yet McFarland argues that the epistemological limits on our knowledge of human personhood and human nature should not lead us to think that all difference is good. McFarland observes that "the story of Jesus suggests that in some cases God's faithfulness to humankind is shown by the elimination of difference. Jesus's practice clearly marks out some manifestations of difference—illness and sin being the most obvious—as incompatible with the integrity of human being, whether understood individually or collectively."[16]

Decisively, Jesus's identity is not infinitely flexible:

> The ascended Christ constantly asserts himself over against our attempts to categorize him, whether or not we prove willing to recognize this fact. If we are bound to acknowledge that Jesus comes upon us as one unknown, however, we also confess that he does not stay that way. Though he stubbornly resists our attempts at definition, he is not a blank slate; and the specificity of his story undermines our attempts to fill it in with whatever content we might wish.[17]

This means that Christ's life determines the shape of every other human's life and not vice versa. Christ is not subject to human malleability, even as his body is not subject to hegemony. So, McFarland asserts: "Our identities, both individually and collectively remain socially constructed; but in the light of the gospel their construction needs to be understood as contextualized by the ongoing story of God's faithfulness to us. This story encloses us on all sides, shaping both the created nature in which we are called and the glorified existence that is prepared for us."[18] What separates the kind of social construction McFarland supports from the examples provided at the start of this chapter is the fact that creatures of God receive their identities, natures, and destinies from God. He agrees that human identities are socially constructed. But these identities cannot be fixed by individual human selves or merely human social contexts.

McFarland's is a suggestive account of human personhood and identity. However, it seems that he draws some inferences that do not follow from his theological arguments. I will focus on his claims about proper

---

15. McFarland, *Difference and Identity*, 94.
16. McFarland, *Difference and Identity*, 139.
17. McFarland, *Difference and Identity*, 163.
18. McFarland, *Difference and Identity*, 143.

epistemic limits, the doctrine of the Trinity, and Christ's presence in the world. McFarland, as noted above, argues that "human beings are not the guarantors of their own identities."[19] Rather, human identities depend upon Jesus Christ. He draws the following inference: "If our identity is 'entire gift,' then it is never something that can be treated as ontological leverage over against non-Christians. It follows that in proclaiming to others the call of Jesus Christ, the Christian should not suppose to be authorized to tell others who they are."[20] It is of course true that the gift of identity cannot be used as "ontological leverage." But it is not true that Christians are unable to tell others something about who they are. Telling someone who they are on the basis of divine revelation is not wielding undue ontological leverage or insisting on an objectionable hegemony so much as it is lovingly inviting that person to contemplate what God has determined to be the case.

Moreover, while McFarland emphasizes the fact that we do not have full knowledge of either Christ or other people, it would be wrong to conclude that we have no clear knowledge of Christ or other people by which we can make some judgments about right and wrong conceptions of human identity. McFarland regularly qualifies his claims to fend off such a critique, but I believe that greater emphasis must be put on the knowledge we have of Jesus Christ and the knowledge we have of ourselves through the gospel. As McFarland himself notes, "The biblical story of the triune God's dealings with the world thus allows for talk of a common humanity."[21] This fact is evidenced by Paul's description of Adam and Christ as instantiating a common humanity even given their very different lives.[22] The appropriate inference to draw from this reality is that there are common features of human existence, based on the doctrine of creation, that bind all humans together without extinguishing our differences. It is not necessary to make difference the primary ontological category in order to allow difference to be important to theological anthropology.

For McFarland, the priority of difference is rooted in the doctrine of the Trinity. However, inferring a general definition of difference from the doctrine of the Trinity is problematic. The Father, Son, and Holy Spirit are identical apart from their relations. And the divine persons share one divine life. In God's life, the Father, Son, and Holy Spirit share a divine identity. Perhaps the distinct personal identities in God may be described

---

19. McFarland, *Difference and Identity*, 93.
20. McFarland, *Difference and Identity*, 93.
21. McFarland, *Difference and Identity*, 138.
22. McFarland, *Difference and Identity*, 137.

as identity-differences, but identity-differences pertain to divine persons in a different way than identity-differences pertain to humans. Furthermore, humans differ from one another in ways that are not analogous to identity-differences in God. Humans differ in identity, attributes, and character. Attribute-differences and character-differences do not apply to God. Therefore, a general definition of difference cannot be established on the basis of the doctrine of the Trinity, unless that definition simply refers to personal distinction. But personal distinction alone does not provide grounds for assessing the goods of attribute-differences or character-differences among humans, which is something McFarland is interested in doing.

If there is an analogy between the divine relations and human relations, it is an analogy that grounds the stability of human identity. Humanity's relation to God establishes stability with respect to humanity's identity and telos. Humans are made in God's image and are expected to reflect God's character in the world. Moreover, humanity's identity and telos are shared by all humans. That humanity's identity and telos are held in common highlights human similarity.

McFarland tries to walk the fine line between the fact that we will be conformed to Christ on the one hand and the fact that our differences are important to our individuality and to the body of Christ on the other. Christ is the head of the body, and all members grow into him. Yet "the head is not the whole body."[23] McFarland states, "Rather than *my* effort to see Christ in my neighbor, discernment is better understood as my openness to Christ's work of disclosing the neighbor to me."[24] But should it not rather be said that the Spirit discloses Christ to me through my neighbor? In this case, the discovery would not terminate in my neighbor but in Christ. And the work of the Holy Spirit in the process of discernment would be highlighted.

So while there is much to learn from McFarland's theological anthropology, certain aspects of his account of human personhood are not justified by the doctrines of the Trinity, creation, or eschatology. McFarland's warnings against hegemony must be taken seriously, and they will be addressed below. But it seems to me that McFarland's account is overly reticent to build on the knowledge we have of Christ and his body. And so his caution becomes overly constrictive for the shape of his anthropology. The purpose of revelation in Christ is to make known—not perfectly known, of course, but sufficiently known—the identity of God and human identity before God.

---

23. McFarland, *Difference and Identity*, 90.
24. McFarland, *Difference and Identity*, 100 (emphasis his).

DIVINE TRANSCENDENCE AS THE KEY TO UNDERSTANDING CREATURELY MALLEABILITY?

Sarah Coakley offers a different way of using divine transcendence to support the malleability of human existence.[25] Coakley frames her discussion as an analysis of desire and the Spirit's work in Christian prayer. Rather than thinking of God as desireless and of our desire as due to creaturely lack, Coakley argues that the perfection of desire is in God, and desire in God "connotes that plenitude of longing love that God has for God's own creation and for its full and ecstatic participation in the divine, trinitarian, life."[26] This claim has direct implications for the analysis of human desire and the ways desire is experienced through human sex and gender. "It follows that, if desire is divinely and ontologically basic, not only is human 'sex' to be cast as created in its light, but 'gender'—which nowadays tends to connote the way embodied relations are carved up and culturally adjudicated—is most certainly also to be set in right subjection to that desire."[27] Pneumatology comes to the fore since the Spirit both "inflames the heart with love (Romans 5.5), and also imparts the (much neglected) 'gift' of 'self-control' (Galatians 5.23)."[28]

Like McFarland, Coakley believes that theology must attend to the marginalized "other." Arguing in favor of her proposal for *théologie totale*, she states that

> the ascetic practices of contemplation are themselves indispensable means of a true attentiveness to the despised or marginalized "other." . . . The moral and epistemic stripping that is endemic to the act of contemplation is a vital key here: its practiced self-emptying inculcates an attentiveness that is beyond merely good political intentions. Its practice is more discomforting, more destabilizing to settled presumptions, than a simple intentional *design* on empathy.[29]

Moreover, *théologie totale* explores "the many mediums and levels at which theological truth may be engaged."[30]

Theologically, Coakley draws upon Gregory of Nyssa and Augustine to ground the importance of human equality and difference.[31] Gregory and

---

25. Sarah Coakley, *God, Sexuality, and the Self: An Essay "On the Trinity"* (Cambridge: Cambridge University Press, 2013).
26. Coakley, *God, Sexuality, and the Self*, 10.
27. Coakley, *God, Sexuality, and the Self*, 10.
28. Coakley, *God, Sexuality, and the Self*, 15.
29. Coakley, *God, Sexuality, and the Self*, 47.
30. Coakley, *God, Sexuality, and the Self*, 48.
31. Coakley, *God, Sexuality, and the Self*, 266–307.

Augustine provide examples of how one can bring together contemplation of the triune God with increased desire and love in a way that affirms the equality and difference of persons but also brings those who practice contemplation to a place where their previous construals of God and themselves are transcended. "There is Gregory's 'apophatic turn' into darkness which upends the world's (and even some of the Bible's) sexual stereotypes, and Augustine's returning and uncontrolled effusions of desire and delight at the divine level in the last chapters of his *De trinitate*."[32] By this movement into contemplation and desire, gender "is made redemptively labile—subject to endless reformulations one can scarcely imagine at the beginning of the spiritual journey. And this occurs precisely by its submission to something more fundamental: the interruptive desire of the trinitarian God for fallen creation."[33] Again, "The contemplative encounter with divine mystery will include the possibility of upsetting the 'normal' vision of the sexes and gender altogether; but it will also include an often painful submission to other demanding tests of ascetic transformation—through fidelity to divine desire, and thence through fidelity to those whom we love in this world."[34] By construing contemplation as "A love affair with a blank," Coakley uses God's transcendence to support apophaticism and uses apophaticism as a means to relativize creaturely "certainties."[35]

Like McFarland's account, Coakley's is theological. And Coakley's theological arguments for human malleability are insightful. Like McFarland, Coakley opens the reader up to new avenues of input—input from the marginalized "other" or from the contemplation of God. But also like McFarland, these avenues primarily encourage apophaticism. The Christian doctrines that offer a stabilizing influence in theological anthropology are downplayed.

AUGUSTINE ON HUMAN IDENTITY AND GOD'S IMMUTABILITY

In his *Image, Identity, and the Formation of the Augustinian Soul*, Matthew Drever provides an account of Augustine's understanding of human malleability and stability.[36] Drever summarizes Augustine's fundamental insight regarding human identity as follows:

---

32. Coakley, *God, Sexuality, and the Self*, 295.
33. Coakley, *God, Sexuality, and the Self*, 59.
34. Coakley, *God, Sexuality, and the Self*, 310.
35. Coakley, *God, Sexuality, and the Self*, 342.
36. Matthew Drever, *Image, Identity, and the Formation of the Augustinian Soul* (New York: Oxford University Press, 2013).

> For Augustine, the primordial identity of the soul is forged in its imaging of God. The image of God is not some "thing," part, or faculty imprinted onto an already existing soul; rather, it characterizes how the soul forms its basic identity out of its existence. . . . The soul exists in a type of reflective immediacy in which its identity is given to it from that which the soul is not (i.e., God). This leads to the paradoxical conclusion that the soul becomes most itself when it is least its own.[37]

For Augustine, then, the human soul's fundamental identity is "image of God."

There are two distinct movements in the soul's formation, one in creation and one in re-creation, namely, "the soul's movement from nothing (*ex nihilo*) to something in its creation and the soul's movement from sin to justice in its redemption."[38] Because these movements are distinct, "it would be erroneous to conflate the basic formation of the soul through the Word with its reformation through Christ,"[39] as this would collapse creation into salvation, thus compromising creation's integrity.

When it comes to humanity's creatureliness, it is both *ex nihilo* but also, more radically, *de nihilo*.[40] Ontologically, humanity is from nothing. "In this way, Augustine draws on the doctrine of *creation ex (de) nihilo* to ground the fluidity, malleability, and fragility that underlies the soul's existence and identity. It also underscores the soul's relational nature: the soul in itself is *de nihilo* and so is only through its relation to God."[41]

While the soul is *de nihilo*, the image of God is grounded in the eternal immutable Son. The Son, the true *imago Dei*, is from God (*de Deo*) whereas creation is *de nihilo*.[42] In God, the Son's vision of the Father is the same as his procession from the Father. Augustine emphasizes that the Son's vision of the Father is "a relation internal to the divine essence that does not violate the doctrines of immutability, eternality, and simplicity. This means that the vision is stable (i.e., eternal, simple) and noncompetitive."[43] Within the divine life, vision is a characteristic of the necessary relations enjoyed by the Father, Son, and Holy Spirit.

Divine vision can be contrasted with human vision, and this comparison illumines humanity's identity as a creature. The particular creaturely

---

37. Drever, *Image, Identity, and the Formation of the Augustinian Soul*, 24.
38. Drever, *Image, Identity, and the Formation of the Augustinian Soul*, 35.
39. Drever, *Image, Identity, and the Formation of the Augustinian Soul*, 36.
40. Drever, *Image, Identity, and the Formation of the Augustinian Soul*, 49.
41. Drever, *Image, Identity, and the Formation of the Augustinian Soul*, 49.
42. Drever, *Image, Identity, and the Formation of the Augustinian Soul*, 70.
43. Drever, *Image, Identity, and the Formation of the Augustinian Soul*, 96.

relations established by physical and spiritual vision are accidental. Due to the instability and mutability of human nature created *de nihilo*, these accidental relations are deeply formative.[44] The soul is shaped by these relations, and by the vision that initiates them, because the soul is conformed in love to that which is envisioned.

When humans love what is changeable with the love due to God, then they are conformed to the fragility and malleability of creation. In a move very much like Athanasius's in the early parts of *On the Incarnation*,[45] Augustine argues that sin draws the sinner back toward the nothingness from which creation was made. "When one succumbs to temptation and so loves the world with the love due to God, one comes to think of oneself in terms of the world and therefore to be conformed to it and have one's identity scattered and dissipated within the *nihil* that grounds it."[46]

When, on the other hand, humans love God above all creaturely things, then they are conformed in an ever-increasing way to God's immutability and stability.[47] The reason for this is that these lovers of God are conformed to that which they see and love—the immutable divine life. The movement of their love is conformed to God, who is love.

For Augustine, Jesus Christ's life and teaching direct the reader of Scripture to the vision of God. And the concrete, individual, body of Christ provides a unified vision of the realities of human nature and the human telos. The goal is conformation to Jesus Christ, through both participation in the *visio Dei* and, through the Spirit, appropriation of the realities of human nature as disclosed by the particularity of Jesus Christ's life, death, and resurrection.

For Augustine, the obstacle to the vision of Christ is not apophatic reservation but sin in the mind.[48] The solution is by grace to enter into the *visio Dei*. Redemption in Christ brings about renewed and growing recognition of God. This renewed and growing recognition of God reshapes one's loves. And as one's loves become fixed on God, who is love, one participates in the life of God. "Humans attain perfection not as they grow or develop in their own nature but when they participate in God's nature, truth, and goodness."[49] The proper response to this conformation to God is worship.

---

44. Drever, *Image, Identity, and the Formation of the Augustinian Soul*, 97.
45. Athanasius, *On the Incarnation*, 3–10.
46. Drever, *Image, Identity, and the Formation of the Augustinian Soul*, 93.
47. See Craig A. Hefner, 'In God's Changelessness There Is Rest': The Existential Doctrine of God's Immutability in Augustine and Kierkegaard," *IJST* 20:1 (2018): 65–83.
48. Drever, *Image, Identity, and the Formation of the Augustinian Soul*, 117.
49. Drever, *Image, Identity, and the Formation of the Augustinian Soul*, 162.

In Augustine's account, therefore, there is an otherness at the heart of human identity, but the "other" is God.[50] The human person can only find stability in God. Insofar as she searches for stability within creation she actually magnifies her fragility and malleability. Jesus Christ, God in the flesh, unites humanity to God and exalts humanity to renewed recognition and love of God. Human recognition and love of God is patterned after the recognition and love God has in his own triune life. Since human beings are different from one another, their own movement into God's life will be different. But the telos toward which they are moving is the same, and this telos is immutable. Thus, God is the source of stability for human identity, both in its creation in the image of God and its end in conformation to God.

CREATED AND CONSTRUCTED HUMAN IDENTITIES

In the rest of this chapter, I will sketch a theological anthropology that applies Augustine's insights to human identity and its relation to human nature and ends. With Augustine, I argue that the *imago Dei* is given stability by the life of God, and therefore human identity as God's image has a stable frame of reference. Progressive conformation to God through vision and love necessitates that humans become what they are through time. Therefore, while the telos is stable, the process of human "becoming" is fluid and flexible.[51]

With McFarland, I affirm that the body of Christ is not intended to be made up of uniform expressions of humanity. From the beginning of life humans are diverse. Therefore, there is good reason to understand this diversity as divinely intended and mutually enriching. I disagree, however, with McFarland's theological justification of human diversity through reference to the divine life. Using the Trinity as the basis for human difference does not provide the necessary theological capital for McFarland's political claims. That capital can be found elsewhere, in the doctrine of creation and humanity's natural mutability.

With Coakley, I affirm that sanctification is intimately tied to desire for God and contemplation of God. These are vehicles to personal transformation in the image of God. However, I do not find contemplation of God to lead so radically to the unknown. It seems to me that there is always an interplay between known and unknown, and this interplay has the effect of providing

---

50. Drever, *Image, Identity, and the Formation of the Augustinian Soul*, 185.
51. Tanner, *Christ the Key*, 42–43.

a combination of stability and fluidity to human becoming. Even if not fully, we do see Jesus Christ and embrace him in love. And since Jesus Christ is God, he is the perfection of the movement of love. Insofar as our love is conformed to him, our movement of love is fulfilled and thereby stabilized (to an imperfect degree prior to the resurrection, but stabilized nonetheless).

Doctrinally, the only way around such movement into stability would be to embrace such a radical doctrine of sin that humanity could not enter the stability established by God in Jesus Christ through the work of the Holy Spirit. In other words, it would demand a denial of the gospel. The doctrine of sin needs to play an important role in theological anthropology, of course. Human sinfulness explains why human mutability is so often a vehicle of deformation and destruction. It also explains why the places from which human life is lived are broken and corrupted. Both the internal and external influences on the soul and its loves are affected by sin from the beginning of postfall human life. Nevertheless, while sin is attendant to all human experience after the fall and prior to the arrival of the fullness of God's kingdom, God's presence as Creator, Redeemer, and Lord is more fundamental still.

HUMAN IDENTITY IN RELATION TO NATURE, TELOS, FACULTIES, AND HABITS

Created identities are those divinely determined realities that (1) make a creature the particular creature that it is, (2) fix the creature's purpose within creation, and (3) fix the creature's appropriate end. A creature's created identity is logically prior to its structural, relational, and vocational features, and this identity shapes the particular features appropriate to that creature. As a creature of God, humanity's identity is located in the *imago Dei*. Humanity is the creature set apart as God's image on earth, patterned in a creaturely way after the eternal Son, since "all things have been created through him and for him" (Col 1:16), and "he is the image of the invisible God" (Col 1:15). Since God's intention to make humanity in his image precedes logically any structural, relational, or vocational features of humanity, then these features should be understood in light of humanity's identity as God's earthly image.

When I refer to human structures, I am thinking of those features that have been understood classically to belong to soul and body. A person's faculties depend upon these structures, including the ability to reason, to will, to remember, to imagine, to love, to perceive, to use language, and so forth. One's individual consciousness is likewise included here. These structures, taken as a whole, are referred to as human nature. From a theological perspective, human nature is the consequence of God's decision to make a creature in God's image. So, the particular structures humans have and the faculties that belong to those structures are intended by God to facilitate human life as God's image.

When I refer to humanity's relational features, I am thinking of the major categories of human relations, namely one's God-human, human-human, and human-world relations. Of course, each of these is a complex reality that demands careful analysis. Though I cannot offer this analysis here, it will be helpful to note a few things about human relations in general. Human relations are shaped by the realities of human faculties and human bodies. God's intention for human identity is the fount of human nature, and human nature conditions human relations. So, the particular way a human relates to God is affected by human nature. The particular ways humans relate to one another are also affected by human nature.

When I refer to humanity's vocational features, I am thinking of the particular ways humans are called to love, and the responsibilities that are entailed by that love. A person's responsibilities in this regard are based upon human identity as God's image, the particular way human nature is shaped by that identity, and the particular identity of the one the subject is related to. While love should form all vocational acts, the form of one's love and the acts appropriate to that love are shaped by the particulars of human identity, nature, and relations. For example, for humans made in God's image, love of God entails worship, imitation, and witness. The aptness of these acts follows from the realities of God's identity and human identity. Love of another human, on the other hand, entails acts of self-sacrificial friendship. This is a broad claim intended to include the demands placed upon any human who loves another human. Friendship, here, is intended to indicate one's commitment to the well-being of another. The particular responsibilities entailed by one's love for another person are determined by the particulars of the person one is related to and the particulars of the relation one has to that person. So while a parent–child relationship entails acts of self-sacrificial friendship, some of the acts of friendship entailed by a loving parent–child relationship differ from the acts of friendship entailed by a collegial relationship. The demands entailed by love can also be conditioned by the other person's situation. So acts of self-sacrificial friendship toward a homeless person may be more extensive materially than acts of self-sacrificial friendship toward a colleague at work. But acts of friendship toward a colleague may be more extensive in other ways. Regarding the human-world relation, love for the world entails care, stewardship, and dominion aimed at creation's flourishing. The key thing to note, once again, is that humanity's identity, nature, and relations shape one's vocational responsibilities. Habits, in this context, should be understood as the settled dispositions to love in certain ways and therefore to also act in certain ways. The regular dynamics of vocational life are conditioned by habits of love and action.

Constructed identities are self-characterizing interpretations of (1) one's particular existence within creation as an individual human being, (2) one's connection to other particular human beings, and (3) the roles and responsibilities one has or ought to pursue. As creatures of God, humans interpret their existence socially and individually before God. This interpretive enterprise is logically posterior to one's created identity. Certain structural, relational, and vocational features *exist prior to* this interpretive work, such as the existence of one's body and soul and one's relation to caregivers. But many structural, relational, and vocational features of one's life *come into existence as one is learning to characterize one's place in the world*. Other features *come into existence because of* one's socially formed self-interpretations, including specific relational or vocational features which are intentionally sought, such as finding a spouse or parenting. Constructed identities are conditioned by the development of settled loves in the context of certain personal and corporate relations through the use of a range of human faculties. They are interpretations of one's structural, relational, and vocational existence. Therefore, they are on the other end of our anthropological analysis from the place had by human identity as the image of God.

The relation of created and constructed identities to human nature, relations, and vocations might be expressed as follows:

God's Creation of Humanity

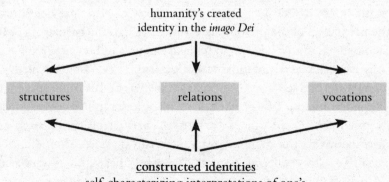

humanity's created
identity in the *imago Dei*

structures   relations   vocations

<u>constructed identities</u>
self-characterizing interpretations of one's
place in the world through consideration of
one's structures, relations, and vocations

THE DIFFERENCES BETWEEN CREATED AND CONSTRUCTED IDENTITIES

Human identity as the image of God conditions human nature, relations, and vocational responsibilities. Constructed identities are conditioned by human nature, relations, and vocations. This means, ultimately, that the term "identity" is being used in two different ways in the two contexts. In the creational context, "identity" refers to God's determination to make humanity what it is, to give humanity its purpose in creation, and to establish humanity's telos. In the context of construction, "identity" refers to one's self-characterizing interpretations of one's place within the world. These can be socially or individually formed interpretations. Most often, they are developed alongside one's significant social and personal experiences.

Constructed identities are efforts to discern some stability across time so that the diverse experiences of life can be made coherent. The problem often faced is that at least some of the person's experiences appear as they do not cohere with the others. When this is the case, the person must decide if these outlying experiences are unusual and therefore ought to be dismissed or if they are unusual and therefore ought to be definitive. People go in different directions with this decision. Coakley's suggestion that contemplation of God helps us to transcend the morass of human experience is right. Contemplation of God helps us transcend our settled convictions about our *identity-constructions*, both social and individual. Our constructions can be transcended because they are often misunderstandings of the realities experienced. Sin and experience of a sinful world confound efforts at self-interpretation. But contemplation of God does not lead us to transcend our divinely determined identity as God's image, our human structures, basic human relations, or basic vocational responsibilities. These are embedded in creation itself, and the contemplation of God confirms them.[52] The gospel provides guidance for redeemed self-characterization since these created realities are drawn into covenantal relationship with God through Jesus Christ and in the Holy Spirit.[53]

Therefore, God's determination of human identity and the fulfillment of that identity in Christ, as these are communicated in Scripture, should guide the self-characterizing interpretations of God's people as we continue to construct personal and social identities. Such guided identity-construction

---

52. See John Webster, *Holiness* (Grand Rapids: Eerdmans, 2003), 99–105.

53. Much more needs to be said here, especially regarding adoption, sonship, and the way these realities affect self-characterization. I anticipate developing this point in more detail in a future publication.

leads toward measured stability because it is directed toward God, who transcends the fragility and malleability of creation.

Created and constructed "identities" are not the same kinds of things. Creational identities are the fundamental truths of who we are as human creatures before God. With respect to the significance of these truths, human particularities are less significant than what God has declared to be true of all humans in common. Constructed identities are our efforts, often fleeting and malleable, to make sense of our personal identities in light of the way we experience human nature and our discreet relations and roles. Christians construct identities along these lines but hopefully with the larger picture of creational identities in view. Those without this transcendent frame of reference may tether their identities to other creaturely realities that appear to be more stable than themselves. But from a Christian perspective, no creaturely reality offers true stability. True stability belongs only to God, since God alone is perfect life and love.

Conclusion

We often conflate our created and constructed identities. Such conflation is dangerous because our constructed identities can then take on hegemonic or absolutized forms, which is a problem about which McFarland and Coakley are rightly concerned. The appropriate response is not to stop participating in identity-construction. We cannot. Rather, we must allow the gospel to condition our self-characterizing interpretations. McFarland and Coakley offer good advice on this front: theology must be allowed to challenge and overthrow erroneous personal and social identities. But since the doctrine of creation is underplayed in their accounts, malleability takes on too large a role in their anthropologies. We need the category of created identities to establish stable guidance for identity-construction. Then identity-construction can be understood as the redeemed effort to interpret our individual places within these stable realities.[54]

This is the vantage from which the ever-present danger of hegemony can be addressed. Stability comes from God and the fulfillment of one's vision, desire, and love in God. Stability is not found in hegemonic cultural norms but in God's life and God's purpose for humanity to participate in that life of vision and love.

---

54. Webster, *Holiness*, 100.

The pressing question related to human identity, then, is not whether there are personally and socially constructed identities, but whether these constructed identities can be judged on the basis of God's intention for the human creature and God's work in creation, judgment, redemption, and consummation.[55] If they can be so judged, then there can be better or worse constructed identities insofar as they are in harmony or in conflict with God's creational/re-creational intent. Social groups play a role in the discovery of a person's place in the world.[56] But movement into the *visio Dei* facilitates the deepest understanding because it reveals one's place before God. Knowledge of God leads to knowledge of self. But due to disordered loves, this process often turns from discovery to sinful projection. Such sinful projections must be arrested by the gospel and conformed to the truth. Before the consummation of God's kingdom there will always be a mixture of harmony and conflict, of right orientation and sin, in our constructed identities. Yet, as part of the process of sanctification, we are called to nurture those aspects of our constructed identities which are in harmony with the gospel and to abandon those aspects which are in conflict—no matter how hard and painful such abandonment might be. We can trust that the Spirit of God is at work aligning our constructed identities to the constellation of theological determinations made about us, so that by the Spirit's work we can be transformed by the renewing of our minds (Rom 12:2).

Often, identity-construction is an effort to establish a secure identity through contemplation of the self and the self's relation to other creaturely realities. It is an act of faith to submit one's self-characterizations to God's determinations as they are revealed in Scripture .By faith, identity-construction can serve human flourishing as groups and individuals find their distinct places inside of broader creational and covenantal realities. Humanity's created identity as the earthly creature made in God's image, created and fulfilled through Jesus Christ and in the Holy Spirit, must ultimately condition and shape constructed identities lest constructed identities become disjoined from the gospel and idolatrous.[57]

---

55. Michael Allen, "Toward Theological Anthropology: Tracing the Anthropological Principles of John Webster," *IJST* 19 (2017): 12.

56. Webster, *Holiness*, 104.

57. Thanks are due to Michael Allen, Craig Hefner, Eric Oldenburg, Timothy Pickavance, Kyle Strobel, and Daniel Treier for their helpful comments on an earlier draft of this chapter. I am also grateful to Biola University for providing financial support for this research.

CHAPTER 8

ADAM AND CHRIST
Human Solidarity before God

FRANCES M. YOUNG

LET'S BEGIN WITH SLIME MOULD.[1] Slime mould spends much of its life as thousands of distinct single-celled units, each moving independently, but under the right conditions, those distinct cells coalesce into a larger organism. In August 2000 a Japanese scientist announced that he had trained slime mould to find the shortest route through a maze, despite it being a very primitive organism with no centralized brain. Here is a natural, self-organizing complex that is greater than the sum of its individual constituent parts—an example of "emergence."

The laws of emergence have had cross-disciplinary impacts—not just on biology and computer science but on sociology and the understanding of collective human behaviour. The collective operates through feedback mechanisms and has no overall directing agent.[2] As the human population multiplies, pollutes its natural environment, causes a fresh mass extinction of species, depletes the resources of the planet, destroys its ecology, and generates climate change, I ask myself whether we might describe ourselves collectively as a kind of slime mould running amok. Do we need to reimagine our human selves as constituting an organism greater than the sum of its individual parts, a collective humanity more disastrously destructive than any single one of us could possibly take responsibility for?

---

1. I owe the slime mould example, and the discussion of emergence in this paragraph, to Steven Johnson, *Emergence* (London: Penguin, 2002).
2. "The behaviour of individual agents is less important than the overall system." Johnson, *Emergence*, 145.

Hold that thought for a moment while I turn to a more conventional opening to a paper on theological anthropology. . . .

In my book *God's Presence*,[3] an important dialogue partner is David Kelsey—his two-volume work *Eccentric Existence*.[4] We share a focus on eschatology, creatureliness, bodiliness and "doxological gratitude." Also I warm to his characterization of sins as "distortions" and concur with his christocentric interpretation of the phrase "image of God." There are more such convergences,[5] but today I want to take up a feature of early Christian thinking that lies right outside the parameters of Kelsey's definition of human being as a "personal living body" with an "unsubstitutable personal identity." It is, I think, telling that he differentiates Jesus from Adam precisely in these terms: "*adam* is not an individual living human personal body," but "humankind, the species," he says,[6] whereas Jesus has an "inalienable quotidian personal identity," which cannot be appropriated by anyone else.[7] Thus, participation in Jesus is ruled out, and Kelsey's challenge to the tradition remains fundamentally coloured by modernity's "turn to the subject." Three sentences reveal a telltale puzzlement: "It is humankind as some sort of corporate whole that is created according to or after the image of God. Humankind as a whole exhibits the image of God in general. However, just what this means, just what the image of God is, remains unclear."[8]

I must confess to a similar puzzlement. It goes back to my student days. In lectures on *The Theology and Ethics of the New Testament*, Professor C. F. D. Moule spoke of Paul's understanding of Christ in terms of "corporate personality." This phrase, startling to post-Enlightenment ears, has stuck with me and remained a persistent question. So this "some sort of corporate whole" is what I want to explore here, first arguing that the idea is fundamental to early Christian understanding of the interlinked themes of anthropology, soteriology, and Christology, then asking how on earth we might make sense of it in our thought-world, implying eventually that

---

3. Frances M. Young, *God's Presence: A Contemporary Recapitulation of Early Christianity* (Cambridge: Cambridge University Press, 2013).

4. David H. Kelsey, *Eccentric Existence: A Theological Anthropology* (Louisville: Westminster John Knox, 2009).

5. E.g., much of Kelsey's careful nuancing of the language of person and self, identity, and individuality, over against post-Enlightenment assumptions about the "autonomous center of self-aware consciousness," could be interpreted as having a similar thrust to my own attempt to identify what the patristic talk of "soul" enabled; while his refusal to set individual and relational models in opposition also correlates with my discussion.

6. Kelsey, *Eccentric Existence*, 922–23.

7. Kelsey, *Eccentric Existence*, 390.

8. Kelsey, *Eccentric Existence*, 922.

we can hardly afford not to—there is, after all, that daunting picture of the potentially destructive, slime-mould-like character of humankind. In any case, I doubt whether it is possible to do justice to either Pauline or patristic thought without taking seriously the corporate whole of humanity, represented both in Adam and in Christ, in each of whom particular instances of humankind do, or may, participate.

ATHANASIUS

Αὐτὸς γὰρ ἐνηνθρώπησεν, ἵνα ἡμεῖς θεοποιηθῶμεν.

He became *anthrōpos* that we might become *theos*.

Possibly one of the most famous sentences in all patristic literature, it is notoriously difficult to produce a satisfactory English equivalent. Should we translate adjectivally: "He became human so that we might become divine"? Or should the force of the verbalised nouns be given greater weight: "He became man so that we might become God"? Neither is without objection. Maybe we get closer by a bit of paraphrastic adaption: "He took humanity that we might share divinity." This translator's conundrum takes us straight into the ambiguities of Athanasius's theology and alerts us to the unavoidable debate as to whether Athanasius thinks of Christ's humanity as that of a particular individual man or humanity in general. Let's put all that in context by considering the overall perspective Athanasius offers in his two-volume work, *Contra Gentes* and *De Incarnatione*.[9] Whether or not this was an early work (I tend to think it was not[10]), it surely provides key background to Athanasius's anti-Arian arguments, illuminating not only his christological thinking but his anthropological and soteriological assumptions.

To grasp the sweep of the overarching story which Athanasius presents, one must take seriously his apologetic concerns in the less well-known volume, *Contra Gentes*. The clash between polytheistic idolatry and knowledge of the one creator God is where he starts, explaining how everything would have been idyllic if human beings had not turned away from contemplating God, as intended, to creating idols, treating nonexistent things as real, led astray by their own bodies, their senses and desires. Adam briefly typifies the general point, but the ongoing description is made to apply to

---

9. Text and ET: Athanasius, *Contra Gentes and De Incarnatione*, trans. and ed. Robert W. Thomson, Oxford Early Christian Texts (Oxford: Clarendon, 1971).

10. For discussion see Frances M. Young with Andrew Teal, *From Nicaea to Chalcedon. A Guide to the Literature and Its Background* 2nd ed. (Grand Rapids: Baker Academic, 2010), 52–56.

"the soul," which could just as well have inclined to the good but actually turned away from it. As we proceed there is oscillation between the plural (human beings) and the singular (the soul), but the point is that humanity invented evil, forgot it was made in God's image, and applied the term "God" to visible phenomena, fabricating nonexistent gods, even raising human beings to divine status.

So at length Athanasius spells out what Paul summarised in Romans 1:20–25:[11]

> Ever since the creation of the world his eternal power and divine nature, invisible though they are, have been understood and seen through the things he has made. So they are without excuse; for though they knew God, they did not honour him as God or give thanks to him, but they became futile in their thinking. . . . They exchanged the truth about God for a lie and worshipped and served the creature rather than the Creator, who is blessed for ever! Amen.

Deduction of the Creator from the harmony of creation, however, is only part of Athanasius's argument; for he has already hinted[12] that if the soul turns back towards God, it can contemplate the image of God's Word/ Logos, which is the image of God the Father, in the mirror that is itself—a point based on Genesis 1:26. And this now becomes the pole around which Athanasius's thinking pivots:[13] inherently unstable, in that they came into being from nothing, God endows created beings with the Logos, from which they receive life and subsistence, harmony, and rationality. The Logos is absolute wisdom, reason itself, the very power of God the Father, absolute light, absolute truth, absolute righteousness, absolute virtue, stamp, effulgence, and image—indeed, the express image of the Father, and this not by participation—for these properties do not accrue to him from outside, in the way of those who participate in him and are given wisdom by him, having their power and reason in him. Rather, he is absolute life, wisdom, and holiness as the true Son of the Father, and nothing exists without him. Yet, even so, human beings in their folly rejected knowledge of him, worshipping the creation instead of the Creator.

Here endeth the first volume; the second, the *De Incarnatione*, not only reveals the significance of this initial exposition but is itself illuminated

---

11. Unless otherwise indicated, Scripture quotations in this chapter come from the NRSVA.
12. *C. Gent.* 34.
13. *C. Gent.* 46–47.

by what we have seen so far. Athanasius is first constrained to go back to the creation of the universe—for its renewal was fittingly effected by the Word who created it in the first place. He highlights, against other views, the points briefly noted—that God made everything from nothing through the Logos, our Lord Jesus Christ, and pitying the human race in particular, made them according to God's own image and gave them a share in the power of the Logos, so making them rational. The result of their turning away, however, he explicitly describes as their sinking back into the non-existence from which they had been brought into being: for effectively they lost the Logos—the source of life and rationality. The incarnation of the Logos is the answer to the tension between God's goodness and God's integrity—for God had declared that, if disobedient, humankind would die. But the Word took a body no different from ours and surrendered it to death on behalf of all so that as all die in him the inevitability of destruction might be dissolved, and he might give them life for death. Athanasius is clear that *all* had to die, that the body taken by the Logos was sufficient exchange for the death of *all*, and because of the indwelling Word its resurrection would bring an end to death for *the whole human race*. He quotes Paul: "For since death came through a human being, the resurrection of the dead has also come through a human being; for as all die in Adam, so all will be made alive in Christ" (1 Cor 15:21–22).

As in the *Contra Gentes* Athanasius affirms that being in the image should have been sufficient for knowing God the Word and, through him, the Father, but human beings failed to recognise God by this means or through the works of creation. God sent the Law and Prophets to school them back. However, their loss of rationality meant they did not look to the truth. If human beings were to know God again, God would have to renew the image again, and that could only happen through the coming of the very image of God, our Saviour Jesus Christ. The Word of God, therefore, took to himself a body and lived as a human being among humans. In two ways the Saviour had compassion through the incarnation: he rid us of death and renewed us and, although invisible and indiscernible, yet by his works, he revealed himself as the Son of God and the Word of the Father. In other words, he reversed both the loss of life and the loss of rationality that led to idolatry. His presence vivified and purified the mortal body.[14]

We need not follow Athanasius as he spells out at some length the result-ant Christology, together with the reasons why Christ died on the cross,

---

14. *De Inc.* 17.

how the resurrection refutes unbelievers and destroys idolatry, and how it was all predicted in Scripture. The point to be underlined is that the death *of all* was fulfilled in the Lord's body, and death and corruption were destroyed because of the Word being in it.[15] The Word of God took a body and used a human instrument to give life to the body and to reveal himself, leaving none deprived of his divinity and knowledge, touching all parts of creation, freeing and undeceiving everything of all error; thus humankind is no longer mistaken about God, but worships God alone, recognizing the Father through him.[16] In his concluding remarks, Athanasius produces, amongst other things, our opening tagline: "He became *anthrōpos* that we might become *theos.*"

Now in my summary—to a large extent a collage of phrases from the translated text—you may have noticed several apparently alternative usages: "the human race," "human beings," "the human," or "the soul," and occasionally "humanity," each used in a generic sense. Their meaning seems indistinguishable. Athanasius refers at least to the human species in general, and possibly to some sort of corporate entity, while the human body taken by the Logos somehow dies the death of the whole human race. This is the reason why I said earlier that I doubted whether it is possible to do justice to patristic thought without taking seriously the corporate whole of humanity.

So how did Athanasius make sense of this corporate whole? The clue lies in a passage from the *Contra Gentes* sketched earlier:[17] as true Son, the Logos is absolute wisdom, reason itself, the very power of God, absolute truth—absolute life, wisdom, holiness—but not by participation, for these properties do not accrue to him from outside as in the case of those who participate in him. Athanasius is not generally regarded as a Platonist, but this passage surely reflects the Platonist intellectual atmosphere of the time. He takes it for granted that particular cases acquire a certain property by participating in its absolute form; the absolute is not just another instance of the quality—it is essentially different, being the principle that allows the participation of other entities in it. So because he is the true Son, embodying absolute life and absolute holiness, particulars can participate in that holiness and life and be adopted into that sonship. This argument, barely explicit in *Contra Gentes* and *De Incarnatione*, becomes the key to his anti-Arian polemic: only because the Logos truly is the Son of God is it possible for humans

---

15. *De Inc.* 20.
16. *De Inc.* 41–45.
17. *C. Gent.* 46.

(women as well as men) to become sons by participation—υἱοποίησις and θεοποίησις depend on the ὁμοούσιος. The Logos is not a creature who merely participates in divinity or Sonship, not another instance of qualities that creatures may share in; rather, he is the very principle of Sonship or divinity which provides the possibility of participation.

Now if that is the kind of philosophical notion that shapes Athanasius's understanding, then, surely, it accounts for his anthropology. The body of Christ, passing through death to resurrection and endowed with the Logos, is absolute humanity, humanity renewed and re-created in God's image, such that other humans may now participate in him, so receiving life, wisdom, holiness. The humanity of Christ is some kind of corporate whole, and Athanasius's entire theological schema would fail if that were not so.[18] It seems undeniable that his soteriology presupposes a twofold corporate anthropology: the human creature lost and the human creature restored, solidarity in sin, solidarity in Christ.

OTHER PATRISTIC MATERIAL

Other early theologians explicitly treated Adam and Christ in typological parallel, implying that each represented a form of corporate humanity. In *God's Presence* I explored at length the pattern of fall and redemption in early Christian theology and its representation in the typology of Adam and Christ, Eve and Mary. Let me avoid repeating my previous discussion and simply underline the corporateness of these representative figures. Irenaeus's account in the *Demonstration of the Apostolic Preaching* may open as a story about the first human creature, explicitly described as weak and immature, but once recapitulation in Christ becomes his focus, he begins to speak of humanity in general, and somehow we are all in Adam. God's Word became flesh so as to "recapitulate in himself the ancient creation of humankind." With some statements Irenaeus clearly anticipates Athanasius:

> The Logos became man, that man united with Logos and receiving his adoption might become the son of God.[19]

---

18. There remains a tension, of course: salvation for the whole of corporate humanity should be implicit in the incarnate absolute, yet υἱοποίησις or θεοποίησις is available only to those who choose to participate, to be baptised into Christ, to become adopted sons and members of the body of Christ. There is also, perhaps, an inconsistency: the general run of humankind falls into corruption, and Adam is cited as an instance of this, yet Athanasius never apparently exploits Adam as a corporate figure for humankind gone-wrong.

19. *Haer.* III.19.

> Because of his measureless love, he became what we are in order to enable us to become what he is.[20]

It might be said that he envisages new creation rather than θεοποίησις, but the overarching story implies that Adam and Christ, Eve and Mary are at least universal types, representing two kinds of truth about humanity; the implication seems to be that we are all incorporated actually in Adam and potentially in Christ.

How each human being may be drawn into this encompassing narrative and find themselves within it becomes evident at a later date in the poetry of Ephrem Syrus, where this typology is a recurring theme. In *God's Presence*, the thirteenth of Ephrem's *Hymns on Paradise* was quoted to show how he fuses biblical stories so as to constitute the story of "everyman." "The king of Babylon resembled Adam, king of the universe," and so did King David: "because it was not easy for us to see our fallen state," he depicted it in that king, "portraying our fall in his fall, and portraying our return in his repentant return." Samson, Jonah, and Joseph appear, each becoming an exemplar of a single human narrative of fall and redemption, Adam and Christ somehow incorporating humanity as a whole.

The same kind of approach underlies the theology of Cyril of Alexandria. In his work *On Worship in Spirit and Truth*, the movement from fall into sin, then through repentance to renewal through God's grace, becomes a universal paradigm, traced out in one narrative after another and applied to "us." It is not hard to see that what happened to Adam happens to each of us, Cyril suggests. The *Glaphyra* treats Adam entirely through the lens of Pauline texts: Christ is the last Adam, recapitulating and reversing the fall of the first, the grace of salvation having been given before the ages began. Cyril's *Commentary on the Gospel of John* is saturated with allusions to Christ as the second Adam, even though that gospel has no reference to Adam at all. "The common element of humanity is summed up in Christ's person, which is also why he is called the last Adam: he enriched our common nature with everything conducive to joy and glory, just as the first Adam impoverished it with everything bringing gloom and corruption."[21] The Adam-Christ typology implies that each figure is somehow corporate, each having a human being in which humans participate. This typology is less

---

20. *Haer.* V. pref.
21. *Comm. Jn.* 1.9 (on John 1:14). ET: Norman Russell, *Cyril of Alexandria*, Early Church Fathers (New York: Routledge, 2000), 106–7.

obviously Platonist, but it surely involves an understanding of humankind as more than simply the aggregate of discreet individuals, something bigger than the sum of its parts. Furthermore, the whole picture of humanity in relation to God stands or falls on whether such a corporate understanding of humankind can work.

PAUL

Cyril's debt to the Pauline material reminds us to return to the question of whether Paul's Christology involves the characterization of Christ as a "corporate personality." The two key texts are Romans 5:12–21 and 1 Corinthians 15:20–23, 45–49.

In 1 Corinthians 15:22, the focus is on resurrection. Here Paul suggests that as in Adam all die, "so all will be made alive in Christ." Later he uses the figures of the first man and the last man to contrast the physical being made from dust and the life-giving spirit come from heaven, suggesting that at the resurrection the physical body, sown in weakness, is raised in power a spiritual body. As we have borne the image of the man of dust, he says, so we will bear the image of the man of heaven. Adam and Christ are at least representative figures, but Paul would appear to suggest more: they typify types of humanity into which humans are, or will be, incorporated.

Turning to Romans 5, Paul hardly meant what Augustine thought he meant—namely, that all humanity inherited from Adam both sin and guilt, these being transmitted through the sexual act. Paul's focus is on death as the consequence of sin. The one man to whom Paul refers is representative of all humanity in that "all have sinned and fall short of the glory of God," the point that Paul has laboured to make clear in his argument up to this point. Paul uses the word "type" in this passage, but not to characterize the way Adam's story typifies the story of the everyman; rather, Adam is a type of the one who is to come. For Adam and Christ go over the same ground, but Paul's rhetoric contrasts the two, a contrast perhaps implicit also in Philippians 2, where not grasping equality with God is the issue. Thus Christ is Adam's antitype. So in Romans, one man occasions death for the many, the other life for the many; one brings condemnation, the other justification. And by an implicit *qal wahomer* argument, righteousness and eternal life are an abundant free gift of grace through the obedience of one man, which was prefigured in the disobedience of one man—the more sin, the more grace, Paul implies, even though he immediately refuses the consequent logic that "we continue in sin in order that grace may abound"

(Rom 6:1). It seems that one is either in Christ or in Adam. Thus they would seem not merely to typify but to incorporate.

There are, of course, other features of Paul's Christology that likewise point in a corporate direction. The most obvious is his use of the body image for the church, found in 1 Corinthians 12 and Romans 12.[22] Then there is Paul's persistent way of speaking about Christians, individually and/or collectively, being "in Christ":[23]

> There is neither Jew nor Greek, there is neither slave nor free, there is neither male nor female; for you are all one *in Christ Jesus.* (Gal 3:28 RSV)

> There is therefore now no condemnation for those who are *in Christ Jesus.* (Rom 8:1)

Thus the corporate character of his conception of Christ's person seems clear.[24] Before God all humanity is in the same case, unless and until they are renewed by coming to be in Christ, and the way to salvation is participation in the new creation which is Christ's humanity. Such incorporation into Christ is also strongly suggested by such statements as 2 Corinthians 5:14–15: "For the love of Christ urges us on, because we are convinced that one has died for all; therefore all have died. And he died for all, so that those who live might live no longer for themselves, but for him who died and was raised for them."

Whether or not some kind of lurking Platonism provides an intellectual framework within which to make sense of it, this corporate perspective, as we have seen, is recaptured in patristic material. Indeed, such corporate thinking seems integral to the grand narrative of creation and salvation that constitute the pattern of early Christian theology. So is there something here which is essential Christian theology?

---

22. The later, possibly post-Pauline, text of Ephesians suggests (4:15) that Christ is the head of the body, which might modify the sense of incorporation somewhat; but it does not negate it, for the text is all about growing up into him.

23. Conversely, though, Paul can speak of Christ being in believers: "But if Christ is in you, although your bodies are dead because of sin, your spirits are alive because of righteousness" (Rom 8:10 RSV). "I have been crucified with Christ; it is no longer I who live, but Christ who lives in me" (Gal 2:20 RSV). The following generalisations have been suggested: (1) that believers exist in Christ, but Christ is active in believers, so the two notions are not exactly parallel, and (2) that while Christ is in the believer individually, believers are often in Christ corporately as God's people. Cf. John Ziesler, *Pauline Christianity* (Oxford: Oxford University Press, 1990).

24. In his little study of *Pauline Christianity*, Ziesler advances reasons for scepticism about the appeal to corporate language in the Hebrew Bible as an explanation, though I suggest it is worth noting that Paul's "I" in Romans 7, so often treated as autobiographical, seems in fact to parallel the "I" of the Psalms, implying a sense of being part of a larger whole, rather like Isaiah's confession that he is a man of unclean lips and lives among the people of unclean lips (Isa 6:5).

THE MODERN INDIVIDUAL SELF

I need hardly point out how inimical today's perspectives are to that whole picture. If the postmodern breakdown of grand narratives were not enough, the "me-society" is reinforced within modern forms of Christianity itself: the evangelical challenge, "Are you saved?" implies that each individual may or may not find personal faith in the Lord Jesus Christ, who died for their own particular failings and sin. Thus it becomes a matter of consumer choice whether you are religious or not, and the majority are increasingly voting with their feet because they feel they cannot personally sign up to the creeds with intellectual integrity. Undergirding the "selfies" of popular culture is, of course, a massive intellectual and philosophical shift dating back to the Enlightenment. I am sure many in my audience will be more *au fait* with how all that has happened than I am, and we need not trace here the whole story through Descartes, Locke, Kant, and others, but let's distil from Charles Taylor's *Sources of the Self: The Making of the Modern Identity* some sense of the crucial shifts which modernity has made, and then note ways in which certain trends have been reinforced, rather than challenged, by so-called postmodernity.[25]

"For us," writes Taylor, "the subject is a self in a way he or she couldn't be for the ancients."[26] He draws out two facets of modern individualism: "self responsible independence" and "recognised particularity." The moral autonomy implied by the first is sharply contrasted with "the great classical moralists," whose "reflection turns us towards an objective order."[27] Rather, "we are defined by purposes and capacities which we discover in ourselves."[28] The order of ideas ceases to be something we find and becomes something we build.[29] He speaks of the "inwardness of self-sufficiency,"[30] of a rationality which is "a property of the process of thinking, not of the substantive content of thought," of freedom and of a "model of reason" that is "exclusive of authority," of "the first person standpoint,"[31] of the inner voice, one's own fulfilment, and of a morality not being imposed from outside.[32]

---

25. Charles Taylor, *Sources of the Self: The Making of the Modern Identity* (Cambridge, MA: Harvard University Press, 1989).
26. Taylor, *Sources of the Self*, 176.
27. Taylor, *Sources of the Self*, 175.
28. Taylor, *Sources of the Self*, 301.
29. Taylor, *Sources of the Self*, 144.
30. Taylor, *Sources of the Self*, 158.
31. Taylor, *Sources of the Self*, 168.
32. Taylor, *Sources of the Self*, 363.

His second facet is the focus on individual difference, on deeper engagement in our particularity,[33] the quest for personal meaning and identity, for self-fulfillment and self-expression—the "self-exploration" that presumes "we don't know already who we are,"[34] by contrast with the old search for one universal human nature. The value put on creative originality, on authenticity, on independence, on one's personal vision, on freedom from social constraint, on privacy, and so on, coheres with the importance for identity of personal narrative, memory, and particular life story. The rise of the novel means that "the general or typical now emerges out of the description of particular people in their peculiarity"—the world is no longer seen as the embodiment of archetypes.[35] "Corresponding to the free, disengaged subject is a view of society as made up of and by the consent of free individuals, and corollary to this, the notion of society as made up of bearers of individual rights."[36]

That paragraph hardly does justice to Taylor's six-hundred-page book, but it does put some of the key themes on the table. It is no accident that Mrs. Thatcher could assert, "There is no such thing as society": we no longer think of ourselves collectively. The autonomous self-directed individual with his own story was once, of course, the white male in a patriarchal society; postmodernism has espoused equality and demanded the same rights for women, for those belonging to the LGBT community, for persons from minority ethnic communities, for those with impairments and disabilities, and even for the child. But note *how* the term "community" has crept in—it is a way of referring to individuals who constitute groups that feel they are in the same boat. In truth, most people take it for granted that relationships are ultimately all about themselves and their own personal fulfilment, whether reflecting shared personal concerns, or furthering one's own profit or self-interest. Postmodernity has exacerbated the fragmentation of society, even as our societies are increasingly globalised.

Psychologically, philosophically, and culturally it seems almost impossible to reclaim a sense of overall human solidarity. So, considering theological anthropology in such a context, are we stuck with the "unsubstitutable personal identity" of Kelsey's, *Eccentric Existence*?

---

33. Taylor, *Sources of the Self*, 182.
34. Taylor, *Sources of the Self*, 178.
35. Taylor, *Sources of the Self*, 287.
36. Taylor, *Sources of the Self*, 106.

BEYOND THE INDIVIDUAL

Recently I reread Primo Levi's *If This Is a Man*,[37] his account of being an inmate in the Auschwitz labour camp. On this second read there was one feature I found particularly striking: the fight for survival meant that each person was on their own, competing for food, warmth, basic necessities, room to sleep. He describes the saved and the drowned. The slightest sign of weakness or self-pity meant a man was shunned and became one of the drowned, and the saved were those who were unscrupulous in their self-interest yet were given respect. This is the starkest account of extreme individualism I have ever read: here was unavoidable autonomy, utter isolation, total self-concern.

Now compare that to a parallel but lesser known story. *The Hunger Angel*, a book by the Nobel Prize–winning novelist, Herta Müller, tells of ethnic Germans from Eastern Europe, who at the end of the World War II were deported by victorious Soviet forces into labour camps to rebuild Russia—in the form of a novel it draws on actual reminiscences.[38] One of the characters is Kati Sentry, a woman described as "born feeble-minded" and completely unaware of where she was: "Kati Sentry wasn't suited for any type of work. She didn't understand what a quota was, or a command, or a punishment. She disrupted the course of the shift." So they found her a sentry job—hence her name.

The persistent refrain of the book is the sheer hunger they suffered, and how they exploited one another to get bread. But no one was allowed to take Kati Sentry's bread.

> In the camp we've learned to clear away the dead without shuddering. We undress them before they turn stiff, we need their clothes so we won't freeze to death. And we eat their saved bread. Their death is our gain. But Kati Sentry is alive, even if she doesn't know where she is. We realize this, so we treat her as something that belongs to all of us. We make up for what we do to one another by standing up for her. We're capable of many things, but as long as she is living among us, there's a limit to how far we actually go.

The camp inmates were redeemed by the presence of a person with learning disabilities.

---

37. Primo Levi, *If This Is a Man*, trans. Stuart Woolf (repr., London: Folio Society, 2000).
38. Herta Müller, *The Hunger Angel*, trans. Philip Boehm (London: Portobello, 2012).

There are ways in which each person with a disability has a more marked "unsubstitutable personal identity" than any of the rest of us. Each is impaired in their own way, particularly those with brain damage or developmental failures. Yet it is those who are absolutely dependent on others, like my son, Arthur,[39] those without self-help skills, with little communication beyond cries and smiles, and needing total care, who most obviously require community for the very sustenance of life. That Arthur has reached fifty years of age is entirely due to the carers who have fed and watered him, kept him clean and free from infection, medicated him to reduce his epileptic seizures—I could go on . . .

In *God's Presence* I discussed theologians, such as Zizioulas and McFadyen, who regard communion and relationships as constitutive of what it means to be human. There is no "self" in itself but only as it is with and for others. Personal integrity is profoundly related to the mutuality involved in communication, trust, and commitment. This view I illustrated by reference to the L'Arche communities, where people live in community with those with learning disabilities, entering into mutual relationships with them. The significance of community, then, I am the first to concede, yet I concluded, with Kelsey, that the "contrast between individualistic and relational concepts of human being as though they are mutually exclusive" is hardly sustainable.

And my point now is this: however necessary it is to counter our individualism with emphasis on the fact that we are social animals and we require community to be what we are, that does not enable us to reclaim the same kind of human corporateness we found in biblical and patristic sources. We seem to need a new conceptuality. Can we find such a thing, and so move to a position where appropriation is possible after all—despite the individualism of modernity and the identity politics of postmodernism?

CONNECTEDNESS

Perhaps a basis for conceptualizing connectedness might be found in the idea of the "collective unconscious." That Freudian analysis and Jungian archetypes have had profound influence on literature and literary criticism, as well as types of counselling and pastoral care, is undeniable. Could it prove a tool in our theological quest?

---

39. For Arthur's story, see Frances Young, *Face to Face* (London: Epworth, 1985; enlarged edition Edinburgh: T&T Clark, 1990); and Young, *Arthur's Call: A Journey of Faith in the Face of Severe Learning Disability* (London: SPCK, 2014).

In *From a Broken Web*,[40] Catherine Keller sets up a binary opposition between the "separative self" and the "soluble self."[41] The "separative self" relates only externally to the other and is identified with both the self of modernity and the *homo incurvatus in seipsum* of Augustine and Luther. The almost inevitable outcome, she claims, is male dominance and a God whose principal characteristic is aseity. The "soluble" or "influent" self, on the other hand, is one that flows into others and feels others flow into itself—there is reciprocal influence, an intertwining, the oceanic feeling of interconnectedness felt by mystics, poets, women, sensitive and religious personalities.[42] Keller suggests that, according to Freudian perspective, this "mass psyche" or "collective unconscious," though universal in infancy, is left behind as the ego matures—Freud thus conspires with the "modern self" and patriarchal norms, whereas Jung "seems to offer a revolutionary, empirically based and psychologically elaborated ground for the non-separative ego."[43] So, "Sacrificing its own illusory claims to autonomy, the ego's task becomes that of reconnecting with the depth and breadth of life from which it had so early cut itself off."[44]

At this point it is tempting to consider the claims of mystics. Let me briefly offer a modern example: Élizabeth-Paule Labat, a trained musician, entered a convent in 1922 and wrote a beautiful little book called *The Song That I Am: On the Mystery of Music*.[45] The English translation appeared in 2014. Self-transcendence, she claims, is "the natural condition of man, who, as man, can only realize himself by going beyond himself."[46] History she sees "as an immense symphony resolving one dissonance by another until the intonation of the perfect major chord of the final cadence at the end of time," and "every being, every thing contributes to the unity of that sublime concert."[47] Christ, she says, "is the leaven of this solidarity in which the collective and the individual are not opposed but rather strengthen

---

40. Catherine Keller, *From a Broken Web: Separation, Sexism, and Self* (Boston: Beacon, 1986).

41. Interestingly, these contrasting types parallel the difference between the "buffered self" and the "porous self" which Charles Taylor describes in his later big book, *A Secular Age* (Cambridge, MA: Harvard University Press, 2007); and he offers a critique of what he calls "excarnation"—the objectification of everything other than the self—which parallels Keller's characterization of the "separative self."

42. Keller, *Broken Web*, 98.

43. Keller, *Broken Web*, 113.

44. Keller, *Broken Web*, 114.

45. Élizabeth-Paule Labat, *The Song That I Am: On the Mystery of Music*, trans. Erik Vardon (Collegeville, MN: Liturgical, 2014).

46. Labat, *The Song*, 103. Inclusive language was not an issue in her time, and the translator has made no effort to alter her voice.

47. Labat, *The Song*, 104.

one another."[48] For her, music enables a foretaste of the joy of universal communion and is a triumphant rediscovery of unity: "By establishing us in a relationship of solidarity with all things, music becomes almost a sacramental of unity."[49] Grace liberates from "the tyranny of egoism."[50] I could go on sharing more of this beautiful little book, but enough! For Keller admits that the mystics, poets, women, and others who experience this oceanic feeling are "all at the margins of society."[51]

Yet perhaps it is the marginalised who through their very difference reveal most effectively our interdependence, given our common, creaturely limitations. Keller claims a profound relationship between connection and individuation: "Authentic individuality can be gained only when I experience myself as fundamentally connected to all of life."[52] "One becomes more and more different by taking in more of what is different."[53] This reminds me of how the founder of L'Arche, Jean Vanier, speaks of the vulnerability and inner brokenness of each of us being exposed by mutual relationship with those with learning disabilities, thus enabling not just communion with them but also a deeper sense of oneself. I find it particularly telling that Jean Vanier does not write "disability theology" but theological anthropology.[54] His interest, like mine, has been in what is revealed about our common human nature by relationship with those with learning disabilities. So I endorse the move made by Deborah Beth Creamer in *Disability and Christian Theology*.[55] Going beyond the models usually employed in disability studies, functional/medical and social/minority, she espouses a "limits model," thus enabling recognition that the complexities of the experience of disability are not satisfactorily captured by a binary contrast with some ideal norm: every one of us is limited in some respect. An approach to theological anthropology through the experience of disability not only reinforces the recent turn to embodment but also, as I have frequently argued myself,[56] shatters the illusion of autonomy by

---

48. Labat, *The Song*, 117.
49. Labat, *The Song*, 66–67.
50. Labat, *The Song*, 83.
51. Keller, *Broken Web*, 98.
52. Keller, *Broken Web*, 114.
53. Keller, *Broken Web*, 136.
54. Jean Vanier has been a prolific writer. From his considerable bibliography I instance here just *The Broken Body: Journey to Wholeness* (London: Darton, Longman and Todd, 1988).
55. Deborah Beth Creamer, *Disability and Christian Theology: Embodied Limits and Constructive Possibilities* (New York: Oxford University Press, 2009)
56. E.g. Frances Young, "The Creative Purpose of God," in *Encounter with Mystery: Reflections on L'Arche and Living with Disability*, ed. Frances Young (London: Darton, Longman and Todd, 1997); cf. Young, *Arthur's Call*; and *God's Presence*.

revealing our common fragility, our limitations, our creatureliness, so revealing our fundamental connectedness, indeed our interdependence.

For Keller the point is that the personal and the collective become permeable, disclosing a level where dichotomies disintegrate. To reclaim the fluid boundaries of the child we must trust that we are already distinctive in and through our connections, she says.[57] So Keller arrives at the idea of a collective or transpersonal psyche, which is the basis of all consciousness.[58] Intriguingly, she thus mirrors the philosophical speculations of antiquity about the universal soul in which each embodied soul participates.

Yet "academic psychology has distanced itself from psychoanalysis";[59] hard-nosed empiricism is suspicious of the whole notion of some kind of "collective unconscious." So can we find more solid ground?

ANTHROPOLOGY

Let's consider anthropology as a secular subject of enquiry. It may seem surprising, given its history of uncovering cultural difference, but it has always presumed commonality in the human race.

> Anthropology has always worked at the intersection of nature and culture, the universal and the particular, patterns and diversity, similarities and differences. . . . Today an anthropologist . . . would be much more likely to argue that the truck and barter of small-scale societies should be treated in the same frame as e-trading in cyberspace.[60]

That quote comes from a little book called *Think Like an Anthropologist*. For all the focus on cultural difference, "difference for difference's sake" is "not the point of anthropology," it states; "while anthropology wants to document differences . . . it also wants to make sense of them."[61] Tracing the history of anthropology, the book acknowledges its early colonialist assumptions, not least its use of categories suggesting evolution from savagery to civilisation, but "the psychic unity of mankind" was always adopted as a principle: "The mental capacities of the savage are the same as those of the civilised gentleman; humanity was one race and, at its core, of

---

57. Keller, *Broken Web*, 147.
58. Keller, *Broken Web*, 150.
59. Jocelyn Bryan, *Human Being: Insights from Psychology and the Christian Faith* (London: SCM, 2016), 5.
60. Matthew Engelke, *Think Like an Anthropologist* (London: Pelican, 2017), 5–6.
61. Engelke, *Think Like an Anthropologist*, 314.

one mind."[62] Levi-Strauss is quoted as saying, "The savage mind is logical in the same sense and the same fashion as ours."[63] For him all the "cultural detail and cultural particularism was nothing more than data that would be used to underscore his true interest, which was the universal structure of the human mind."[64]

Such a position would now be reinforced by basic biology. The study of the human genome, as more and more data is crunched, proves that "we share all our ancestry with everyone on Earth. We are all cousins, of some degree. . . . Our DNA threads through all of us."[65] Indeed, "None of the ways in which we talk about race today stands up to the scrutiny that genetics has enabled."[66] We are all interconnected, genetically related to every other human person. There is one modern human species, as distinct from earlier human species identified through bones and fossils.

THE UNIVERSAL

Scientific study, then, upholds a notion of universal human nature. Furthermore, this is the basis of the Universal Declaration of Human Rights. Often treated as upholding the rights of each individual, thus conspiring with the assumptions implicit in the modern sense of the autonomous self and the self-oriented claims of self-identified groups, it is actually an attempt to protect in law those humans whose rights might be threatened—the oppressed, the exploited, the vulnerable, the different, those living with disabilities, women and children—and it does this on the basis of common human being. Charles Taylor, in *A Secular Age*, notes how the goal of universal human rights and universal welfare are aspirations pointing to solidarity and in tension with the modern focus on the self.[67] That tension between the one and the many, the universal and the particular, remains cogent.

And, certainly, it takes us some way towards solidarity, even more so if we note the intertwining of stories. As a pregnant woman at a maternity clinic, I had to acknowledge the reality that this experience was both profoundly personal, affecting my very being both physical and spiritual, yet it

---

62. Engelke, *Think Like an Anthropologist*, 69–70.
63. Engelke, *Think Like an Anthropologist*, 286.
64. Engelke, *Think Like an Anthropologist*, 47.
65. Adam Rutherford, *A Brief History of Everyone Who Ever Lived: The Story in Our Genes* (London: Weidenfeld and Nicolson, 2016), 166.
66. Rutherford, *A Brief History of Everyone Who Ever Lived*, 266.
67. Taylor, *A Secular Age* (Cambridge, MA: Harvard University Press, 2007), 608–9.

was common to all the women there and the majority of women across the globe. History and "social narratives of family, society and culture also intersect with and influence our personal stories and become integrated into who we are and become."[68] Our need for engagement with the human interest of news stories, not to mention novels and biographies, reveals our capacity to sense identity with many different particular stories, to become an imaginative player in another's story, indeed another's culture and history. To care for someone with profound disabilities is an experience that brings you right down to the common basics of human existence, feeding and defecating, washing and dressing, protecting and keeping warm. Many particular stories intertwine with the story of someone like my son, Arthur—indeed, for some, caring for him has been life-changing, even a catalyst for discerning their vocation. The coinherence of narratives, rather than some abstract Platonic entity, makes sense of the dynamic relationship between the particular and the universal.

But the idea of universality does not yet conceptually incorporate each into a larger whole, which is surely required to appropriate early Christian theology.

INCORPORATION

So back to slime mould—for the concept of "emergence" might take us further. As one moves from subatomic particles to chemical combinations, living cells, complex organisms, and human consciousness, each whole is clearly more than its parts.[69] No extra component is added, yet "what happens at a higher level is not completely derivable from what happens on the level beneath it."[70] In their self-organizing capacity, swarms of starlings, bees, and locusts, and even ant colonies and human cities, are similar to slime mould.[71] Through feedback mechanisms individuals become part of a larger whole with its own patterns of behaviour. In "emergence," I suggest, we have the concept which enables appropriation of the idea of a corporate humanity. Myriads of acts of free will, generating and responding to feedback from those close by, produces collective thought and action. The analysis of

---

68. Bryan, *Human Being*, 29.

69. John Polkinghorne, *One World—The Interaction of Science and Theology* (London: SPCK, 1986), 80. It is this concept of "emergence" that most fundamentally challenges anthropological dualism, the view defended in ch. 4 by Hans Madueme.

70. John C. Lennox, *God's Undertaker: Has Science Buried God?* (Oxford: Lion, 2007), 56.

71. Johnson, *Emergence*.

group dynamics describes individuals being caught up in behaviours beyond anything they would consent to rationally and individually, such as mob lynchings, while participation in small self-directed singing or instrumental groups enables individual performance to be taken up into something much greater than itself. Such experience, writ large, coheres with the notion of an emergent corporate personality engaged in patterns of coherent activity. This has, of course, generated dangerous sectional collectivities, distinguishing themselves from others in hostile ways. But put the slime mould analogy alongside the story of Kati Sentry, and what we have is the potential either for corporate condemnation or corporate redemption.

In fact, as is clear in early Christian theology, divine judgement is the context in which human solidarity makes the most sense, solidarity in sin and solidarity in salvation. Humanity stands together in its gonewrongness, in its failure to be God's representative on earth, in its failure to tend the garden of creation rather than exploiting it. All together we are slime-mould-like, polluting and corrupting the natural world. And not for nothing have campaigners spoken of "*institutional* racism" and theologians of "*structural* sin"; both are ways of acknowledging the same idea: that corporately sin is greater than the minor misdeeds of most of us, greater even than the horrors perpetrated by individuals to whom the media loves to attribute "pure evil." Liturgical confession should perhaps move from its implied individualism to a greater awareness of how a congregation might take responsibility before God for humanity's corporate mess. Is that not what it means to be a kingdom of priests and a holy nation? (1 Pet 2:9).

And corporate sin surely needs a corporate answer. So if it is possible to conceptualise solidarity in sin in such terms, so too it must be possible to have some comprehension of a new corporate creation in Christ, a renewal of humankind with the potential to transform its corporate behaviour. This surely implies some process of participation in Christ as each separate cell of Christ's body interacts with others, all being assimilated into the emerging superorganism. Thus, this too is realized bottom-up, by feedback mechanisms, by mutual inspiration to different behaviours, like the response of those labour camp inmates to Kati Sentry. Dare we affirm the necessity of tragedies such as profound disability, of vulnerability, and even death—not least the death of Christ—to evoke from us transformed collective responses capable of redeeming humankind as a whole? Dare we point to Christ and the Spirit as catalysts for such transformation?

The process of incorporation into Christ's body takes place over time, through ecclesial feedback mechanisms—the church's stories, its saints, its communal and liturgical life. Indeed, for Cyril of Alexandria the partaking was conceived in remarkably physical terms: in the eucharist the holy body of Christ is mingled with our bodies, like the insertion of a glowing ember into a pile of straw.[72] The genesis of self-transcendence, of being taken up into something bigger than ourselves, is knowing ourselves as an element in the whole story of the God who created us, each and every one, and so as part of the whole human race, both now and over time. Redemption, in the end, is about how all stand together before God at the final judgement—*simul justus et peccator*, in Christ who redeems Adam and Eve, and all of us in them.

---

72. *Comm. Jn.* 3.6 (on John 6:35); 4.2 (on John 6:54).

CHAPTER 9

LIFE IN THE SPIRIT
Christ's and Ours

LUCY PEPPIATT

*"Spirit-christology is after all a model that
exegetes the divine economy."*[1]

PROPONENTS OF SPIRIT CHRISTOLOGY claim that it functions as a useful dogmatic foundation for theological anthropology. There are several reasons for this claim, chiefly that Spirit Christology gives an account of the incarnate life of Christ as a human existence lived out in dependence upon the empowering, guidance, and comfort of the Holy Spirit. This not only reflects the accounts of Christ's life in the biblical narratives but affords a direct ontological connection between Christ's life and our own.[2] With this emphasis on the fully human Christ, we are able to give an account of how he is like his brothers and sisters "in all things" or "in every respect" (Heb 2:17), sin excepted (Heb 4:15). Jesus's life thus functions as a model for Christian existence. Notwithstanding the complicating factor that the term Spirit Christology can encompass almost any account of Christ and the

---

1. Ralph Del Colle, *Christ and the Spirit: Spirit-Christology in Trinitarian Perspective* (New York: Oxford University Press, 1994), 29.
2. There are now numerous works on Spirit Christology. For a selection of orthodox Spirit Christologies see David Coffey, *Deus Trinitas: The Doctrine of the Triune God* (New York: Oxford University Press, 1999); Del Colle, *Christ and the Spirit*; Myk Habets, *The Anointed Son: A Trinitarian Spirit Christology* (Eugene, OR: Pickwick, 2010); Gerald F. Hawthorne, *The Presence and the Power: The Significance of the Holy Spirit in the Life and Ministry of Jesus* (London: Word, 1991); Alan Spence, *Incarnation and Inspiration: John Owen and the Coherence of Christology* (London: T&T Clark, 2007).

Spirit (including adoptionist, post-Trinitarian, and revisionist Christologies), in itself this is not an unreasonable claim. However, as Ralph Del Colle astutely observes, those seeking dogmatic coherence when constructing a Spirit Christology within the parameters of christological and Trinitarian orthodoxy soon find that "theological problems begin to multiply"![3] What ostensibly sounds like a simple claim based on biblical evidence is not dogmatically unproblematic.

However, I do not think that the problems are insurmountable, and given both the strong scriptural foundation for Spirit Christology and the growing interest in pneumatology in relation to Christology, it is worth endeavoring to work towards some solutions. This paper is an attempt to think through a particular challenge associated with Spirit Christology, the question of agency in the person of Christ, a question that is clearly at the heart of claims relating to Christ's life as analogous to our own. In order to do this, I will consider the highly sophisticated pneumatic Christology of John Owen, who himself is at pains to explain the work of the Spirit in Christ within the bounds of orthodox christological and Trinitarian formulae. From this dogmatic foundation, he builds a rich theological anthropology. I borrow some of his insights on the work of the Spirit in humanity and conclude with some implications for models of spiritual formation with reference to Pentecostal and charismatic spirituality.

THE QUESTION OF AGENCY IN OWEN'S CHRISTOLOGY

Regarding the work of the Spirit in the two natures of Christ in relation to their distinct properties and operations, Owen's claims are both bold and complex. He is clearly aware of any criticism that might come his way, so he begins *Christologia* with a robust defense of his account of the two natures as having both a scriptural foundation and Chalcedonian support.[4] Owen's theology is characterized by his conviction that the doctrine of the two natures must be treated in conjunction with a strong account of the inseparable but also clearly distinct economic roles of the persons of the Trinity. It is often noted that his innovation in Christology (giving rise

---

3. Del Colle, *Christ and the Spirit*, 5.
4. See the preface of Owen's *Christologia*, where he argues for a clear distinction between the properties and operations of the two natures as the most faithful account of the person of Christ. John Owen, *Christologia*, in *The Works of John Owen* (Dublin: Richard Moore Tims, 1831), xxx. Throughout the preface, Owen defends his Christology as both biblical and rooted in the traditions of the Fathers.

to its retrospective identification as Spirit Christology) is due to the very distinct roles that Owen assigns to the Son and the Spirit in the one person of Christ, affording a prominent and indeed, constitutive, role for the Holy Spirit.[5] What follows is a brief summary of his most famous and oft-quoted claims, which are directly relevant to the question of agency in Christ.

First, he claims that the "only immediate [peculiar] *act* of the person of the Son on the human nature was the *assumption* of it into subsistence with himself."[6] He elaborates, "All other actings of God in the *person of the Son* towards the human nature were voluntary, and did not necessarily ensue on the union mentioned; for there was no transfusion of the properties of one nature into the other, nor real physical communication of divine essential excellencies unto the humanity."[7] He concludes, therefore, that it is the person of the Holy Spirit and not the Son who is "the *immediate, peculiar, efficient cause* of all external divine operations: for God worketh by his Spirit, or in him immediately applies the power and efficacy of the divine excellencies unto their operation. . . . It is the Spirit who is the immediate operator of all divine acts of the Son himself, even on his own human nature."[8] Owen, however, is not without his critics.

CRITICISMS OF OWEN

In Owen's day, John Biddle, Owen's Socinian nemesis, questioned whether this insistence on the operation of the Holy Spirit in Christ implies that the divine nature is in the "mean time idle and useless?"[9] Matt Jenson echoes this concern, wondering whether this model leaves us "with a non-operative divinity in Jesus that is functionally identical to . . . kenoticism."[10] Oliver Crisp, similarly, sees "no metaphysical room for the interposition of another divine person between the intentions of God the Son (i.e., his agency) and

---

5. Del Colle writes, "If the pneumatological dimension of Christian salvation is to be fully articulated—e.g., that the Christian life is life in the Spirit—then it is necessary to explicate how the being and event of incarnation/redemption is pneumatological. Spirit-christology affirms the constitutive agency of the Holy Spirit in the confession of Jesus Christ and in those homologies and eventual doctrinal constructions that express the meaning of his person and deed" (*Christ and the Spirit*, 78).

6. John Owen, *The Works of John Owen*, vol. 3, *Pneumatologia*, ed. William H. Goold (Carlisle, PA: Banner of Truth, 1972), 160.

7. Owen, *Pneumatologia*, 161.

8. Owen, *Pneumatologia*, 160–61.

9. John Biddle, *XII Arguments Drawn out of the Scriptures where in the commonly-received opinion touching the Deity of the Holy Spirit is clearly and fully refuted* (London, 1647), 27ff. cited in Alan Spence, "The Significance of John Owen for Modern Christology," in *The Ashgate Research Companion to John Owen's Theology*, ed. Kelly M. Kapic and Mark Jones (Farnham: Ashgate, 2012), 171–84, at 178.

10. This is a criticism aimed at Spence's use of Owen. Matt Jenson, review of *Incarnation and Inspiration*, by Alan Spence, *Journal of Reformed Theology* 2, no. 3 (2008): 299–300, at 300.

the intentional actions brought about in his human nature."[11] Crisp's concern is that Owen's doctrine generates a "distinction between God the Son and his agency 'in' or 'through' his human nature at all moments after the first moment of the assumption of human nature" after which "his divine nature does not act directly upon his human nature, but only mediately, via the agency of the Holy Spirit." This is a fair assessment of Owen, whose position on this point Crisp deems to be "theologically dubious."[12]

Owen, aware of potential opprobrium, identifies the two threads of criticism that will come his way and distinguishes two related but distinct questions. He writes, first, "For could not the Son of God himself, in his own person, perform all things requisite both for the forming, supporting, sanctifying, and preserving of his own nature, without the especial assistance of the Holy Ghost?" and second, "Nor is it easy to be understood how an *immediate work* of the Holy Ghost should be interposed, in the same person, between the one nature and the other."[13] These two issues will be the focus of this paper.

OWEN'S PREMISES

Before we summarize Owen's basis for defending his Christology, I wish to draw attention to the three foundational premises upon which Owen's Christology rests. This highlights some foundational christological principles within Owen's thought in terms of what he thinks must be said and what cannot be said. If one accepts his premises, then his christological construction follows as the only plausible explanation for the work of God in and through Christ.

1. Christology must be able to account for the fully human life of Christ in every respect, first to be faithful to the biblical witness, and second because this is the heart of the gospel as he understands it.
2. Although there is one person of Christ, if we were to ascribe sole agency to the divine Son in the one person of Christ, without

---

11. Oliver D. Crisp, *Revisioning Christology: Theology in the Reformed Tradition* (Farnham: Ashgate, 2011), 105.

12. Crisp, *Revisioning Christology*, 100. Piet Schoonenberg poses the same questions of Spirit Christology in general: "How can the divine person of the Spirit mediate between the other divine person of the Logos and his humanity without interrupting their hypostatic union? Or, if we prefer to see the [Spirit] Logos (*sic.*) at work alongside of the Logos, do we avoid making Jesus's human nature a sort of condominium of two persons?" Piet Schoonenberg, SJ, "Spirit Christology and Logos Christology," *Bijdragen* 38 (1977): 350–75, at 366, cited in Del Colle, *Christ and the Spirit*, 150.

13. Owen, *Pneumatologia*, 160.

accounting for his rational soul and all that this entails, we would be compromising on his fully human existence. This is often expressed as a theological intuition that the divine might overwhelm or eclipse the human.[14] We will return to this point below. For now, it should be noted that holding to this principle is an attempt to resist Apollinarism, monoenergism, or a flawed distinction between acts done in Christ's divine nature and acts done in his human nature such as we find in Cyril of Jerusalem or Leo's Tome.[15]

3. The Holy Spirit is the person of the Trinity, without exception, who works in and through created terms. There are multiple reasons given for this in Owen, all related to the issues above, namely, remaining faithful to Scripture, the safeguarding of the full humanity of Christ, the efficacy of the atonement, and the conditions under which human beings may flourish.

The only way to ensure Christ's *human* agency in his one person, as Owen sees it, is through a faithful exposition of Chalcedon and by insisting that the two natures function in Christ without change and without confusion, thus giving credence to Christ's full humanity. In summary, Owen's Christology is a portrayal of the way in which he understands God the Trinity to act both upon and within human nature in a way that (a) represents Christ's life as depicted in the New Testament, (b) is explanatory of the efficacy and power of his atoning sacrifice, and (c) respects the dignity and worth of humanity in general.

THE DIVINE SON AS MEDIATOR

Does Owen's Christology imply that the divine Son is no longer the origin of all his own actions?[16] Some of Owen's statements give this impression;

---

14. Owen claimed that if Christ's human nature had been filled with the immenseness and omniscience of God, that it would have been destroyed and not exalted. See Owen, *Christologia*, 33.

15. See Cyril of Jerusalem, *Catechetical Lectures* 4.9 (*NPNF*[2] 7:22). Here Cyril assigns different actions and attributes to the distinct natures, that is, what is seen to his human nature, what is not seen to God. Christ ate like us, but fed the five thousand as God. He slept in the ship as man, and raised the dead and walked on water as God. This bifurcated attribution of Jesus's acts occurs again in Leo's Tome. Ian McFarland calls this thinking succumbing to the "Leonine temptation" and makes the point that "association of Jesus's divinity with his miracles is deeply problematic" as there is "no observable difference between the miracles performed by Jesus and those performed by other people in his name." Ian A. McFarland, "Spirit and Incarnation: Toward a Pneumatic Chalcedonianism," *IJST* 16, no. 2 (2014): 143–58, at 147.

16. Crisp asserts that "for the actions of Jesus of Nazareth really to be the actions of God the Son Incarnate, they must be actions that originate with God the Son." Crisp, *Revisioning*, 105.

however, his answer to this question would be an emphatic *no*. How does Owen answer the charge that his Christology renders the agency of the divine Son in Christ somehow inoperative?

To answer his own questions cited above, while remaining faithful to a two nature Christology, Owen makes certain key distinctions. These include (1) an appeal to the principle of inseparable operations with certain acts of the Trinity *ad extra* ascribed eminently to distinct persons, (2) a distinction between the notions of assumption and union (3), a distinction between the grace of union and habitual grace,[17] and (4) a distinction between the works of the Son and the effects of those works.[18]

We cannot explore all of these in detail, but these distinctions serve as explanatory concepts given to account for Christ's fully human mediating office, which is the key to understanding Owen's Christology. Although Owen's soteriology encompasses a range of metaphors for the atonement,[19] Christ is, above all, the Mediator. The pivotal concept at the heart of Owen's soteriology is the perfect obedience of the Son in his humanity even unto death. Out of this Owen develops the themes of oblation/sacrifice, intercession, trust, suffering, endurance through trials and temptations, vulnerability, and faith. The necessary covenant between the Father and the Son for our salvation can only be enacted if we can account for the dialogical and relational space between the two persons of one essence.

---

17. Owen is reliant on Aquinas for this distinction. "Likewise, inasmuch as He was the Word of God, He had the power of doing all things well by the Divine operation. And because it is necessary to admit a human operation, distinct from the Divine operation, as will be shown (III:19:1), it was necessary for Him to have habitual grace, whereby this operation might be perfect in Him." *ST* III, Q. 7, A. 1, ad. 2. Also, "The humanity of Christ is the instrument of the Godhead—not, indeed, an inanimate instrument, which nowise acts, but is merely acted upon; but an instrument animated by a rational soul, which is so acted upon as to act. And hence the nature of the action demanded that he should have habitual grace." *ST* III, Q. 7, A. 1, ad. 3.

18. In addition to this Owen distinguishes between acts of Christ in his mediation as immediate actings of his distinct natures, which he calls ἐνεργήματα, and the effects or outcome of those actings as acts of his whole person, which he calls ἀποτελέσματα. "As in the person of a man, some of his acts, as to the immediate principle of operation, are acts of the body, and some are of the soul; yet, in their performance and accomplishment, are they the acts of the *person*: so the acts of Christ in his mediation, as to their ἐνεργήματα, or immediate operation, were the actings of his distinct natures,—some of the divine and some of the human, immediately; but as unto their ἀποτελέσματα, and the perfecting efficacy of them, they were the acts of his *whole person*." Owen, *Works*, 5:255, cited in Kelly M. Kapic, *Communion with God: The Divine and the Human in the Theology of John Owen* (Grand Rapids: Baker Academic. 2007), 143–44, (emphasis Kapic's). So Kapic writes, "Thus, Jesus's obedience was 'performed in the human nature; but the *person* of Christ was he that performed it.'" Kapic, *Communion with God*, 143. Spence also refers to this distinction in Owen, noting that Owen's use of "person" is problematic for the modern reader "in the light of a psychological model of human personhood," and adds, "But this model is clearly inadequate to express the agency of one who is God-man acting through his two natures, even though it might have value in clarifying what it means for that one to be and act as a human." Spence, *Incarnation*, 141.

19. See, e.g., John Owen, *The Death of Death in the Death of Christ*, for a multifaceted description of the atonement.

Referring to John 1:1, he makes the point that it is only possible for Christ to be our representative if he not only *is* God but is also *with* God.[20] However, the only means by which he, as the Word, is able to enter properly into this covenantal and sacrificial relation with the Father is in and through his humanity.[21] This is how Christ discharges his mediatorial and sacerdotal office.[22]

In order to construct an account of Christ as the fully obedient Son and second Adam, Owen draws and builds on Thomist thought, where we find an insistence on the need for habitual grace in Christ, designated as a work of the Spirit.[23] Interestingly, in *Christ and the Spirit* Del Colle undertakes a remarkably similar project to Owen with precisely the same focus.[24]

HABITUAL GRACE

Owen is indebted to Aquinas who argued before him that it was necessary for Christ to have habitual grace, first, "because it is necessary to admit a human operation, distinct from Divine operation," and second, because habitual grace is the means whereby this human operation "might be perfect in Him."[25] In neither Aquinas's nor Owen's nor Del Colle's view, does this compromise the agency of the one person. It is illustrative of the different ways God acts in and through the Son, and explanatory of the way God works in and through humanity *in toto*. As Aquinas writes, "The humanity of Christ is the instrument of the Godhead—not, indeed, an inanimate

---

20. Owen, *Christologia*, 52.

21. Owen, *Pneumatologia*, 178–80. Del Colle makes the point that the only dialogical relationship in the New Testament is the Father/Son relation. Del Colle, *Christ and the Spirit*, 150.

22. "The Lord discharged his office and work of revealing the will of the Father in and by his human nature, that nature wherein he 'dwelt among us,' John i.14; for although the person of Christ, God and man, was our mediator, . . . yet his human nature was that wherein he discharged the duties of his office and the "principium quod" of all his mediatory actings, 1 Tim. ii.5." Owen, *Works*, 19:30.

23. For an example of this in Owen see John Owen, "Sermon XI. The Humiliation and Condescension of Christ," November 9, 1681, in *The Sermons of John Owen*, Christian Classics Ethereal Library, https://www.ccel.org/ccel/owen/sermons.i.html. Although Aquinas refers mostly to "habitual grace" as "grace," he also refers to this as a work of the Spirit. He first cites Isaiah 11:2, "The Spirit of the LORD shall rest upon Him," as proof of habitual grace at work in Christ and later writes, "but the principle of habitual grace, which is given with charity, is the Holy Ghost, who is said to be sent inasmuch as He dwells in the mind by charity" (*ST* III, Q. 7, A. 13). In support of his view, he references Augustine, who in himself writes, "grace is signified by the Holy Spirit" (*Enchridion de ide, spe, et caritate* 12.40).

24. Del Colle has no references to Owen in his work, but as they share the same roots in Aquinas, their work develops in a remarkably similar fashion. It is interesting to see the same theological developments in both the Roman Catholic and Reformed traditions. See especially Del Colle, *Christ and the Spirit*, 69–70.

25. *ST* III, Q. 7, A. 1, ad. 2. Del Colle defines habitual grace as "that radical active potency enabling the operations of the human soul of Christ." Del Colle, *Christ and the Spirit*, 70.

instrument, which nowise acts, but is merely acted upon; but an instrument animated by a rational soul, which is so acted upon as to act. And hence the nature of the action demanded that he should have habitual grace."[26] The concept of habitual grace as a work of the Spirit provides us, I suggest, with the means to answer a number of questions in relation to Owen's and other theological anthropologies based on Spirit Christology. We should not lose sight, however, of the fact that Owen's Christology is driven by his soteriology, which is what ultimately leads him to the conclusion that it is necessary to claim a particular role for the Spirit in the humanity of Christ.

There are, therefore, several interwoven issues in relation to the need for habitual grace in Christ, the Mediator. The existence of the rational soul in Christ accounts for the limitations and frailty of his humanity, which for Owen includes a noetic dimension. In other words, we are able to account both for Christ's lack of knowledge of all things and his capacity to increase in wisdom and knowledge.[27] Thus, the incarnate Son in his humanity receives the knowledge and love of the Father in the manner that all human beings receive the knowledge and love of God, via habitual grace, or the work of Spirit. The uncreated act of knowledge and love of the Father in the Son that is his by nature is communicated to the human nature/soul in a different manner (a created act of grace), which can account for a response of human willing and obedience.[28] This takes us back to premise two that I mentioned earlier regarding the potential for the overwhelming of the human by the divine in Christ due to the asymmetric nature of the hypostatic union. How can the infinite join with the finite and not eclipse the created term? In answering this, Owen rightly eschews any form of kenoticism. The human nature of Christ is the human nature of the Son and is only given existence because it is his human nature eternally filled to the fullness of God. This is not in question. Owen is, rather, referring to the *way* humanity is filled with divine excellencies in the economy—that is, voluntarily by the Spirit—in order to accord humanity with dignity and worth and to account for an obedient human response. The alternative is that if sole agency were to be accorded to the Son, humanity would immediately be divinized through union with the divine so as to render the human response of Christ nonexistent. Hence the need for the knowledge and love of the Father to the Son to be imparted by grace/the Spirit to the

---

26. *ST* III, Q. 7, A. 1, ad. 3.
27. Owen, *Pneumatologia*, 170.
28. *ST* III, Q. 7, A. 1, ad. 2.

rational soul in the same way that it is imparted to all creatures.[29] This is the foundation of Owen's pneumatological theological anthropology.

Aquinas and Owen come to the same conclusions. If the Son's response to the Father is not a human response by grace, then his link with the rest of humanity is severed and his role as Mediator is annulled.[30] We will return to these themes in relation to anthropology. Before we do, I wish to mention briefly some further principles in Owen's Christology that demonstrate that he does not draw as strict a line between the agency of the Son and the Spirit as might be supposed.

INSEPARABLE OPERATIONS

Owen sees the work of the Spirit as inextricably linked to the work of the Father and the Son, and he is wholly committed to the principle of inseparable operations—that all the works of the Trinity *ad extra* are undivided. Whereas this does not resolve the problems with agency per se, it does soften the sharp distinctions of the works of the Father, Son, and Spirit that are evident in Owen's work. Owen's dual insistence on the one essence and will of the Godhead *and* ascribing certain works of God eminently to the Father, Son, and Spirit is consistent with the principle of inseparable operations in its entirety, where the second clause reads that "the order and distinction of the persons [be] preserved."[31] So as far as Owen is concerned, it is wholly proper to speak of the Spirit as a person with a will and a "personality," thereby acknowledging the hypostatic individuation of the Spirit.[32] And given, for example, that the incarnation is ascribed eminently

---

29. *ST* III, Q. 7, A. 1, ad. 3. Although Owen clearly draws on Aquinas, Owen develops his pneumatology in a much more personal direction than Aquinas, who equates the work of the Spirit with a form of grace.

30. *ST* III, Q. 7, A. 1.

31. Henri Blocher cites a second half of the rule of inseparable external operations, "*servato discrimine et ordine personarum* (the distinction and order of the Persons being preserved)" in "Immanence and Transcendence in Trinitarian Theology," in *The Trinity in a Pluralistic Age*, ed. Kevin J. Vanhoozer (Grand Rapids: Eerdmans, 1997), 104–123, at 120, citing Emil Brunner, *Dogmatique I: la doctrine chrétienne de Dieu*, French trans. Fréderic Jaccard (Geneva: Labor & Fides, 1964), 253. I am unclear as to the origins of this precise wording used by Blocher/Brunner. The principle of inseparable operations is normally associated with Augustine. In *On the Trinity* 4.5.30, Augustine claims that the Father, Son, and Holy Spirit "act inseparably." He goes on, "But they cannot be manifested inseparably by creatures which are so unlike them, especially material ones." He adds, the "trinity together produced both the Father's voice and the Son's flesh and the Holy Spirit's dove, though each of these single things has reference to a single person. Well, at least the example helps us to see how this three, inseparable in itself, is manifested separately through visible creatures" (Augustine, *The Trinity*, ed. John E. Rotelle, OSA, trans. Edmund Hill, OP [Hyde Park, NY: New City, 1991], 183). Owen is adhering also to this latter principle.

32. Owen, *Pneumatologia*, 77–81. "Hereunto the act of willing is properly ascribed, and he in whom it is proved to be a person" (81).

to the Son,[33] making a similar claim for works of the Spirit in relation to other works of the Trinity *ad extra* is perfectly acceptable.[34] When we speak of the Spirit's proper mission, we are referring to the Father and the Son's Spirit, who through his will is enacting the one divine will. Thus Owen has no compunction in ascribing certain works of the Trinity eminently to the Holy Spirit—in this case, the formation of the human nature of Christ.[35]

Secondly, we are referring to the Son's own Spirit. He writes, "Whatever the Son of God wrought in, by, or upon the human nature, he did it by the Holy Ghost, who *is his Spirit*."[36] This is, incidentally, why he is also so insistent on maintaining the *filioque* clause, a point we will return to below. My point here is that Owen portrays the work of the Spirit as in some senses derivative of both the Father and the Son and certainly as a continuation and completion of the works of the Trinity *ad extra*. "The collation of the Spirit is a *continued act*, in that he was given [to Christ] to abide with him, to rest upon him, wherein there was a continuance of the love of God towards and his care over him in his work."[37] For this reason, the idea that the Spirit is "interposed" between the divine and human nature is a misleading concept, and although Owen himself anticipates the use of this word, it is, in my opinion, infelicitous.

The need for habitual grace in the formation of the human nature of Christ is not a hiatus in divine agency, according to Owen, but a continuation of the works of God in and through the incarnation. The Word assumes the human nature in an immediate act, which is the ground of Christ's being. The act of union, which follows, is mediate by virtue of the assumption.[38] Habitual grace (or the work of the Spirit) galvanizes the human acts of Christ. The Word thus sustains the person of Christ in

---

33. See esp. *Christologia*, 124ff. and *Pneumatologia*, 66ff.

34. Owen, *Pneumatologia*, 162.

35. Owen apportions the distinct actions to the persons of the Trinity as follows: "As unto authoritative designation—it was the act of the Father; As unto the formation of the human nature—it was a peculiar act of the Spirit; As unto the term of the assumption—it was the peculiar act of the person of the Son." *Christologia*, 241.

36. Owen, *Pneumatologia*, 162, emphasis added. Note Owen's use of "hence" in the following quotation: "The Holy Spirit is the *Spirit of the Son*, no less than the Spirit of the Father. . . . And hence is he the immediate operator of all divine acts of the Son himself, even on his own human nature. Whatever the Son of God wrought in, by, or upon the human nature, he did it by the Holy Ghost, who is his Spirit, as he is the Spirit of the Father." *Pneumatologia*, 162. And further, the work of the Spirit is "not his own work, but rather the work of the Son, by whom he is sent, and in whose name he doth accomplish it: John xvi. 13–15." *Pneumatologia*, 195. In my view, this is a satisfactory response to Cyril's ninth anathema where he anathematizes those who claim that the Spirit at work in Christ is other than his own. Del Colle expresses it thus: "The Son adorns or anoints his humanity with the Holy Spirit." *Christ and the Spirit*, 53.

37. Owen, *Pneumatologia*, 173.

38. Owen, *Christologia*, 241.

subsistence, but the Spirit is both behind and within the human actions of Christ.[39] This mediating work of the Spirit between the two natures serves both to prevent attributing human characteristics improperly to the divine nature, *and* to affirm Christ as the mediator and high priest. So, according to Owen, the divine nature has no concurrence in the human acts of the divine Son because the divine nature did not act in hungering, thirsting, weariness, bleeding, and dying; "it cannot do so."[40] He concludes, while the acts of "the divine nature on the human were acts of sustentation, whereby he acted these things,"[41] the acts themselves are human acts.

Thus, with reference to the execution of his office of mediation, Owen distinguishes between the agent, Christ the God-man, who is the *principium quo* (the principle by which Christ acts that gives life and efficacy to the whole work) and that which operates in both natures distinctly considered which he calls the *principium quod*.[42] This culminates in the ἀποτέλεσμα, "the effect produced, which ariseth from all, and relates to them all: so resolving the excellency [spoken of] into his personal union."[43] On the question of divinity as a causative principle, Ian McFarland writes, "The confession that the Word is the *subject* of Jesus's thoughts and actions (since Jesus *is* the Word) must be distinguished from the claim that the Word is the *cause* of Jesus's human operations."[44] As I see it, this is precisely Owen's aim. I turn now to the theological anthropology that arises from Owen's Spirit Christology and the interplay of theology, Scripture, and experience in his work that gives his Christology a particular pastoral significance.

OWEN'S PNEUMATOLOGICAL THEOLOGICAL ANTHROPOLOGY

It seems strange somehow to connect Owen's theology to Pentecostal and charismatic (hereinafter P/c) spirituality, as many of the practices in P/c churches in relation to spiritual gifts and styles of worship would, I think,

---

39. In one sermon, Owen makes the point that human nature is not "self-sufficient," even the human nature of Christ. It "eternally lives in dependence on God and by communications from the divine nature." Owen, "Sermon XI," 496.

40. Owen, "Sermon XI," 498.

41. Owen, "Sermon XI," 498.

42. Owen, *Of Communion with God the Father, Son and Holy Ghost* (1657), 2.2, https://www.ccel.org/ccel/owen/communion.i.vii.ii.html.

43. Owen, *Of Communion with God the Father, Son and Holy Ghost*, 2.2.

44. Echoing Owen, McFarland writes, "In short, crucial to a proper understanding of the hypostatic union is the principle that the divine hypostasis—the Word—is the subject who wills and acts, but within the realm of time and space the Word's willing and acting are properties of his human nature." McFarland, "Spirit and Incarnation," 151–52.

have appalled him! However, there is no doubt in my mind that Owen has far exceeded any theological reflection on the Spirit so far undertaken within the P/c churches. Thus, in this section I explore what a seventeenth-century English Puritan divine, who describes the Christian life as "life in the Spirit" and is himself committed to the person, presence, power, and work of the Holy Spirit might offer to twenty-first-century Christians with the same commitments.

Despite some significant differences between Owen and P/c perspectives on the purpose and implications of the gift of the Spirit to the church, there are also some remarkable similarities. In respect to this paper it is the shared conviction that it is the Spirit whose particular task it is to form human nature, both Christ's and ours in precisely the same way, with precisely the same effects, that is the focal point. In this regard, the difference between Christ and humanity is only in degree but not kind.[45] In addition to this, Owen's language and concepts will be familiar to Pentecostals and charismatics: the anointing, unction, filling, and baptism of the Spirit first to Christ and from Christ to us.[46] The filling of the Spirit that brings with it the knowledge of the love of God, the impartation of extraordinary powers and gifts, great and miraculous works, prophetic witness, priestly and kingly offices, wisdom, joy, comfort, support, and peace.[47] Notwithstanding that Owen himself did not hold to the view that everything conferred on Christ's human nature by the Spirit would or could be conferred on his followers, the logic of his argument takes us in that direction, and the implications of his basic claims are vast. For now, I have chosen to focus only on three topics in relation to spiritual formation: human willing and response, the Spirit of Sonship, and the role of experience.

HUMAN WILLING AND RESPONSE

Christian accounts of spiritual formation answer the question of how it is that human beings are formed or re-formed in the image and likeness of Christ. Answers to this question vary, but central to any account of spiritual

---

45. He writes, "For although believers are so, as to measure and degree, unspeakably beneath what Christ was, who received not the Spirit by measure, yet as he is the head and they are the members of the same mystical body, their unction by the Spirit is of the same kind." Owen, *Pneumatologia*, 61.

46. See esp. *Pneumatologia*, ch. 4.

47. In addition to this, he writes of the anointing on Christ as king, priest, and prophet being given to us: "How, by virtue of an unction, with the same Spirit dwelling in him and us, we become to be interested in these offices of his, and are made also kings, priests, and prophets to God." Owen, *Of Communion with God the Father, Son and Holy Ghost*, 3.247.

formation is the question of grace and effort, or gift and response. In line with Maximus centuries before, Owen has a strong account of how Christ's human willing is in concert with the divine will. As we have seen, he utilizes the two-wills doctrine as a corollary of the two-natures doctrine to underpin his soteriology. Owen also sees this as the key to Christ's connection with the rest of humanity, and it is through a discussion of the will that he develops his theology of grace and response. Space precludes a detailed discussion of Maximus and Owen, but it appears Owen is indebted to him in at least two important ways. The first is his emphasis on the self-determining nature of the human will, [48] and the second his view of the receptivity of the human soul, softened by grace, which becomes "the dwelling-place of God" (Eph 2:22).[49] Moreover, these two aspects of human being are empowered by the Spirit.

When discussing the self-determining aspects of Christ's human nature (viz., his willing), we must also affirm that Christ was a human being in whom the fullness of God dwelt in bodily form. The Spirit is given to him "without measure." He is *full* of grace and truth. Tradition has it, however, that this fullness of God does not overwhelm his human response but enlivens and shapes it to perfect obedience. This work of God in his human nature is ascribed to habitual grace, or the work of the Spirit, which works in precisely the same way in us. It is worth quoting Owen in full.

> I say, then, that by the habit of grace and holiness infused into us by the Spirit of sanctification, the will is freed, enlarged, and enabled to answer the commands of God for obedience, according to the tenor of the new covenant. This is that freedom, this is that power of the will, which the Scripture reveals and regards and which by all the promises and precepts of it we are obliged to use and exercise, and no other.[50]

Despite the obvious disanalogies of Christ's life and our own in relation to sanctification in particular, the point here is that God works by his Spirit

---

48. Maximus writes, "The great Gregory, says, 'with divine authority, he gives the nature time, when it wishes, to perform what belongs to itself.' For if it is only as God that he wills these things, and not as himself being a human being, then either the body has become divine by nature, or the Word has changed its nature and become flesh by loss of its own Godhead, or the flesh is not at all in itself endowed with a rational soul, but is in itself completely lifeless and irrational." Maximus, *Opuscule* 7, 77B, in *Maximus the Confessor*, ed. Andrew Louth (London: Routledge, 1996), 184. Louth makes the point that this has not been found in Gregory's extant works (n15). For further references to the self-determining aspects of the soul, see also Maximus, *Two Hundred Texts on Theology and the Incarnate Dispensation of the Son of God*, §11.

49. Maximus, *Two Hundred Texts*, §12.

50. Owen, *Pneumatologia*, 496.

first in Christ and then in us to accord worth and dignity to the human soul. Thus, God's will is enacted through a freely willing human will.[51]

What can Owen's account offer P/c theology? First, this is not a blunt account of free will often found in P/c circles, but the freedom of humanity to be wooed and not coerced by the Spirit of God, who in turn leads human beings to follow freely. The Spirit does not override the human will but is able to move the will to act in accordance with God's will.[52] Owen describes a subtle interplay of the Spirit and the human will so that the will grows (freely) in obedience to God. Furthermore, according to Owen, the Spirit does not and cannot act contrary to a person's own nature, endowments, or qualifications; he likens this work of the Spirit in a person to a master musician skilfully playing several notes of music on different instruments, variously tuned.[53]

Thus, Owen's is an account of the Spirit-led life that accommodates the passing of time and the work of the Spirit through natural processes. The believer is united to Christ by faith through Christ's blood and then formed by the Spirit over the course of time, as we see in the life of Christ. And so there is room for growth in wisdom and grace. Although many aspects of P/c accounts of spiritual formation are entirely in line with these views in general, Owen's theology has emphases that are often muted in P/c accounts of spiritual formation, notably his emphasis on the work of the Spirit in the natural processes of human growth and development and through the passing of time. A predilection to focus on signs and wonders in P/c traditions risks a disavowal of this aspect of the Spirit's work as it becomes expected that natural processes will be overridden or subverted through miraculous events. To this, Owen's pneumatology acts as a welcome corrective.[54]

THE SPIRIT OF SONSHIP

As we have seen, Owen's commitment to the *filioque* is the basis on which he claims that we both receive the Spirit *of* the Son and receive the Spirit

---

51. The Holy Spirit "acts our wills so that they also act themselves, and that freely." Owen, *Pneumatologia*, 320. Owen cites Augustine's Second Letter against Pelagius 1.19 in support of his position.

52. Owen explains that God works in us to stir up the exercise of grace that he has given us. He cites Phil 2:13, "It is God who worketh in you both to will and to do his good pleasure." *Pneumatologia*, 535.

53. Owen, *Pneumatologia*, 145.

54. The second is the interpretation of life in the Spirit or the concept of walking in the Spirit as primarily a life of obedience, which in my experience has gone out of fashion in charismatic circles. See Owen, *Pneumatologia*, 533.

from the Son.[55] As the bearer of the Spirit, Christ is also the sender of the Spirit. Through this we are endowed with the Spirit of adoption or sonship that establishes us as sons and daughters of God. In an Owenesque manner, Del Colle claims, "The pneumatological relation of Jesus to God *intensifies* rather than substitutes for Jesus's filial relation even as the Spirit's presence in believers makes them daughters and sons in the Son. The inseparable but nonidentical relations of the Son and Spirit to Christ reinforce the notion that the believer's status by adoption proceeds from the same Spirit who forged the identity of Jesus over the course of his life, ministry, and death."[56]

Foundational to any P/c account of spiritual formation is the gift of the Spirit to the believer to impart the Spirit of sonship, or rather the assurance of the believer's status as a daughter or son of God, with Romans 8:14–17 as a seminal text. The Spirit is the one who allows us to cry with Christ, "Abba, Father," as the Spirit witnesses with our spirit that we are indeed children of God. The knowledge and love of the Father, however, in line with all we have discussed of Christ's life as analogous to ours, is not comprehended solely in the mind but is apprehended in the heart and the spirit. This brings me to my final point on which Owen, Del Colle, P/c spirituality and many proponents of Spirit Christology agree—namely, the role of experience and the affective in the Christian life and, most specifically, the experience of the knowledge and love of God at the heart and as the foundation of Christian existence.

THE ROLE OF EXPERIENCE

According to Owen, Christ experiences the apotheosis of all human experience with an intensity that is beyond merely human capacity. The purpose of this is his formation as our mediator and intercessor. In his humanity, he feels every pain and sorrow, shame, fear, and grief to the highest degree of sense and tenderness. Through this intense trial of human experience, he is supported with the "thoughts of his present glory that was set before him" by the gift of the Spirit.[57] Christ as the incarnate Son feels compassion and mercy that he could not feel as the impassible eternal Word, and through this he is moved to rescue and save a desperate humanity.[58] In his exposition

---

55. Owen, *Pneumatologia*, 61–64.
56. Del Colle, *Christ and the Spirit*, 184, emphasis added.
57. Owen, *Works*, 19:485.
58. See Owen, *Works*, 19:468, 480–84; 20:421–24.

of Christ in the garden of Gethsemane and in the cry of dereliction, Owen describes Christ as an example of patience, faith and prayer, submission, trust, and dependence,[59] with his point being that this is nothing that is not available for believers today. If Christ was supported and carried through his sufferings by the power of God, we can expect to be also.[60]

The hope and promise for believers, according to Owen, is that this is given as a real experience in times of testing and hardship, alleviating distress and imparting joy and peace. The Spirit gives

> unto the minds and souls of believers a spiritual, sensible experience of the reality and power of the things we do believe. He doth not comfort us by words, but by things. Other means of spiritual consolation I know none; and I am sure this never fails. Give unto a soul an experience, a taste, of the love and grace of God in Christ Jesus, and be its condition what it will, it cannot refuse to be comforted. And hereby doth he "shed abroad the love of God in our hearts," Rom. v. 5, whereby all graces are cherished and increased.[61]

That the Spirit is the one who sheds abroad the love of God into our hearts is a central plank of charismatic and Pentecostal spirituality. Frank Macchia, the Pentecostal theologian writes, "The highest description possible of the substance of Spirit baptism as an eschatological gift is that it functions as an outpouring of divine love."[62] Here, he too cites Romans 5:5. Owen describes the Spirit-filled life as a celebration of the joy, delight, vigour, power, and hope that is imparted to the believer, as well as an expectation that there will be a felt intimate communion with God.[63] All of these are normative claims in contemporary P/c theology. There is a note of caution, however, for P/c spirituality that arises from Owen's insights on the purpose of the gift of the Spirit to the church. Where P/c teaching tends to focus almost exclusively on the gift of the Spirit for rescue from or elimination of suffering, hardship, trials and temptations, weakness, and frailty, Owen sees the gift of the Spirit for obedience, endurance, and faith *through* suffering, hardship, trials, and temptations. There are many pastoral implications of this shift in emphasis to be explored on another occasion.

---

59. Owen, *Works*, 20:513.
60. Owen, *Works*, 20:507, 509.
61. Owen, *Pneumatologia*, 391.
62. Frank Macchia, *Baptized in the Spirit: A Global Pentecostal Theology* (Grand Rapids: Zondervan, 2006), 17.
63. Owen, *Of Communion with God the Father, Son and Holy Ghost*, 3.242–47.

SUMMARY

The purpose of this paper has not been to prove that Owen was some kind of closet charismatic. (Although he often refers to the bestowal of spiritual gifts upon believers in the postapostolic church, it appears that he is not referring to the more extraordinary gifts.) It is, rather, first, to demonstrate that it is possible to construct a strong dogmatic foundation for the claim that Spirit Christology gives us an orthodox christological model of how Christ's life in the Spirit is like ours and, second, to begin to explore some of the implications of this for what we understand as "life in the Spirit." There is much potential for developing a pneumatological theological anthropology on this foundation and significant scope for a theology of the person, power, presence, and work of the Spirit in a human being. As an insider to the P/c world, my view is that we would do well to attend to Owen's insistence on the gift of the Spirit for much that has gone out of fashion in our accounts of spiritual formation: obedience, suffering, holiness, comfort and strength through trials and temptations, frailty and vulnerability, and gifts of endurance and perseverance. This, I suggest, would be a welcome counterbalance to the docetic tendencies to which P/c spirituality is so prone and would certainly be in the spirit of Owen, who saw the *whole* of Christ's life as a model for our own.

CHAPTER 10

FLOURISHING IN THE SPIRIT

Distinguishing Incarnation and Indwelling for Theological Anthropology

Joanna Leidenhag and R. T. Mullins

THERE ARE TWO CENTRAL CLAIMS of the doctrine of humanity that we wish to focus on in this paper. (1) To understand what it means to flourish as a human being we have to look to the incarnation of Jesus Christ. (2) Part of the biblical witness is that the Holy Spirit is "poured out" on all flesh. One thing that can be learnt by integrating these two claims is that to flourish as a human person is to be indwelt by the Holy Spirit, who is the Spirit of Christ. However, a problem arises in this approach to theological anthropology as there are yet no clear differences between accounts of incarnation and indwelling. In this paper, we propose a substantive distinction between the incarnation of the Son and the indwelling of the Spirit, which elucidates how the humanity of Christ unlocks flourishing for the rest of humanity.

In order to argue our case, we shall proceed in six steps. In section 1, we shall explain why the incarnation of the Son and the indwelling of the Holy Spirit matter for theological anthropology, and why it matters that they are clearly demarcated. In section 2, we shall briefly explain the basic Chalcedonian doctrine of the incarnation. In section 3, we shall articulate the difficulty of demarcating the incarnation of the Son from the indwelling of the Holy Spirit. In section 4, we will explain how the neo-Chalcedonian

Christology of the fifth ecumenical council can help solve the demarcation problem. In section 5, we shall use these christological insights to develop a clear and distinct account of the indwelling of the Holy Spirit. Then, in section 6, we shall offer concluding thoughts reiterating the importance of this demarcation between incarnation and indwelling for theological anthropology.

WHY INCARNATION AND INDWELLING MATTER FOR THEOLOGICAL ANTHROPOLOGY

John Calvin famously argued at the beginning of *Institutes of the Christian Religion*, that knowledge of God and knowledge of humanity "are bound together in a mutual tie."[1] Although reflection upon the nature of humanity can be addressed from any number of perspectives, the *theological* articulation of what it means to exist and flourish as a human is primarily an expression of the relationship between humanity and the triune God. The profession of the Christian faith is that this relationship finds its central pivot in the incarnation and the belief that Jesus of Nazareth lived, died, and lives again as fully human and fully God. To understand what it means to be "fully human," to flourish as a human being, theologians must look to the incarnation of Jesus Christ. As Marc Cortez's work continues to teach us, christological anthropology is multifaceted and has been done in a variety of ways throughout the Christian tradition.[2] The continuing challenge for this aspect of christological anthropology is the scandal of Jesus's particularity, both due to his human existence as a first-century Jewish male *and* due to the uniqueness of the incarnation. There has never been and never will be another Jesus Christ. Although some theologians have extended the concept of the incarnation so that other human beings might be said to be "incarnate" or to become incarnate at the eschaton, the standard view, which we uphold, is that Jesus alone is God incarnate. Although we hope one day to fully flourish as human, this flourishing will never mean that we will be fully God as Jesus is.

All is not lost for the rest of us, however. The biblical witness clearly outlines that subsequent to Jesus's ascension, God's own Spirit dwells within individual human beings bringing them into closer union with God and

---

1. *Inst.* 1.1.3.
2. Marc Cortez, *Christological Anthropology in Historical Perspective: Ancient and Contemporary Approaches to Theological Anthropology* (Grand Rapids: Zondervan, 2016).

each other, thereby perfecting their created nature to become "the body of Christ" and to be identified with Christ before the Father. To flourish as a human being in light of the incarnation, then, is to be indwelt by the Spirit of Christ. We can see already from this brief description that the indwelling of the Holy Spirit cannot be viewed apart from the incarnation of Jesus Christ and that the interaction between indwelling and incarnation presupposes a clear demarcation of these two relations. As such, we argue that upholding a clear distinction between the two God-human relations, "incarnate" and "indwelt," is fundamental for developing an adequate doctrine of humanity. However, there is a problem prevalent in Christian theology: this distinction between incarnation and indwelling can collapse in either direction.

If incarnation is subsumed within the category of indwelling, then the uniqueness of the person of Jesus Christ is easily lost, and the ability of Jesus's death and resurrection to save all of humanity is placed in question. One theologian who falls victim to this concern is Geoffrey Lampe. In his 1976 Bampton lectures, Lampe argued that "God has always been incarnate in his human creatures, forming their spirits from within and revealing himself in and through them."[3] Here, although the language of incarnation is used, it is applied to every human being. The only difference for Jesus of Nazareth is that "in Jesus the incarnate presence of God evoked a full and constant response of the human spirit."[4] Lampe here reveals his lack of demarcation between incarnation of the Son and the indwelling of the Spirit when he goes on to say that the presence of God in Jesus "was not a different divine presence, but the same God the Spirit who moved and inspired other men, such as the prophets."[5]

Lampe's view might be described as a radically exclusive form of Spirit Christology, since it does not state that the incarnate Son was indwelt by the Spirit but that the *only* theologically significant fact about Jesus Christ is found in his response to the indwelling of the Holy Spirit. This is an example of how the relation of incarnation can be subsumed within the relation of indwelling. Jesus may still be considered fully human in the way that, in the postresurrection state, we might all expect to constantly and fully respond to the indwelling Spirit, but Lampe's Jesus cannot be considered fully God. Not only (as Lampe's Gifford lectures went on to

---

3. G. W. H. Lampe, *God as Spirit: The Bampton Lectures 1976* (Oxford: Clarendon, 1977), 23.
4. Lampe, *God as Spirit*, 23.
5. Lampe, *God as Spirit*, 23–24.

advocate) does this radically exclusive version of Spirit Christology demolish the doctrine of the Trinity, but it has severe consequences for salvation and theological anthropology as well. If Jesus is not fully God, then Jesus should not be worshiped, and Jesus cannot forgive sins; these are things only God can do. This places into question the sinlessness and full humanity of Jesus because Jesus accepts worship in the Gospels (Matt 28:9, 17; Luke 24:52; John 9:38; 20:28) and offers forgiveness (Matt 9:1–8; Mark 2:5–12; Luke 5:20). The logic follows that if sin prevents us from becoming fully human, and Jesus sinned by blaspheming in this way, then Jesus is not fully human. If Jesus is neither fully God, nor fully human, theological anthropology has lost its central pivot, and the hope for human flourishing we have through Jesus vanishes entirely.

Alternatively, indwelling can be subsumed under the category of incarnation. When the collapse goes in this direction, all human beings, or at least all Christian believers on more exclusive views, either are already or have the potential to become God incarnate. Thomas P. Flint has proposed the *theory of final assumption*, which says that the "ultimate end of all human beings who attain salvation is to be assumed by the Son."[6] On this eschatology, all redeemed human persons will eventually become incarnated by the Son just "as truly and as completely as" the Son is incarnated in Jesus Christ.[7] What this means is that all redeemed human persons will cease to be *persons* because the only person left will be God the Son.[8] All redeemed human persons will become human natures that are assumed by the person of the Son. We find many things troubling about the theory of final assumption, not least of which is the seeming eradication of redeemed human persons.[9] Yet, for the purposes of this paper, we shall simply say that this is quite obviously not God's plan for humanity as laid out in Scripture. Scripture says that God is pouring out his Spirit on all flesh (Acts 2:16–17, 38). It does not say that the Son is assuming all persons. Scripture says that human persons will one day receive glorified and resurrected bodies that are fully embraced by the Spirit (1 Cor 15:42–44). It does not say that the Son will eliminate all human persons. To be sure, Flint is envisioning the incarnation as the closest possible relationship between God and humanity,

---

6. Thomas P. Flint, "Molinism and Incarnation," in *Molinism: The Contemporary Debate*, ed. Ken Perszyk (Oxford: Oxford University Press, 2011), 198.

7. Flint, "Molinism and Incarnation," 198.

8. Flint, "Molinism and Incarnation," 199.

9. Cf. R. T. Mullins, "Flint's 'Molinism and the Incarnation' Is Too Radical," *Journal of Analytic Theology* 3 (2015): 109–23; R. T. Mullins, "Flint's 'Molinism and the Incarnation' Is Still Too Radical—A Rejoinder to Flint," *Journal of Analytic Theology* 5 (2017): 515–32.

and surely God and humanity will have an intimate relationship in the eschaton. However, we think that Flint is vastly underappreciating the role of the Holy Spirit in God's eschatological plan for human flourishing.

So far, we have argued that it is fundamental for a doctrine of humanity that two forms of God-human relation—incarnation and indwelling—remain conceptually and metaphysically distinct. However, we have not yet outlined what these two relations are and how one might distinguish between them. As we outline the traditional views on this matter, it will quickly become apparent that a clear demarcation is sorely lacking and faces some serious obstacles.

CHALCEDONIAN INCARNATION: THE BASICS

On the standard story, the most significant aspects of ecumenical Christology come from the Council of Chalcedon in 451. What does Chalcedonian Christology look like? Oliver Crisp summarizes five relevant desiderata from the Chalcedonian Creed:[10]

1. Christ is of one substance (*homoousious*) with the Father.
2. Christ is eternally begotten of the Father according to his divinity and temporally begotten of the Virgin Mary according to his humanity.
3. Christ is one theanthropic (divine-human) person (*hypostasis*) subsisting in two natures (*phuseis*), which are held together in a personal union.
4. Christ's two natures remain intact in the personal union without being confused or mingled together to form some sort of hybrid entity or *tertium quid*.
5. Christ's two natures are a fully divine nature and a fully human nature, respectively, his human nature consisting of a human body and a "rational" soul.

For the purposes of our paper, the fifth point is quite important since it allegedly lays out the requisite understanding of theological anthropology. If the requisite requirement for Christ to have a human nature is for him to possess a human body and a rational soul, the same goes for the rest of humanity. However, historians like G. L. Prestige often point out

---

10. Oliver D. Crisp, "Incarnation," in *The Oxford Handbook of Systematic Theology*, ed. John Webster, Kathryn Tanner, and Iain Torrance (New York: Oxford University Press, 2007), 161.

that Chalcedon left its terms disastrously ambiguous.[11] As such, we will need to tighten up what it means for Christ to have a human body and a rational soul.

To start, one will notice that the language of a "rational soul" presupposes some version of substance dualism. This is because substance dualism was the predominant view during the early church.[12] On substance dualism, a human person is a rational soul with a physical body. Today, many Christian thinkers reject dualism in favour of a physicalist anthropology. We shall not focus on physicalism since one of us has elsewhere dealt with the undesirable consequences of physicalism for Christology.[13] For this paper, we shall affirm a generic version of substance dualism about human persons.

If a human person is a rational soul with a human body, we must ask what it means for Christ to become a human person. Following the contemporary taxonomy of christological models, we shall speak of composite Christologies.[14] The main idea behind compositional approaches to the incarnation is to specify how many "parts" our incarnate Lord is composed of in order to be a human person. For example, a two-part Christology says that Jesus is composed of the immaterial Son and a material body. This is the Logos-sarx Christology of thinkers like Athanasius. The Son is a rational soul and becomes a *human* person by being appropriately related to a human body. On a three-part Christology, Jesus is composed of the immaterial Son, an immaterial soul, and a material body. Nestorius and Pope Leo endorsed this view.[15] Surprisingly, Apollinaris also endorses a three-part Christology since he claims that Jesus is composed of the Son (who counts as a rational soul), an animal soul, and a human body.[16] Yet the three-part Christology of Nestorius and Pope Leo has been the most influential view in Christian thought, so we shall focus our attention on it. On this three-part Christology, the Son becomes a human person

---

11. G. L. Prestige, *Fathers and Heretics* (New York: Macmillan, 1940), 239.

12. Paul L. Gavrilyuk, "The Incorporeality of the Soul in Patristic Thought," in *Christian Physicalism? Philosophical Theological Criticisms*, ed. R. Keith Loftin and Joshua R. Farris (London: Rowman & Littlefield, 2018), 1–26.

13. R. T. Mullins, "Physicalist Christology and the Two Sons Worry," in *Christian Physicalism? Philosophical Theological Criticisms*, ed. R. Keith Loftin and Joshua Farris (Lanham: Lexington, 2018), 153–74.

14. Cf. Oliver Crisp, *Divinity and Humanity: The Incarnation Reconsidered* (Cambridge: Cambridge University Press, 2007). Anna Marmodoro and Jonathan Hill, "Composition Models of the Incarnation: Unity and Unifying Relations," *Religious Studies* 46.4 (2010): 469–88.

15. Cf. Richard Norris, *The Christological Controversy* (Philadelphia: Fortress, 1980), 149.

16. Apollinaris says, "If, then, a human being is made up of three parts, the Lord is also a human being, for the Lord surely is made up of three parts: spirit and soul and body." Norris, *Christological Controversy*, 110.

by becoming appropriately related to a numerically distinct human soul and a human body.

With that being said, we must specify what it means for the Son to be appropriately related to a human soul and a human body. Unfortunately, this is not so straightforward. Any student of theology might find this a bit surprising. On the standard story, Nestorianism affirms that there are two people in Jesus Christ, whereas Pope Leo and Chalcedon affirm that there is only one person in Christ. The problem with this standard story is that Nestorius, Pope Leo, and Chalcedon affirm that Jesus Christ has the same three parts, so the difference between Nestorius and Chalcedon is not clear in the slightest. After the Formula of Chalcedon is framed, many Christians in the East remained unconvinced that there is a clear difference between the defenders of Chalcedon and the Nestorians.[17] Christopher Beeley explains that the Chalcedonian definition "left the basic identity of Christ and the nature of the union disastrously ambiguous from the point of view of the more unitive traditions. It is no wonder that Nestorius reportedly felt vindicated by the result."[18] According to Prestige, Nestorius thought that Chalcedon and Pope Leo's *Tome* "expressed exactly what he himself had always believed."[19] Given this, the inability of Eastern Christians to see a difference between Chalcedon and Nestorianism is understandable.

This creates a serious problem for us. What we need is a clear account of the unity of the person of Christ, but this is exactly what Chalcedon failed to provide. What exactly is this appropriate relation that the Son has to his human soul and body such that there is only one person in Christ and not two? Nestorians, like Theodore of Mopsuestia, affirmed that this appropriate relation is a functional unity. On this view, the Son works so well together with the soul and body of Jesus that they function as one person.[20] A bit of background will help one understand this view.

It was common for the patristics to say that the Word indwells his "man" in the way God indwells the temple, prophets, or saints. One can find such statements in Apollinaris, Athanasius, Eustathius of Antioch, Diodore, Theodore of Mopsuestia, Nestorius, and Cyril of Alexandria.[21] Apart from the Logos-sarx Christology of Athanasius, it is not entirely clear what it

---

17. See J. N. D. Kelly, *Early Christian Doctrines* (London: Black, 1958), 340–42.
18. Christopher A. Beeley, *The Unity of Christ: Continuity and Conflict in Patristic Tradition* (New Haven, CT: Yale University Press, 2012), 284.
19. Prestige, *Fathers and Heretics*, 269.
20. Norris, *The Christological Controversy*, 113–22.
21. Kelly, *Early Christian Doctrines*, 283–320.

means for the Son to indwell a human soul and a body in such a way that there is only one Son and not two in Christ. Cyril asserts that the Son and his human nature are hypostatically united, but it is never made clear what this means. According to Cyril, the hypostatic union is an ineffable mystery.[22] In the Eastern churches, the union between the Son and the humanity is not made much clearer. Sergius the Monophysite proclaims that the union is inexpressible or ineffable.[23] Even though Sergius thinks very little of Cyril's Christology, they seem to agree that the hypostatic union is an ineffable mystery. But can we say anything more about this ineffably mysterious union?

Theodore of Mopsuestia gives us one of the lengthier treatments of the Son's union by indwelling. Theodore says that God only indwells the saints, but not by God's essence, nor by God's active operation. According to Theodore, we cannot say that God indwells the saints by essence since that would limit the essence of God to a few spatiotemporally located things. We gather that Theodore thinks it is absurd to limit the essence of God in this way. Theodore also says that indwelling cannot be God's active operation because God is actively present in all things as he gives them existence.[24] In other words, indwelling cannot be mere omnipresence. Instead, Theodore says that God is present in the saints according to his "good pleasure." God only exercises his good pleasure towards those with whom he is pleased—those who are zealously dedicated to God. Since an omnipresent God is present to everyone, Theodore thinks that the active presence of "good pleasure" can make sense of the fact that God is closer to some than he is to others. This, according to Theodore, is how God indwells the saints and apostles. However, Theodore is clear that this is not exactly how God is present in Jesus. According to Theodore, God indwells Jesus in the way of good pleasure as in a son. What this means is that by God's active good pleasure, God gave Jesus all honour and dominion through union with the Son. The Son has all honour and dominion by nature. Through the indwelling, Jesus is able to share in this honour with the Son and thus "be counted one person in virtue of the union" with the Son.[25] Through this union of indwelling and the cooperation between Jesus and the Son, Jesus and the Son count as one person.[26]

---

22. See Cyril's second letter to Nestorius in Norris, *The Christological Controversy*, 132–33.

23. Iain R. Torrance, *Christology after Chalcedon: Severus of Antioch and Sergius the Monophysite* (Norfolk: Canterbury, 1988), 143.

24. Theodore of Mopsuestia as quoted in Norris, *The Christological Controversy*, 114–15.

25. Theodore of Mopsuestia as quoted in Norris, *The Christological Controversy*, 115–17.

26. Theodore of Mopsuestia as quoted in Norris, *The Christological Controversy*, 118.

The proponents at Chalcedon thought that this unity through good pleasure and cooperation clearly entailed two persons in Jesus Christ. As such, they condemned it as a merely functional unity.[27] What the pro-Chalcedonian theologians wanted was an ontological unity in Christ such that there is only one person with two natures. However, this ontological unity is not articulated at Chalcedon. As Prestige reminds us, Chalcedon provided "no positive and convincing rationalisation of the right faith."[28] This lack of a clearly articulated ontological unity was even a worry at the Council of Chalcedon for the Illyrian and Palestinian delegates, who had to be convinced that Pope Leo was not a Nestorian. The Tome of Leo, as endorsed by Chalcedon, appears to affirm a merely functional unity between the two natures. In reflecting on the "sickness of Chalcedon," Severus of Antioch says that Leo's hypostatic union is a "bastard partnership and of a relationship of friendship."[29] It is not a true union in Severus's eyes. Again, this creates a serious demarcation problem for us since we have not specified what the appropriate relationship is between the Son and his soul and body such that there is only one person and not two in Jesus.

To be sure, this account of unity that we see in Theodore has a precedent in the Christology of Origen who also affirms a unity through coopera-tion. Origen offers a challenge to anyone who does not like this account of the union—if you don't like it, find a better view of the incarnation and confirm it with Scripture.[30] In response to Origen's challenge, we say that we do not like it, and we can offer a better account. But first, we need to explain a deeper worry about this lack of unity as it relates to the indwelling of the Holy Spirit.

THE DEMARCATION PROBLEM

According to Alan Spence, the patristic theologians see this demarcation problem, but they remain vague on outlining the difference between incarnation and indwelling.[31] Consider the following from Gregory of Nazianzus: "For it was fitting that as the Son has lived with us in bodily form—so the Spirit too should appear in bodily form; and that after Christ

---

27. Thomas G. Weinandy, *Does God Change? The Word's Becoming in the Incarnation* (Still River, MA: St. Bede's, 1985), 36–37.

28. Prestige, *Fathers and Heretics*, 239.

29. Torrance, *Christology after Chalcedon*, 154.

30. Origen as quoted in Norris, *The Christological Controversy*, 81.

31. Alan Spence, *Christology: A Guide for the Perplexed* (London: T&T Clark, 2008), 45.

had returned to His own place, [the Spirit] should have come down to us."[32] Gregory's view of indwelling follows exactly his view of incarnation. Although these are temporally distinct, they seem to remain the same type of relation, just one after the other.

One can find similar remarks in later theologians like Jonathan Edwards. According to Edwards, "The incarnation, or the union of the divine nature with the human nature, is by the Holy Spirit dwelling in the human nature."[33] This makes any difference between incarnation and indwelling somewhat obscure. When Edwards unpacks his idea elsewhere, it only adds to the confusion. Edwards writes, "By sending the Spirit, assuming his flesh into being and into the person of the divine Logos, at the same time and by the same act, the Father sent him into the world, or incarnated him by an act of sanctification; for the incarnation was assuming flesh, or human nature, into the person of the Son, or giving communion of the divine personality to the human nature, in giving that human nature being. And this was done by giving the Holy Spirit in such a manner and measure to that human nature in making it."[34] Edwards's emphasises the idea that the Spirit had an important role in the incarnation, and this seems an important theological point. However, without demarcating the type of union which the human Jesus Christ had to the Son and to the Spirit respectively, Edwards's worthy theological goal is almost impossible to achieve effectively.

Think of the problem this way: Oliver Crisp is a rational soul with a human body. As Christians, most of us wish to affirm that Oliver has a very interesting relationship with Jesus Christ. However, we would like to know why Oliver is not identical to Jesus Christ. Oliver is a soul and a body that is interestingly related to God the Son. Why is the Son not incarnate in Oliver, and yet is incarnate in Jesus Christ? Chalcedonian Christology does not appear to provide any satisfying answers. Following the lead of the early fathers, one might say that the Son indwells the soul and body of Jesus, and does not indwell the soul and body of Oliver. But that leaves us wondering about Oliver's relationship to the Holy Spirit. It seems to us that the Holy Spirit indwells Oliver. So why isn't Oliver one person with the Holy Spirit?

Things are further complicated by the fact that the Holy Spirit indwells Jesus too. It is not simply the Son who indwells Jesus. What is the difference

---

32. *Or.* 41.11.

33. Jonathan Edwards, "Miscellanies," no. 1043, in *The Works of Jonathan Edwards*, vol. 20, ed. Amy Plantinga Pauw (New Haven: Yale University Press, 2002), 383.

34. Edwards, "Miscellanies," no. 709, in *Works* 18:334.

between the Son's and the Holy Spirit's relationship to Jesus? At this point, we are still working with the christological deposit given to us at Chalcedon. Therefore, the conceptual resources for demarcating the indwelling of the Holy Spirit from the incarnation of the Son seem to be dim.

Of course, one could appeal to the ineffably mysterious assumption relation. One could say that the Son assumes Jesus, which entails that the Son and Jesus are the same person. Then say that the Holy Spirit indwells Jesus such that the Spirit and Jesus are not the same person. One could also deny that the Son assumes Oliver, which is why Oliver and the Son are not the same person. These are all affirmations which we think Christian theologians should want to make. However, our ability to make such assertions in a meaningful way is undercut if the "assumption relation" does not specify what the appropriate relationship is between the Son and the soul and body of Jesus.[35] It is in danger of becoming a black box that fails to demarcate the difference between Jesus and Oliver. At the end of the day, if technical concepts like "assumption" and "hypostatic union" are nothing but ineffable mysteries, it remains unclear what the true difference is between orthodoxy and heresy, and between the Son and the Spirit's relation to Jesus and Oliver. This exemplifies a serious demarcation problem between the incarnation and the indwelling of the Holy Spirit.

For the sake of clarity, it might be helpful to use a metaphor from simple mathematics. Without expressing how "assumes" and "indwells" express different types of relation, we are in danger of saying something like, $1 + 1 = 2$ in the case of Oliver, and $1 + 1 = 1$ in the case of Jesus Christ (or $1 + 1 + 1 = 2$ if we remember that Jesus Christ was assumed by the Son and indwelt by the Spirit). What we need is to say that $1 + 1 = 2$ in the case of Oliver and that $1 \times 1 = 1$ in the case of Jesus Christ (or again $1 \times 1 + 1 = 2$ in the case of Jesus Christ's additional indwelling by the Spirit). The outcome is the same, but the logic works because the relations (here represented as addition and multiplication) are clearly differentiated. This metaphor should not be taken to mean that addition and multiplication are good ways of understanding incarnation and indwelling—that would be rather silly. We use this metaphor only to show that in order to get different outcomes, parts have to be related in different ways, and these relations have to be specified. We do not need to understand everything about the assumption relation (indicated by the plus sign), and the indwelling relation (indicated by the multiplication sign). They may equally be beyond

---

35. R. T. Mullins, *The End of the Timeless God* (Oxford: Oxford University Press, 2016), ch. 7.

192

our ken. However, we do need some sort of way of demarcating between them in order to avoid the problems represented by Geoffrey Lampe and Thomas Flint.

NEO-CHALCEDONIAN CHRISTOLOGY TO THE RESCUE

Not to worry because there is another way to understand the incarnation, which doesn't face this demarcation problem, and which has been developed in the tradition after Chalcedon. In the aftermath of Chalcedon, various Nestorian parties felt that they could interpret Chalcedon in such a way that they could agree to the formula. In the sixth century, the emperor Justinian could see right through these moves and condemned a merely semantic hypostatic union as falling victim to the worry that there are two persons in Christ. He notes that Nestorians can and do affirm that there are "two natures and one person in Christ" as Chalcedon claims. In fact, *many* Nestorians in the early church affirmed this. But Justinian argues that the content and meaning of their theology does not in fact support this claim. Instead, he argues that the way they use these terms entails that there are in fact two persons in Christ. This, says Justinian, is heresy.[36] What one sees here in Justinian is a demand for an underlying metaphysical account for the hypostatic union instead of a merely verbal affirmation of the union of the person of Christ.

One of the main motivations for the fifth ecumenical council, Constantinople II (553), is to give a proper interpretation of Chalcedon that fully excludes Nestorianism.[37] The Christology that eventually emerges from this is often called *neo-Chalcedonian*. It is this Christology that is adopted by the Council of Constantinople II and that has left a huge mark on the way subsequent generations of Christians have thought about the incarnation. Most Christology today is not in fact Chalcedonian because it bears the marks of the much-needed clarifications that neo-Chalcedonian Christology developed.

One of the most important developments during this time for our discussion is the *anhypostasia* and *enhypostasia* distinction, which is used to

---

36. Richard Price, *The Acts of the Council of Constantinople of 553 with Related Texts on the Three Chapters Controversy*, vol. 1 (Liverpool: Liverpool University Press, 2009), 149.

37. Fred Sanders, "Introduction to Christology: Chalcedonian Categories for the Gospel Narrative," in *Jesus in Trinitarian Perspective*, ed. Fred Sanders and Klaus Issler (Nashville: B&H, 2007), 27–35.

rid Christology of Nestorianism.[38] This is a distinction that developed in the aftermath of Chalcedon leading up to the fifth ecumenical council. Though the terms *anhypostasia* and *enhypostasia* are not used by the council, the theology is adopted and affirmed by the fifth ecumenical council as the proper interpretation of Chalcedonian Christology.[39]

The fifth ecumenical council took place because of a controversy over Adoptionism, Nestorianism, and Origenism—views that many at the time believed entailed two sons or persons. These views seemed to entail the possibility of the human nature of Christ being a complete, separate person apart from God the Son. In order to avoid this, the neo-Chalcedonian Christology of the council claims that the human nature of Christ cannot have a *hypostasis* (person) of its own. Christ's human nature is said to be *anhypostasis*, which means that it is not a person.[40] In fact, the *anhypostasis* claim is even stronger—Christ's human nature would not exist without the incarnation. The *enhypostasia* claim is that the Son's human nature only exists because of the incarnation. Further, the *hypostasis* of the Son is brought to the assumed human nature, thus giving the human nature a hypostatic and personal reality.[41] In other words, the Son brings his personhood to the assumed human nature. The human nature is not, nor could have been, a person independent of the Son's assumption.[42]

Fred Sanders explains that this is where the strength of the distinction comes into play in ridding ecumenical Christology of Nestorianism. The distinction excludes the very possibility that the human nature of Christ could have formed some person from coming into existence if the Son had not assumed this nature.[43] The human nature of Christ cannot form a person apart from the incarnation. The human nature of Christ is a person only because it is assumed by the person of the Logos. The human nature

---

38. Thomas F. Torrance, *Incarnation: The Person and Life of Christ* (Downers Grove, IL: InterVarsity, 2015), 84; Crisp, *Divinity and Humanity*, 74.

39. Price, *The Acts of the Council of Constantinople of 553*, 1:73; Sanders, "Introduction to Christology," 30.

40. Demetrios Barthrellos, *Byzantine Christ: Person, Nature, and Will in the Christology of Saint Maximus the Confessor* (Oxford: Oxford University Press, 2005), 34–35.

41. Jaroslav Pelikan, *The Christian Tradition*, vol. 2 (Chicago: University of Chicago Press, 1974), 84–85, 88–89.

42. David Brown, *Divine Humanity: Kenosis and the Construction of a Christian Theology* (Waco: Baylor University Press, 2011), 24; Ivor Davidson, "Reappropriating Patristic Christology: One Doctrine, Two Styles," *Irish Theological Quarterly* 67 (2002), 225; Davidson, "Theologizing the Human Jesus: An Ancient (and Modern) Approach to Christology Reassessed," *IJST* 3 (2001): 135. This entailment of the assumption relation is why, in the case of Thomas Flint's "Theory of Final Assumption," redeemed human persons lose their personhood in their assumption to the Son (see above).

43. Fred Sanders, "Introduction to Christology," 30–35.

exists only because of the incarnation. Wolfhart Pannenberg sums up the neo-Chalcedonian theology as follows: "By itself Jesus' humanity would not only be impersonal in the modern sense of lacking self-conscious personality, but taken by itself Jesus' human being would be non-existent."[44]

Since this is not true for the ordinary Christian believer, this opens up a potential difference between incarnation and indwelling. Since, with indwelling, there is already a human person existing, prior to the union of indwelling. The indwelling seems to presuppose that there is a human person that already exists for the Spirit to indwell. When the Holy Spirit indwells a believer, she does not bring personhood and existence to a human nature that lacks it. Instead, she comes to indwell a human nature that already has existence and personhood. Again, consider Oliver. We take it as obvious that Oliver can exist without being incarnated by a divine person. He is currently existing without being incarnated by the Son. Oliver's existence and personhood are not dependent upon the Son in the same way that Jesus's existence and personhood are according to neo-Chalcedonian Christology. Further, nothing about the indwelling of the Holy Spirit demands that the Spirit bring her personhood to Oliver's human nature. Oliver is not a person only because the Holy Spirit brought her personhood to Oliver's human nature. It seems like we are starting to make some progress in demarcating the incarnation from indwelling.

SOLVING THE DEMARCATION PROBLEM: A MODEL OF INDWELLING

If part of what it means for Jesus to be God incarnate is that there is no human person without the incarnation and that the person Jesus exists only as a result of the incarnation, then we have taken a significant step towards demarcating incarnation from indwelling. The majority view on indwelling is that it happens at some midpoint in a person's life: either at conversion, water baptism, or a subsequent spirit-baptism. This is clear merely from the fact that Jesus tells his disciples, who are already a motley crew of human persons, to wait for the Holy Spirit who will indwell them (Acts 1:1–7). Regardless of when or under what conditions a human person is said to receive the Holy Spirit, we should all be able to agree that a human person of some description existed prior to their reception of the Holy Spirit. Even for views whereby the Spirit indwells all humanity,

---

44. Pannenberg, *Jesus: God and Man* (Philadelphia: Westminster, 1964), 338.

the relation of indwelling is a matter of human flourishing, not a matter of human existence.[45]

One way to elucidate what is entailed by the indwelling of the Holy Spirit is to suggest that this is the type of relationship between God and humanity Nestorians, such as Theodore of Mopsuestia, articulated with regards to the incarnation: two persons, one with a divine nature and the other with a human nature, remaining ontologically distinct but functionally united.[46] This is quite the turn in doctrinal events: the condemned view, which has become known as Nestorianism is not all bad, it should only be used to refer to the indwelling of the Spirit, and not the incarnation of the Son. This functional unity can be strengthened, even to the point of sharing the two subjectivities, but not collapsing that into one subjectivity. This is the model of indwelling which we find in recent articulations of indwelling by analytic theologians like William P. Alston and Marilyn McCord Adams.

William Alston's essay, "The Indwelling of the Holy Spirit" instigated the discussion by identifying two constraints upon the concept of indwelling.[47] The first constraint is that indwelling must uphold a "division of labour" between the Holy Spirit and the created subject in bringing about the sanctification of the human individual. There is no immediate communication of divine properties to the human person, but the attributes of Jesus Christ can be worked out by the believer themselves in this division of labour to produce the fruits of the Spirit in the believer's life (Gal 5:22–23). Already in this first constraint, we can see that Alston presupposes two interacting agents or two persons acting in consonance. This fits well with the demarcation we are suggesting from the neo-Chalcedonian Christology. On neo-Chalcedonian Christology, the Son brings his personhood to a human nature that lacks personhood in order to become incarnate. This entails that there is only one person in Jesus Christ. With the indwelling of the Holy Spirit, the Holy Spirit does not negate the personhood of the human being that she is indwelling. As such, there is one divine person and one human person acting in consonance with each other. It may be

---

45. It should be noted that the model of indwelling offered in this section is in no way intended to limit the activity of the Holy Spirit within the divine economy to indwelling alone. We regard the Holy Spirit to have many functions, probably including the creation of persons and the gift of life. However, this is a separate activity of the Holy Spirit from indwelling, which requires an already existing person, albeit created and sustained by God, to be indwelt.

46. Bertrand R. Brasnett, *The Suffering of the Impassible God* (London: MacMillan, 1928), 60.

47. William P. Alston, *Divine Nature and Human Language: Essays in Philosophical Theology* (Ithaca, NY: Cornell University Press, 1989).

possible on this model of indwelling to assert that sanctification is an essentially relational process, which requires at least two persons and cannot be achieved in isolation.

Alston's second constraint regards the "internality" of the Holy Spirit's presence. This constraint demarcates the type of presence connoted by the term *indwelling* both from God's omnipresence throughout the universe and from the type of physical presence that human beings share with the world around them, which is external to them. Instead, Alston uses the biblical language of "filled, permeated, pervaded" to suggest that indwelling constitutes the interweaving of subjectivities, which he calls "the sharing model."[48] On this model there is "a literal merging or mutual inter-penetration of the life of the individual and the divine life, a breaking down of barriers that normally separate one life from another."[49] Although the barriers separating persons is broken down in Alston's model of indwelling, the person of the Holy Spirit and the human person remain two persons who share, and do not fuse into one Divine-human person.

This is made clearer in how Marilyn McCord Adams has rearticulated and developed Alston's "sharing model." McCord Adams articulates the indwelling of the Holy Spirit and the sanctification of the human person who flourishes through this indwelling in the following way: "[The] Holy Spirit enters into lived partnership with psychic agencies of the created person so that they *work together* to manage inputs from the outside and impulses on the inside and so coordinate the person's interactions with the world."[50] This is a clear expression of a cooperative relationship between two persons.

It may be important to note that this type of divine-human cooperation does not require the human partner to have the highest human capacity for agency or rationality. A living consciousness is all that is required with inputs of awareness and experience from the outside world. A person can be said to be indwelt by the Holy Spirit in their internal life, no matter how traumatized, disabled, developed, or corrupt, that internal life may be or may appear. More importantly for the argument in this paper, McCord Adams models indwelling as a functional union between God and humans, which does not bring about the existence of a new human being but instead

---

48. Alston, *Divine Nature and Human Language*, 242, 244.
49. Alston, *Divine Nature and Human Language*, 246.
50. Marilyn McCord Adams, "The Indwelling of the Holy Spirit," in *The Philosophy of Human Nature in Christian Perspective*, ed. Peter J. Weigel and Joseph G. Prud'homme (New York: Lang, 2016), 96, emphasis added.

empowers an already existing human person to grow and flourish through experiential engagement with the world in embodied particularity.

Importantly, this distinction between indwelling and incarnation means that we can affirm that Jesus of Nazareth was *both* incarnate by the Son and indwelt by the Spirit, since the incarnation creates the divine-human person Jesus Christ, which the Spirit indwells fully through a seamless, sinless, cooperative life-sharing. By considering the unique case of Jesus, who alone enjoys both types of divine-human relationship, we can see that this demarcation between incarnation and indwelling is not, at its core, a temporal distinction whereby one follows the other in time. It is not the same relation at different temporal points but more properly described as a metaphysical distinction, since indwelling and incarnation are two different kinds of relation. Thus, Jesus may well have been indwelt by the Spirit from the moment that the Holy Spirit overshadowed the Virgin Mary, but this in no way undermines our demarcation.[51]

CONCLUDING THOUGHTS

This paper opened with an affirmation that to flourish as a human being is to be indwelt by the Spirit of Christ. This brief statement already tells us that ordinary human beings can be indwelt by God the Spirit and that this relation is logically dependent upon another type of God-human relation. This prior relation is captured in the shorthand "Christ" and refers to the incarnation. We then showed that if indwelling and incarnation are collapsed—either by maximising the concept of indwelling, as Geoffrey Lampe has done, or universalising the incarnation, as Thomas Flint has proposed—the result is disastrous for theological anthropology. Turning to the tradition, we explored how Chalcedon provides woefully few resources for understanding the metaphysics of the incarnation, which is a necessary first step in demarcating incarnation and indwelling. How is Jesus of Nazareth's human nature related to God the Son, and different to the ordinary believer's relationship to God the Spirit, in such a way that allows

---

51. Due to brevity, we offer no reflections in this paper on differences in the indwelling of the Holy Spirit between the Old and New Testaments or pre- versus post-Pentecost believers. Suffice to say that on our model there is no reason that the Spirit could not come alongside, share in the conscious life of, and act in functional unity with Old Testament persons. We see no reason however that the indwelling of the Holy Spirit in different epochs in salvation history need be a metaphysically different kind of relation, although there may be other kinds of difference (permanency of union, depth of internality as a result of justification, the putting on of the mind of Christ in the believer through indwelling, etc.).

us to affirm that Jesus's relationship to the Son provides salvation, whereas our relationship to the Spirit allows us to receive salvation?

Fortunately, neo-Chalcedonian Christology does make significant progress in this area. By affirming that Jesus of Nazareth does not exist as a human person without the incarnation of the Son, a space starts to open up between indwelling and incarnation. The relationship of indwelling presupposes the existence of a human person prior to this relationship. Put more starkly, incarnation creates a new human person, whereas indwelling allows already existing human persons to flourish by God's grace. Whereas incarnation is an ontological unity of two natures in one person, the indwelling is a functional partnership between a divine person and a human person. Here, then, we have thankfully and finally come to propose a meaningful distinction between incarnation and indwelling, and in doing so, shown why this demarcation is a matter of utmost importance for the doctrine of humanity.

CHAPTER 11

MAPPING ANTHROPOLOGICAL METAPHYSICS WITH A DESCENSUS KEY

How Christ's Descent to the Dead Informs the Body-Mind Conversation

MATTHEW Y. EMERSON

IN *EMBODIED SOULS, ENSOULED BODIES*, Marc Cortez argues that the presence of an intermediate state would rule out all kinds of physicalism and some kinds of dualism. But he seems to be ambivalent about the presence or absence of an intermediate state in Scripture and therefore does not adjudicate between physicalism and dualism, at least not via appeals to the intermediate state.[1] If, however, the biblical data teaches that Christ, in his human soul, descended to the place of the dead, this means that Christ experienced an intermediate state between his death and resurrection.[2] Because Christ's humanity is paradigmatic for all humans, this would also entail an intermediate state and thus, more than likely, some kind of anthropological dualism for all human beings. This essay will first map

---

1. Marc Cortez, *Embodied Souls, Ensouled Bodies: An Exercise in Christological Anthropology and Its Significance for the Mind/Body Debate* (London: T&T Clark, 2008), 89–91, 183–85.
2. Cortez acknowledges this in *Embodied Souls, Ensouled Bodies*, 91n48.

the different views of Christ's descent and what kinds of anthropological metaphysics they could entail. It will then make an attenuated biblical and theological argument for an understanding of Christ's descent that entails an intermediate state and thus some form of anthropological dualism.

In spite of Cortez's point about the *descensus* and its implication of an intermediate state, Christ's descent is typically ignored in constructive accounts of theological anthropology. Interestingly, apart from Cortez's work mentioned above, many discussions of theological anthropology do not mention Christ's descent in their adjudication between forms of physicalism and anthropological dualism.[3] Three notable exceptions here are John Cooper's *Body, Soul, and Life Everlasting*, Cortez's aforementioned *Embodied Souls, Ensouled Bodies*, and Jason McMartin's essay, "Holy Saturday and Christian Theological Anthropology." Cooper discusses the descent briefly in his chapter on personal eschatology in the New Testament and notes that positing either immediate resurrection or cessation of personhood between death and resurrection has serious, perhaps insurmountable, christological problems.[4] Jason McMartin builds on these observations by Cooper, noting that physicalist accounts of theological anthropology present at least three philosophical and theological problems ("gappy existence," "alternative time," and "immediate resurrection") for accounting for Christ's time in the tomb.[5]

---

3. See, for instance, on the anthropological dualism side of the debate, William Hasker, *The Emergent Self*, Cornell Studies in the Philosophy of Religion (Ithaca, NY: Cornell University Press, 2001), esp. 232–36; and Eleonore Stump, "Non-Cartesian Substance Dualism and Materialism without Reductionism," *Faith and Philosophy* 12, no. 4 (1995): 505–31. Likewise, on the nonreductive physicalist side, neither Joel Green nor Nancey Murphy mention the descent in their defense of nonreductive physicalism. For Green, see "'Bodies—That Is, Human Lives': A Re-Examination of Human Nature in the Bible," in *Whatever Happened to the Soul? Scientific and Theological Portraits of Human Nature*, ed. Warren S. Brown, Nancey Murphy, and H. Newton Malone (Minneapolis: Augsburg Fortress, 1998), 149–73; as well as the discussions of biblical anthropology, resurrection, and the intermediate state (or lack thereof) in Green, *Body, Soul, and Human Life: The Nature of Humanity in the Bible*, Studies in Theological Interpretation (Grand Rapids: Baker Academic, 2008), 46–71, 140–70. For Murphy, see *Bodies and Souls, or Spirited Bodies?*, Current Issues in Theology (Cambridge: Cambridge University Press, 2006), esp. 24–26 and 137–41. And Oliver Crisp, in an analytic exploration of the compatibility of materialist Christologies with the Chalcedonian definition, does not mention the descent in his essay. See Oliver D. Crisp, "Materialist Christology," in *God Incarnate: Explorations in Christology* (London: T&T Clark, 2009), 137–54. Given that the thrust of Crisp's essay concerns how materialist Christologies relate to the Chalcedonian definition, and therefore to (in part) its response to Apollinarianism, it is interesting that Crisp does not mention the possible (probable?) anti-Apollinarian purpose of the descent clause in the Apostles' Creed. On this, see Justin W. Bass, *The Battle for the Keys: Revelation 1:18 and Christ's Descent into the Underworld*, Paternoster Biblical Monographs (Eugene, OR: Wipf and Stock, 2014), 7; Jeffery L. Hamm, "*Descendit*: Delete or Declare? A Defense against the Neo-Deletionists," *Westminster Theological Journal* (2016): 106; and Catherine Ella Laufer, *Hell's Destruction: An Exploration of Christ's Descent to the Dead* (Farnham: Ashgate, 2013), 28, 199.

4. John W. Cooper, *Body, Soul, and Life Everlasting: Biblical Anthropology and the Monism-Dualism Debate* (Grand Rapids: Eerdmans, 1989; repr., 2000), 129–32.

5. We will return to these problems later in the essay. See Jason McMartin, "Holy Saturday and Christian Theological Anthropology," in *Christian Physicalism? Philosophical and Theological*

Thus in the remainder of this essay I hope, first, to fill out the details of Cortez's comments regarding the implications of the *descensus* for the body-mind, or body-soul, debate by mapping exactly which views of the descent entail and/or rule out which kinds of theological anthropology. Second, I wish to push Cortez a bit on his view of Christ's descent and experience of the intermediate state, which he says is ambiguous in the biblical data. Instead of positing ambiguity and therefore leaving open the question of which kinds of theological anthropology are entailed by Christ's descent, I will argue that Scripture does speak, albeit relatively softly, on what happens to Jesus between his death and resurrection. I will also argue that even if one takes the view that anthropology, the intermediate state, and/or Christ's descent are biblical *adiaphora*,[6] the christological stakes are still too high with respect to Christ's human nature and the continuity of the hypostatic union to adopt current versions of nonreductive physicalism or monism. I will conclude, therefore, that the biblical data about and theological implications of Christ's descent to the dead entail an anthropological dualism that allows for an intermediate state.

MAPPING THEOLOGICAL ANTHROPOLOGY USING A DESCENSUS KEY

We begin by associating historical views of the descent with the theological anthropologies they might entail. Because most of Western thought until the modern period assumed an anthropological dualism,[7] most views of the descent are (at least implicitly) predicated on anthropological dualism. This does not mean, however, that they all necessarily entail anthropological dualism. The earliest Christian view of the descent, which gave rise to both the Roman Catholic and Eastern Orthodox positions, posits that "he descended to the dead" means that Jesus experienced death like all humans do—his dead human body went to the grave while his human soul

---

Criticisms, ed. by R. Keith Loftin and Joshua R. Farris (Lanham: Lexington, 2017), 117–36. This book was released after I had finished a first draft of this paper, and less than two weeks before its presentation. There is significant overlap in my argument and McMartin's. Three factors, though, suggest that our essays are complementary rather than identical. First, McMartin places emphasis only on addressing physicalist accounts, whereas this essay, in part, maps a number of different options for theological anthropology given particular views of the descent. Second, McMartin spends most of his essay arguing in detail points I only make briefly (see below in my response to a physicalist account of the descent). Finally, McMartin leaves open the question of the biblical data regarding the descent, whereas this is an integral part of my essay. For these reasons, my hope is that our essays are read as complementary to one another, not in competition.

6. Murphy suggests this about anthropology in *Bodies and Souls, or Spirited Bodies?*, 4.

7. See, e.g., the comments in Crisp, "Materialist Christology," 139, 153.

experienced a conscious intermediate state in paradise, or Abraham's bosom, the righteous compartment of the place of the dead. By the hypostatic union, Christ's experience of human death is victorious, and during his descent Jesus proclaimed his victory and transformed paradise from a place of expectation for the coming Messiah to a place in which he is present with the faithful dead.[8]

While later Roman Catholic and Eastern Orthodox positions expand this view and, in my estimation, depart from the biblical witness in significant ways,[9] this core affirmation stands at the heart of their respective positions. It should be apparent from the above description that neither the early Christian view nor the subsequent Roman and Orthodox positions allow for physicalism, and they also cannot allow for some kinds of dualism (e.g., property dualisms or a hylemorphic dualism of the animalist sort).

During the Reformation, three views emerged. First, Luther retained the earlier view in many ways, affirming that Christ visited the place of the dead in victory,[10] while rejecting what he considered to be aberrations (e.g., the implicit universalism in Orthodoxy, the "Harrowing of Hell," and its relation to purgatory in Roman Catholicism). Luther's view is not entirely univocal with the early Christian view, however, as Luther may or may not affirm a conscious intermediate state.[11] Rather than Christ "descending" in victory via his human soul on Holy Saturday, "Luther taught that after Christ's burial, after He became alive again in the grave and before His emergence from the grave, the God-man descended to hell in a supernatural manner, conquered the devil, destroyed hell's power, and took from the devil all his might."[12] Luther adopts the view that the soul is

---

8. On the early Christian view of the descent, see, e.g, Metropolitan Hilarion Alfeyev, *Christ the Conqueror of Hell: The Descent into Hades from an Orthodox Perspective* (Crestwood: St. Vladimir's Seminary Press, 2009), 1–101; Bass, *The Battle for the Keys*, 1–19; and Jared Wicks, SJ, "Christ's Saving Descent to the Dead: Early Witnesses from Ignatius of Antioch to Origen," *Pro Ecclesia* 17, no. 3 (2008): 294–309. I do not find the universalist tendency in Alfeyev and others to be persuasive, but that is not the focus of this essay. For my views on the (limited) salvific scope of the descent, see my *"He Descended to the Dead": An Evangelical Theology of Holy Saturday* (Downers Grove: IVP Academic, 2019).

9. Especially with respect to the Eastern Orthodox tendency to imply universal salvation from it and the Roman Catholic attachment of the doctrine of purgatory and the "Harrowing of Hell" (Limbo) to it.

10. See Luther, Third Sermon at Torgau, April 17, 1533, in *LW* 57:127–38.

11. On Luther's view of the intermediate state, in which he repeatedly uses the term and description of "sleep" to describe it, see, e.g., *LW* 4:312; 8:318; and 15:147–50. Based on Luther's commentaries, it does not appear to me that his position is soul sleep *per se*, although there is a resemblance. Thiselton, on the other hand, seems to think that Luther posits soul sleep. See Anthony C. Thiselton, *Life after Death: A New Approach to the Last Things* (Grand Rapids: Eerdmans, 2012), 68–69, citing *LW* 28:110, 200.

12. Richard Klann, "Christ's Descent into Hell," *Concordia Journal* 2 (1976): 43.

"asleep" during the period between bodily death and bodily resurrection to explain the intermediate state. If one takes a Lutheran, and thus bodily, view of the descent, then either anthropological dualism, whether or not it includes soul sleep, or a form of nonreductive physicalism or anthropological dualism that allows for immediate resurrection are permissible.

The other two innovations in the Reformation regarding the descent come from Martin Bucer and John Calvin. Bucer, along with proto-Reformer Leo Jud, argued that the creedal phrase "he descended to the dead" was synonymous with "he was buried."[13] For Bucer, and for many modern theologians, confessing Christ's descent entails nothing more than redundancy with the confession that "he was buried," that is, that he experienced human death. This view is thus not conclusive regarding theological anthropology, since it only states that Jesus died and tells us nothing about the anthropological import of that confession. Calvin, while rejecting Bucer's and Jud's view and instead arguing that each line in the creed must be there for a reason, also departed from the early Christian view. The Genevan reformer stated that the descent clause means that Christ experienced the torments of hell on the cross on Good Friday, thus shifting the meaning of the clause from victory to torment and its timing from Saturday to Friday.[14]

On the face of it, Calvin's view does not *prima facie* require a particular theological anthropology since he stresses that Christ experienced the wrath of God on the cross in his human nature, going no further (in his explication of the clause) on the exact constitution of that nature or where in it torment is experienced. Later, though, in the context of drafting the Westminster Confession of Faith, post-Reformation Reformed theologians felt as though the clause needed to be retained in order to combat incipient Apollinarianism since, for them, it affirmed that Christ experienced the torments of hell in his human soul.[15] This means that, at least for the Westminster Confession drafters, Reformed theologians have interpreted Calvin's view as implying anthropological dualism.[16] If this is the proper interpretation of Calvin's view, then this Reformed position requires some kind of anthropological dualism. If, on the other hand,

---

13. Bass, *The Battle for the Keys*, 17–18.
14. On Calvin's view of the descent, see *Inst.* 2.16.8–12.
15. On which see Chad B. van Dixhoorn, "New Taxonomies of the Westminster Assembly (1643–52): The Creedal Controversy as Case Study," *Reformation & Renaissance Review* 6, no. 1 (2004): 93.
16. This is due in part to the fact that Calvin was an anthropological dualist. See *Inst.* 1.15.1–8.

the "anti-Apollinarian" understanding of Calvin's statements is not the only possible interpretation, and one could instead simply state that Christ experienced God's wrath in his human nature without specifying it took place in his human soul, then it is possible to affirm a Calvinian understanding of the descent along with either a nonreductive physicalism or an anthropological dualism.

A modern riff on the descent that attempts to combine the Calvinian (and later, Barthian), early Christian, Roman, and Orthodox views comes from the Roman Catholic theologian Hans Urs von Balthasar. In his understanding of the descent, Christ experienced the torments of hell in his human nature on Holy Saturday to such a non-Nestorian extent that there is an existential separation between the *hypostases* of Father and Son. This existential separation is bridged by the love of the Holy Spirit, and thus the triune God gains victory over the forces of darkness, namely sin, death, hell, and Satan.[17] Balthasar, as a Roman Catholic, affirms that Jesus's human nature experiences death via the intermediate state and so is an anthropological dualist. Balthasar's position thus requires an anthropological dualism since his articulation is grounded, in part, in the Roman Catholic understanding of the reality of the intermediate state and of the human person as constituted by a body and a rational soul.

MODERN THEOLOGICAL ANTHROPOLOGIES AND THEIR RELATION TO THE DESCENT

While a few of these views may allow for physicalism, their original proponents were all, at least implicitly, anthropological dualists. We do not find Calvin or Luther or early Christians arguing for nondualist understandings of the human person. And thus most of the views above require anthropological dualism of some sort if we understand their positions on the descent in conversation with their articulations of theological anthropology. Nevertheless, it will also be useful to mention how some modern theological anthropologies, including ones that draw on the historical figures mentioned above, relate to the descent and work with or against various views of it.

An important point to make initially is that, as Cortez argues, physicalism is ruled out by a view of the descent that entails Christ experiencing

---

17. On Balthasar's view of the descent, see, e.g., *Theo-Drama: Theological Dramatic Theory*, vol. 4, *The Action*, trans. Graham Harrison (San Francisco: Ignatius, 1994), 317–19. For a critical analysis of Balthasar's position on the descent, see Alyssa Lyra Pitstick, *Light in Darkness: Hans Urs von Balthasar and the Catholic Doctrine of Christ's Descent into Hell* (Grand Rapids: Eerdmans, 2007).

an intermediate state in his human soul. This means that if one adopts the early Christian, Roman Catholic, Greek Orthodox, Balthasarian, or Westminster-translated Calvinian position, physicalism of any sort is not an option. It is also reasonable to suggest that, given Luther's affirmation of a "soul that is asleep" and therefore some kind of anthropological dualism,[18] the Lutheran view *as a whole* is not an option.[19]

The only view of the descent that clearly allows for physicalism or versions of dualism that deny an intermediate state is Jud's and Bucer's, where the descent is merely redundant with "he was buried" and thus simply affirms that Christ experienced human death and particularly bodily burial. But even here there is no demand, for one could still say that experiencing human death entails an intermediate state and therefore anthropological dualism. On the other hand, one could say that experiencing human death means the human being ceases to exist until God raises him from the dead.[20] If we take the latter option, though, we must return to Christology. Is this really an appropriate position given what it implies? For if humans cease to exist between death and resurrection, then the human nature of Jesus ceases to exist between Friday and Sunday.[21]

Thus, among the more immediate problems that would be raised with a nonreductive physicalist or monist view of Christ's time in the tomb, the problem of the cessation of Jesus's human nature, and thus the problem of two incarnations, is the most pressing. It seems to me that if God the Son, who, as the second person of the one God acting in time in the economy, is temporarily disunited from the human nature of Jesus of Nazareth because of the cessation of its existence upon death, then this necessarily implies the cessation of the hypostatic union. While nonreductive physicalists have provided some potential answers to the problem of the continuity of personal

---

18. Again, whether or not Luther affirmed soul sleep is ambiguous in his actual comments on the experience of the soul during death. Even if one concludes he did affirm soul sleep, though, that position still posits an intermediate state that the soul (i.e., one of two substances) experiences, even if the experience is not *conscious*.

19. Of course, one could always adopt Luther's view of the descent—that is, a victorious, postresurrection, predisentombment, bodily descent—without adopting his anthropology. But this would require (1) explaining how Christ could descend to the place of the dead to proclaim victory if there is no one there (in a theological anthropology that denies an intermediate state) and (2) defending intermediate resurrection for Jesus and the rest of humanity, a view I find questionable at best.

20. So according to Kevin Corcoran, "Human persons are *essentially* constituted by the biological bodies that do in fact constitute them. Therefore, if my body should ever cease to exist, I would cease to exist." Kevin Corcoran, "The Constitution View of Persons," in *In Search of the Soul: Four Views of the Mind-Body Problem*, ed. Joel B. Green and Stuart L. Palmer (Downers Grove, IL: InterVarsity, 2005), 160.

21. McMartin calls this problem "gappy existence" and responds to it in detail in "Holy Saturday and Christian Theological Anthropology," 123–25.

identity,[22] I fail to see how the continuity of personal identity upon Jesus's resurrection maintains the continuity of his human nature and therefore the continuity of the hypostatic union during the period between Good Friday and Easter Sunday. Further, this discontinuity seems to imply that Christ's resurrection is also a new instance of incarnation. God the Son ceases to be hypostatically united to the human nature of Jesus upon his death and thus has to hypostatically unite with a human nature, or become incarnate, for a second time—even if to the same human nature—at Jesus's resurrection.[23] Suffice it to say that the problem of two incarnations only multiplies the christological and soteriological problems from there.[24]

We are thus in a position where we either posit the cessation of the hypostatic union for three days, or we turn to immediate resurrection.[25] The former is fraught with christological and soteriological difficulties, and the latter is logically and biblically questionable (at best).[26] This is not the place to make a detailed argument against immediate resurrection, but suffice it to say that a view which requires Jesus to leap in time from Friday to Sunday, and us to leap from the moment of death to the moment of the final judgment, is one which strains the biblical language about death, both Christ's and our own. We could point to the fact that Scripture affirms time and again that Jesus was in the tomb for three days and to Paul's language about those who are dead being asleep at the present moment (e.g., 1 Thess 4:13–14). These statements are little more than phenomenological fancy if, for instance, Christ only *appeared* to be in the tomb for three days but instead inhabited the tomb for little more than a few minutes (or seconds?). And if we are immediately raised, why even entomb people in the first place? In fact, why is there a body in front of us at all? Perhaps one could say that the "immediateness" of the resurrection is from the perception of the believer, not of those "left behind." But if that is the case, are we positing that the

---

22. See, for instance, Nancey Murphy's and Kevin Corcoran's respective contributions to *In Search of the Soul: Four Views of the Mind-Body Problem*: Murphy, "Nonreductive Physicalism," 115–38; Corcoran, "The Constitution View of Human Persons," 153–76.

23. See also McMartin, "Holy Saturday and Christian Theological Anthropology," 121.

24. See particularly McMartin's points about soteriological patterns in "Holy Saturday and Christian Theological Anthropology," 121–22, 25, 28–29.

25. On physicalist accounts of immediate resurrection and the christological problems it entails, see McMartin, "Holy Saturday and Christian Theological Anthropology," 127–29.

26. For an attempt at defending immediate resurrection from the standpoint of hylemorphic dualism and what Turner calls an "Eschatological Presentism" view of time, all while rejecting views of immediate resurrection dependent on "gappy existence" and eternalist and four-dimensionalist views of time, see James T. Turner Jr., "How to Lose the Intermediate State without Losing Your Soul," in *Christian Physicalism? Philosophical Theological Criticisms*, ed. R. Keith Loftin and Joshua Farris (Lanham: Lexington, 2018), 271–93.

human being—including Jesus—does not exist between the moment of their death and their resurrection (more on this below)? Or are we saying that there are two bodies, one lying before us dead, and one—the same one—raised to new life in the eschaton?[27] Suffice it to say that I find this position fraught with logical difficulties. In any case, the only views of the descent that allow for the cessation of human existence between death and resurrection or for immediate resurrection are Calvin's, Luther's, and Bucer's. But to adopt cessation of existence or immediate resurrection under a Calvinian or Lutheran *descensus* garb would entail adopting only their view of the descent, not their anthropology. On the other hand, while physicalists and other monists may find Jud's or Bucer's view of the descent compatible with their theological anthropology, it is difficult to ascertain how it works with classic Christology and the biblical affirmations about his death.

A BIBLICAL CASE FOR THE CLASSIC VIEW OF CHRIST'S DESCENT

These historical, philosophical, and theological considerations are sufficient to suggest that the most christologically sensible views of the descent are ones that at least imply, if not require, an anthropological dualism. Nevertheless, in the remainder of this essay I will return to the biblical data in order to make an abbreviated case for a view of Christ's descent that does require an anthropological dualism that allows for an intermediate state.[28]

Often discussions of Christ's descent center on 1 Peter 3:18–22, and many commentators and theologians opt against the doctrine being taught in that particular text. While I do believe that an argument can be made for the traditional view of the descent from this passage,[29] it is better in this limited space to discuss less exegetically difficult passages. While each of the passages discussed contains its own interpretive challenges, my goal here is to provide a summary of the biblical data, not a comprehensive exegetical argument.[30]

---

27. In this regard, see Thiselton's discussion of death as "sleep" in *Life After Death*, 69–70.

28. I want to stress the attenuated nature of the argument. It is not intended to be a full discussion of all the relevant passages, issues, or exegetical points under consideration. For that kind of analysis, see Justin Bass, *The Battle for the Keys*; see also my forthcoming *"He Descended to the Dead"*.

29. See, e.g., Bass, *The Battle for the Keys*, 84–96; and Hamm, "*Descendit*: Delete or Declare?," 108–15.

30. For such an argument see Bass, *The Battle for the Keys*. The entire book is important for a biblical and historical defense, but pages 62–114 in particular contain Bass's exegesis of the relevant New Testament texts.

Aside from 1 Peter 3:18–22, there are at least five texts that bear on how we understand Christ's time in the tomb in the New Testament: Matthew 12:40; Acts 2:27; Romans 10:7; Ephesians 4:8–9; and Revelation 1:18. While it would be beneficial to examine each of these in detail, I will focus my attention here on Romans 10:7 and Matthew 12:40. I have chosen these two passages, first, because they contain explicit language about the fact and manner of Christ's existence between his death and resurrection. While I believe that Acts 2:27;[31] Ephesians 4:8–9; and Revelation 1:18[32] also contain similar language about the fact and manner of Christ's existence between Good Friday and Easter Sunday, it would take considerable exegetical argumentation, for which I do not have space here, in order to gain common assent. It is much less difficult to gain common assent to the claim that Matthew 12:40 and Romans 10:7 speak of Christ's time in the tomb, given Jesus's analogy to Jonah in the fish's belly in the former and Paul's use of "abyss" in the latter.

MATTHEW 12:40

With respect to Jesus's words in the Gospel of Matthew, we need to consider the allusion to Jonah 2 and what it entails for Jesus's experience of death. First, from the context both of Jesus's statement and of Jonah's experience, Jonah's three days and three nights in the belly of the fish is analogous to Jesus's experience of death between Good Friday and Easter Sunday. Those dealing with the biblical data regarding Christ's intermediate state (or lack thereof) commonly acknowledge at least this much, but many are unwilling to go further than the simple recognition that the text affirms that Christ remained dead for three days. But when we examine Jonah 2, it appears that there is more to the analogy than this.

Jonah 2[33] contains Jonah's prayer after the fish swallows him. In it, Jonah describes the belly of the fish as Sheol, the abyss, the place of the

---

31. It should be noted, though, however briefly, that Acts 2:27 does assume that Jesus experienced death as all humans do. And given that assumption, it is reasonable to conclude that Luke has some kind of content associated with the claim that Jesus experienced death *as all humans do*. For a careful study of the kinds of beliefs that Luke (and other New Testament writers) may have held about the afterlife in their first-century context, see N. T. Wright, *The Resurrection of the Son of God*, Christian Origins and the Question of God 3 (Minneapolis: Fortress, 2003), 32–206. For a comprehensive survey of views of the afterlife in the ancient Near Eastern, Greco-Roman, Second Temple Jewish, New Testament, early Christian, Islamic, and rabbinic cultures and traditions, see Alan F. Segal, *Life After Death: A History of the Afterlife in Western Religion*, Anchor Bible Reference Library (New York: Doubleday, 2004).

32. Rev 1:18 implies that Christ took the keys from Death and Hades, which also implies that he visited them in order to do so. See Bass, *The Battle for the Keys*, 97–114.

33. The following paragraph is taken from my forthcoming book, *"He Descended to the Dead"*.

dead.[34] While "belly of the fish" and "belly of Sheol" differ with respect to the exact terms used, they are still used here as metaphorical synonyms.[35] In fact, the phrases that are repeated in Matthew 12:40 occur in Jonah 2:4 (LXX) and 2:7 (LXX), both of which make reference or are parallel to Hades/Sheol (2:4 and 2:3 LXX).[36] Consider the following: Matthew 12:40 reads, ὥσπερ γὰρ ἦν Ἰωνᾶς ἐν τῇ κοιλίᾳ τοῦ κήτους τρεῖς νύκτας, οὕτως ἔσται ὁ υἱὸς τοῦ ἀνθρώπου ἐν τῇ καρδίᾳ τῆς γῆς τρεῖς ἡμέρας καὶ τρεῖς νύκτας. The quotation is from Jonah 1:17 (2:1 LXX), but the other phrases in Matthew 12:40 also parallel portions of Jonah 2.[37] First, while Jesus says he will go into the heart (καρδίᾳ) of the earth, Jonah is cast by the LORD into the heart (καρδίας) of the sea (Jonah 2:3 [2:4 LXX]). Further, this reference is parallel to "the belly of Sheol" in 2:2 (2:3 LXX; ἔκ κοιλίας ᾅδου, literally "belly of Hades"). Notice how this phrasing thus lexically connects "belly of the fish" (1:17 [2:1 LXX]), "belly of Sheol" (2:2 [2:3 LXX]), and "heart of the sea" (2:3 [2:4 LXX]).[38] Finally, and perhaps most importantly, Jesus's statement that he will be three days and three nights "in the heart of the earth" (καρδίᾳ τῆς γῆς) finds a clear parallel in Jonah 2:6 (2:7 LXX) with the phrase κατέβην εἰς γῆν ("I went down to the land").[39] Both Jesus and Jonah descend to the depths of the pit, Hades, Sheol, the abyss.[40] These are all synonymous terms in Jonah 2,[41] and the lexical similarities between

---

34. Billy K. Smith is worth quoting at length here: "The term 'Sheol' was used in various ways. It may be said with certainty that in Hebrew thought the term referred to a place of the dead. It was spoken of as located under the earth (Amos 9:2). Normally those who were in Sheol were seen as separated from God (Ps 88:3; Isa 38:18), yet God was shown to have access to Sheol (Ps 139:8). Sheol was used as an expression for being in the grave (Pss 18:6; 30:3; 49:14; Isa 28:15). With this imagery Jonah here described his experience of being 'at the very brink of death.' Fretheim agrees that the language used here goes beyond the literal sense, especially regarding Sheol: 'Inasmuch as Sheol was believed to be under the floor of the ocean, Jonah was spatially near the place.' It also helps to understand at this point that in the Old Testament death is understood to be more a process than an event. As for Jonah's place in that death process, life had ebbed so much that he could have been reckoned more among the dead than among the living." Billy K. Smith and Frank S. Page, *Amos, Obadiah, Jonah*, New American Commentary 19B (Nashville: B&H, 1995), 245–46.

35. Marvin A. Sweeney, *The Twelve Prophets*, vol. 1: *Hosea, Joel, Amos, Obadiah, Jonah*, ed. David W. Cotter, Berit Olam: Studies in Hebrew Narrative and Poetry (Collegeville, MN: Liturgical, 2000), 320.

36. John Woodhouse, "Jesus and Jonah," *The Reformed Theological Review* 43, no. 2 (1984): 36.

37. On the exegetical points that follow, see Woodhouse, "Jesus and Jonah," 36.

38. Note the parallels with chaos (Gen 1:2) in Jonah 2:6 (2:6 LXX). See Sweeney, *The Twelve Prophets*, 1:321–22.

39. "'In the heart of the earth' [is] a reference to Sheol, the Hebrew underworld." Dominic Rudman, "The Sign of Jonah," *Expository Times* 115, no. 10 (2004): 325. See also Sweeney, who says that "verse 7 [NRSV: 6] employs the imagery of descent to Sheol or the netherworld, i.e., he is going down to the world of the dead who are barred from reentering the world of the living." Sweeney, *The Twelve Prophets*, 1:321.

40. It should be obvious that for Jonah, the abyss is a place where a person can be conscious and have a continuous identity. Otherwise the comparison, and particularly the invocations of YHWH's faithfulness, makes no sense.

41. As indicated by the intertextual parallels noted in the exegesis above. See also Rudman,

that chapter and Matthew 12:40 indicate that "the primary meaning of the 'sign of Jonah' . . . is . . . the correspondence between Jonah's experience in the belly of the sea creature, and Jesus' experience in death, *his* descent to Hades."[42] Further, Hades, Sheol, and the abyss were commonly understood in the ancient Near East and in first-century Palestine not merely as the grave but as the dwelling place of the souls of the departed. For these reasons, we could accurately say that Jonah's descent into the belly of the fish is figuratively portrayed as his descent to the place of the dead, namely, the intermediate state. And so, as Nolland puts it, "Both [the belly of the sea monster and the heart of the earth] represent liminal states connected with death."[43] Jesus and Jonah thus both descend to the place of the dead.[44]

ROMANS 10:7

In Romans 10:7 Paul asks, "Who will bring Christ up from the dead?" In Greek, this reads, Τίς καταβήσεται εἰς τὴν ἄβυσσον; τοῦτ' ἔστιν Χριστὸν ἐκ νεκρῶν ἀναγαγεῖν. For our purposes, we need to make at least three exegetical points here. First, the word "abyss" is significant. It is used contrastively with "heaven" in verse 6 and so is intended to refer to the realm opposite of heaven. Further, according to Bales, "The word ἄβυσσος is used in parallel with νεκρῶν, 'the dead,' here as a synecdoche for Hades."[45] Given the use of "abyss" in synonymity with "the dead" and in contrast to "heaven," it is most likely that it refers to the place of the dead—the intermediate state. A second important exegetical feature of the passage, the word νεκρῶν, heightens this likelihood. It is a plural participle, meaning that Paul's description of raising Christ up could be translated as "bringing him up from *among the dead ones*." He was one of the dead, νεκρῶν, but God raised him up.

Finally, Paul quotes Deuteronomy 32:12–14 in Romans 10:6–7, which is important for understanding the passage. The phrase parallel to verse 7, "beyond the sea" (πέραν τῆς θαλάσσης; Deuteronomy 30:14 LXX), was

---

"The Sign of Jonah," 326: "It is clear that Jonah's psalm [2:3–10] links imagery of being engulfed by water and of being imprisoned in Sheol."

42. Woodhouse, "Jesus and Jonah," 36.

43. John Nolland, *The Gospel of Matthew: A Commentary on the Greek Text* (Grand Rapids: Eerdmans, 2005), 511.

44. The comparison between the sea (as represented by the fish) and death is made in various other places throughout the Old Testament. As Rudman explains, this is because "the Deep and Sheol could therefore be seen by Israelite writers as comparable in the sense that both were places of chaos and non-creation." Rudman, "The Sign of Jonah," 327.

45. William Bales, "The Descent of Christ in Ephesians 4:9," *Catholic Biblical Quarterly* 72 (2010): 98.

commonly used for the place of the dead in the ancient Near East.[46] Paul does not ignore the meaning of Deuteronomy 32:14 here by inserting "abyss" for "beyond the sea"; rather, both terms can refer to the place of the dead. We see this not only in the ancient Near East but also in the Septuagint. "Abyss" is commonly used in parallel with both "the sea" and the place of the dead in the Old Testament.[47]

HADES, THE ABYSS, SHEOL, AND THE PLACE OF THE DEAD

What Romans 10:7 and Matthew 12:40 affirm, then, is that Jesus experienced death as all humans do. That is, his body was buried and his soul went to the place of the dead—Hades, the abyss, Sheol. This is what Acts 2:27 affirms as well, and it is implied by Revelation 1:18.[48] Further, given the intertextual relationship between Ephesians 4:8–9 and Romans 10:7,[49] it is plausible that it also refers to Jesus in the place of the dead. So the question remains: What exactly does "the place of the dead" refer to?[50] While some

---

46. See Richard Bauckham, *The Fate of the Dead: Studies on the Jewish and Christian Apocalypses*, Supplements to Novum Testamentum 93 (Atlanta: SBL, 1998), 9–48; Bass, *The Battle for the Keys*, 45–61.

47. On the synonymous relationship of the sea and the underworld in Rom 10:7, as well as their equivalency in Jewish thought, see James D. G. Dunn, *Romans 9–16*, WBC 38B (Dallas: Word, 1988), 606. Additionally, Dunn notes that the phrase εἰς τὴν ἄβυσσον... ἐκ νεκρῶν ἀναγαγεῖν "echoes that of Ps 71 [LXX 70]:20—ἐζωοποίησάς με καὶ ἐκ τῶν ἀβύσσων τῆς γῆς ἀνήγαγές με; Wisd Sol 16:13—'you have power of life and death, and you lead down to the gates of hell and back again (ἀνάγεις).'" Dunn, *Romans 9–16*, 606. See also Schreiner, *Romans*, Baker Exegetical Commentary on the New Testament (Grand Rapids: Baker, 1998), 559.

48. On the implications of this passage regarding Christ's descent to Death and Hades and the forcible removal of the keys from their possession, see, e.g., David F. Aune, *Revelation 1–5*, WBC 52A (Dallas: Word, 1997), 104; G. K. Beale, *The Book of Revelation*, New International Greek Testament Commentary (Grand Rapids: Eerdmans, 1999), 215; and Bauckham, *The Fate of the Dead*, 39.

49. On the syntactical and lexical relationship between the two passages, see Bales, "The Descent of Christ in Ephesians 4:9," 98.

50. Space does not permit an in-depth exploration of terms and concepts such as Sheol, Hades, and *nephesh*, so here I would simply point to good introductions to both sides of that debate. For arguments that the biblical data is ambivalent regarding the nature of the intermediate state, and thus at least allowing for nonreductive physicalism and other kinds of anthropological monism, see Green, "'Bodies—That Is, Human Lives,'" 149–73; as well as Green, *Body, Soul, and Human Life*, 46–71, 140–80. See also the discussion of Sheol in Philip S. Johnston, *Shades of Sheol: Death and Afterlife in the Old Testament* (Downers Grove: IVP Academic, 2002). Johnston's book is referenced repeatedly by Green and others in support of their contention that death was equivalent to nonexistence for ancient Israel. For a response to Green's biblical arguments (as well as Murphy's in *Bodies and Souls*) and a constructive account of a conscious intermediate state, see Matthew Levering, *Jesus and the Demise of Death: Resurrection, Afterlife, and the Fate of the Christian* (Waco: Baylor University Press, 2012), 97–108. For a fuller picture of the Old Testament's view of death in the context of the surrounding Mesopotamian, Egyptian, and Ugaritic backgrounds, see Christopher B. Hays, *A Covenant with Death: Death in the Iron Age II and Its Rhetorical Uses in Proto-Isaiah* (Tübingen: Mohr Siebeck, 2011; repr., Grand Rapids: Eerdmans, 2015). The portraits given of the ancient Near Eastern background (see esp. pp. 55–56, 89–91, 131–32) suggest a very different picture of the afterlife, one in which persons are assumed to carry on and possibly (through various means of intervention) have a somewhat happy postmortem existence. Hays goes on to demonstrate that the

want to argue that it is synonymous with "the grave," it is not clear that this is either the only or the best option, both biblically and theologically. A few points warrant consideration.

First, while contemporary common convention seems to rest on the idea that Sheol in the Old Testament and Hades in the New Testament are simply synonymous with "the grave," (i.e., bodily burial), there is significant evidence marshaled to the contrary. Perhaps most notably and most recently, Richard Steiner has made a thorough, detailed, exegetical, and historical investigation into the term *nephesh* and its use in the Hebrew Bible, arguing that both it and Sheol should not be relegated to simply mean "life" or "grave," respectively.[51]

Additionally, the dominant cultural backgrounds for the New Testament—Greco-Roman Hellenism and Second Temple Judaism— affirmed, in many cases, a nonbodily afterlife, even if their conceptions of it differed in significant respects.[52] It is important to note here, as N. T. Wright does, that both Greco-Roman and Second Temple Jewish views of the afterlife were varied. But, as Wright also points out, the belief in *some kind* of conscious, personal afterlife was the common view in both Hellenistic and Jewish systems of thought. Further, as Wright repeatedly states, the Second Temple Jewish belief in the resurrection of the dead (which, of course, was not unanimous but nevertheless predominant[53]) was both widespread[54] *and* entailed a belief in an intermediate state.[55] As Wright puts it, "Any Jew who believed in resurrection, from Daniel to the Pharisees and beyond, naturally believed also in an intermediate state in which some kind of personal identity was guaranteed between physical death and the physical re-embodiment of resurrection."[56] Thus, *contra* Green, who cites Wright in support of his position that Greco-Roman thought and Second Temple Judaism were too varied to indicate any kind of common ground

---

ancient Israelites encountered and adopted many of these ancient Near Eastern beliefs and practices, and thus the Old Testament authors' references to death and the afterlife, and particularly their insistence that YHWH is Lord over death and that dead persons are relatively inactive, are polemics against the ancestor cults, deification of the dead, and the like in other ancient Near Eastern cultures (see 153–201, and esp. 190–92). This is a much more nuanced picture than the often-employed narrative that the Old Testament does not care about the afterlife and that the Second Temple Jewish views of the dead are mostly the products of Hellenization.

51. See Richard Steiner, *Disembodied Souls: The "Nefesh" in Israel and Kindred Spirits in the Ancient Near East, with an Appendix on the Katumura Inscription,* Ancient Near East Monographs (Atlanta: SBL, 2015).

52. On which see Wright, *The Resurrection of the Son of God,* 32–206.

53. Wright, *Resurrection of the Son of God,* 131–40.

54. Wright, *Resurrection of the Son of God,* 129, 147.

55. Wright, *Resurrection of the Son of God,* 130, 133, 134, 142, 164, 177, 203.

56. Wright, *Resurrection of the Son of God,* 164.

for the New Testament authors' view of humanity and the afterlife,[57] the New Testament authors all presume one *particular* Second Temple Jewish view—the resurrection of the dead. And it is a position that, as Wright says, also entails an intermediate state (in Second Temple Jewish thought). Thus the supposed ambiguity of the biblical data, so often invoked by those who wish to discard more traditional views of theological anthropology and the intermediate state, is not as ambiguous as is often claimed.

"Hades" and "paradise" also had fairly well-defined meanings in the first century, which sheds yet more light on Jesus's use of "paradise" in Luke 23:43. In Second Temple Judaism, the place of the dead (commonly referred to as Hades) was typically compartmentalized: paradise or Abraham's bosom (cf. Luke 16:16–31) contained the righteous dead.[58] This compartmentalization of the place of the dead and Jesus's references to it lead us to a second consideration regarding the New Testament's conception of the afterlife, namely the repeated use of από νεκρῶν.[59] As discussed earlier, this phrase (and similar ones using different prepositions) should be translated "among the dead ones." It is a reference to a place where the dead reside. This fits with many of the common Greco-Roman and Second Temple Jewish understandings of the afterlife, which often included conscious (albeit shadowy, to varying degrees) existence in a spiritual state. It also implies that Jesus's personal identity remains personally and consciously intact—and not merely possible to be reinstated upon resurrection—while dead.

Here again one may be tempted to assume that "among the dead ones" could just refer to dead bodies being buried in their respective graves. We could counter initially by returning to the biblical data: this does not accord with Matthew's and Paul's statements that Jesus was "in the heart of the earth" and "the abyss," respectively. Both phrases would have been understood as references to the place of the dead (i.e., the intermediate state) in first-century Palestine. But as we have already traversed that ground, this objection brings us to a third and explicitly theological issue. If one assumes that the phrase, along with the other biblical passages marshaled, merely means that Jesus's dead body was buried, and therefore that some form of physicalism or materialism is permissible for theological anthropology, we return once again to the problem of the cessation of existence of Jesus's human nature. Here we once more encounter the issue of the hypostatic

---

57. E.g., Green, *Body, Soul, and Human Life*, 60, 146.

58. See the discussion of compartments in Bass, *The Battle for the Keys*, 45–61; as well as Bauckham, *The Fate of the Dead*, 9–48.

59. See on this phrase Bass, *The Battle for the Keys*, e.g., 94n149.

union as it relates to Christ's existence between Good Friday and Easter Sunday. And again, for the reasons detailed earlier, neither cessation of existence or immediate resurrection is a plausible way to think about the period between Christ's death and resurrection. Regarding the former, it would appear we have two incarnations; regarding the latter, we encounter several biblical and logical problems, most notably that Christ would have only *appeared* to remain in the tomb for three days.

CHRIST'S DESCENT AND ANTHROPOLOGICAL DUALISM

Given these biblical and theological concerns about Christ's descent, it appears to me that the clear way forward in theological anthropology is to affirm some form of anthropological dualism that allows for an intermediate state. I do not have the space to speculate about precisely which form is best here, and so I offer instead a few biblical and theological parameters. First, any affirmation of dualism needs to be at the same time an affirmation of the biblical picture of the wholeness of the human person.[60] Second, it seems to me that much of the pushback against dualism comes from scientific perspectives, particularly neuroscience. While I do not wish to posit some kind of "soul of the gaps" theory, science does not and never can tell us everything about everything, and there remain significant scientific problems with physicalism of any variety, particularly with respect to consciousness.[61] Scientific problems exist for both anthropological dualisms and monisms, if we are honest.[62]

---

60. Affirmation of an intermediate state that includes a disembodied existence in the presence of Christ does not necessarily entail the problematic elements of Platonic or Cartesian dualism, where the soul is valued above the body. Instead, we can say with, for instance, Aquinas, Levering, and McMartin, that the intermediate state is not the same thing as the beatific vision, the new heavens and new earth, or our natural state. It is impermanent and imperfect. For Aquinas's view (and Levering's), see Levering, *Jesus and the Demise of Death*, 15–26. McMartin says in his essay that "if we endure an intermediate state . . . , it is not comfortable or 'natural' for us (2 Cor. 5)." McMartin, "Holy Saturday and Christian Theological Anthropology," 122. For a recent affirmation of the wholeness of the human person from an anthropological dualist, see John W. Cooper, "Whose Interpretation? Which Anthropology? Biblical Hermeneutics, Scientific Naturalism, and the Body-Soul Debate," in *Neuroscience and the Soul: The Human Person in Philosophy, Science, and Theology*, ed. Thomas M. Crisp, Steven L. Porter, and Gregg A. Ten Elshof (Grand Rapids: Eerdmans, 2016), 238–57.

61. In this regard, see Eric LaRock, "Neuroscience and the Hard Problem of Consciousness," in *Neuroscience and the Soul*, 151–80.

62. For instance, both Terence Nichols and Joseph Ratzinger point out that there are just as many scientific issues (and particularly related to physics) with resurrection and new creation as there are with an intermediate state. Nichols, *Death and Afterlife*, 77–90, 135–50; and Joseph Ratzinger, *Eschatology: Death and Eternal Life*, 2nd ed. (Washington, DC: Catholic University of America Press, 1988), 106.

Finally, the surveys above and the first two considerations just mentioned indicate that Christ's descent to the dead demands some form of theological anthropology that allows for an intermediate state while also maintaining a holistic view of the human person and rejecting problematic forms of anthropological dualism. In this regard, I find Eleonore Stump's articulation of a "non-Cartesian substance dualism" that draws on Thomas's hylemorphic account of the human person to be most compatible with affirming Christ's descent to the dead. Other, better options may be present of which I am unaware, and other options may arise which currently do not exist. Additionally, since Stump also argues that her position has affinity with "materialism without reduction," it is possible that some form of monism or physicalism may exist or be posited in the future that allows for all the considerations outlined above. Because the monist and physicalist positions of which I am aware reject the intermediate state, though, it seems that this option is not currently on the table. Such an account would need to allow for an intermediate state in which the mind exists apart from the body. For these reasons I conclude that affirming Christ's descent to the dead, which is warranted by both historical and biblical considerations, should lead one to affirm some form of anthropological dualism.[63]

---

63. I am grateful to Luke Stamps and Porter Taylor for their constructive comments on earlier versions of this essay.

CHAPTER 12

"THE UPWARD CALL"
The Category of Vocation and the Oddness of Human Nature

IAN A. MCFARLAND

CHRISTIANS SPEAK OF HUMAN BEINGS having their end in God. As Augustine states at the outset of the *Confessions*, "You have made us for yourself, and our heart is restless until it rests in you."[1] Such a claim suggests that human nature is ontologically odd, since it implies that what is "natural" to human beings is not to have a "nature," in the sense of a clearly defined, self-contained type of being. Instead, it is characteristic of human beings that they should become, in the words of 2 Peter 1:4, "participants in the *divine* nature"—that is, that they should share in a type of being that is *not* natural to them—to be most fully human. Nor is this "eccentric" character of human nature simply a matter of the future hope of eschatological transformation.[2] It is also a feature of this-worldly human teleology, for, in contrast to other creatures for which maturation involves growing into a predictable type (acorns into oaks, foals into horses, and so on), human life is inherently open in that the particular end (or combination of ends)—astronaut, parent, baker, monk—that defines the unique

---

1. Saint Augustine, *Confessions*, trans. Henry Chadwick (New York: Oxford University Press, 1998), 1.1 (3). Cf. *The Shorter Catechism*, in *Book of Confessions: Study Edition* (Louisville: Geneva, 1996), Q. 1 (229): "Man's chief end is to glorify God, and to enjoy him forever."
2. The term "eccentric" is taken from David Kelsey, who develops the point exhaustively in his *Eccentric Existence: A Theological Anthropology*, 2 vols. (Louisville: Westminster John Knox, 2009).

mode of a person's humanity, and thus the unique way they will ultimately participate in the divine nature, is not predictable.[3]

Although this open-endedness may be understood in terms of humans lacking the kind of self-enclosed ontology other creatures have, this "lack" can also be associated with an identifiable feature of human nature, namely, the fact that human beings have *wills*. The character of the will is, of course, a contentious one in the history of Christian theology and in Western thought more generally. I use the term in a minimalist (and I hope correspondingly uncontroversial) way, such that to have a will is to experience oneself as an *agent*, that is, as a kind of entity who ineluctably refers to herself as "I" and thereby characterizes her being and actions as precisely *hers*. In this way, to have a will is to "own" oneself and one's deeds in the colloquial sense of that term. So understood, the assertion that human beings have wills entails no claim one way or the other about whether or not the will is "free" in a libertarian sense. Nor does it mean that human beings experience all their actions as subject to their conscious control. Evidently, they do not: my blinking or sweating, for example, is not subject to my control in the way that my eating or speaking is. It remains the case, however, that a human will say, "I blinked," or "I sweated," just as naturally—and legitimately—as "I ate," or "I spoke." The upshot of the claim that human beings have wills is simply to register this point and thereby to identify the will as, so to speak, the locus of human nature's ontological oddity: that aspect of human nature by virtue of which a human being is irreducible to her nature.[4] That I should be a professor rather than a pastor, a parent rather than childless, is certainly not reducible to my decision, but it is inseparable from my willing, so that the will may be characterized as that feature of human nature that renders it "naturally" open-ended.[5]

---

3. To be sure, other species also exhibit diverse individual teleologies (e.g., the difference between queen, worker, soldier, etc. in an ant colony), but this diversity is strictly circumscribed and takes the form of limited, predictable types. By contrast, humans, like pots, "take their identities from the uses to which they put themselves" rather than from uses to which they are antecedently determined. Kathryn Tanner, *Christ the Key* (Cambridge: Cambridge University Press, 2010), 44. Cf. Ingolf U. Dalferth, *Creatures of Possibility: The Theological Basis of Human Freedom* (Grand Rapids: Baker Academic, 2016).

4. See the discussion in Ian A. McFarland, *In Adam's Fall: A Meditation on the Christian Doctrine of Original Sin* (Malden: Wiley Blackwell, 2010), ch. 5, esp. 126–27; cf. Tanner, *Christ the Key*, ch. 1.

5. While angels, too, have wills and are thus also properly characterized as agents, the fact that angels are (at least on a Thomist account) pure form means that each angel is its own species. Thus, like an acorn, an angel's "maturation" involves its conformity to a particular predetermined type, even though (unlike an acorn) this conformity is mediated through an act of will. In other words, an angelic will has only a single possible mode of self-realization, serving only to confirm (or, in the case of fallen angels, to disconfirm) that angel's status as the particular species it is. As such, the angelic will is not a sign of open-endedness, since an angelic species, unlike the human, is not open

Conceived in relation to this understanding of the will, the church's traditional emphasis on human freedom is best understood not as a claim about a special ability human beings possess (of the "Invictus," "I am the master of my fate," variety) but rather as a further way of highlighting human nature's inherent open-endedness.[6] That is, to speak of the will and its freedom as constitutive features of humanity does not so much define human nature as signal that this nature is distinctive precisely in eluding the possibility of definition. In comparison with other creatures, human beings stand out by virtue of the absence of the sorts of defining characteristics that tie the realization of the human to any particular form. In this context, Kathryn Tanner has suggested that the biblical claim that humanity was created in God's image (Gen 1:26–27; cf. 5:1; 9:6) should be understood in just these terms: that is, because God's transcendence of the world precludes any definition of the divine essence, we human beings image the divine in that our nature, by virtue of its open-endedness, is also incapable of definition.[7] Indeed, insofar as human beings achieve ultimate fulfillment as the particular kind of creatures they are only as they come to participate in the divine nature, living in glory by somehow sharing the power of God's own life, humanity's reflection of the divine is a matter of content as well as form. In other words, it is not simply that a human life has no predetermined form but that it finds its ultimate fulfillment precisely in sharing that very infinity of the divine nature that renders the latter incapable of definition.[8]

THE PROBLEM OF NATURE AND GRACE

This close relationship between human fulfillment and the divine nature, however, raises some tricky theological questions. For Christians want to affirm that the life of glory by which we participate in the divine nature is a matter of grace and thus a gift of God that is beyond or in excess of

---

to an indefinite number of forms of self-realization; rather, the angelic form is identical with (and thus defined by) the nature.

6. See Tanner, *Christ the Key*, 48–50. For example, Irenaeus contrasts the Christian emphasis on human freedom or agency with what he takes to be the ontological determinism of the Gnostics. See *Haer.* 4.37 (*ANF* 1:518–21); cf. 1.6 (*ANF* 1:323–25).

7. See Tanner, *Christ the Key*, 53–54: "An apophatically-focused anthropology forms the natural consequence of an apophatic theology."

8. Of course, this does not mean that human life in itself becomes infinite, as though the boundary between creature and Creator were dissolved; it is rather that our finitude takes the form of an endless exploration of the inexhaustible fullness of the divine life that Gregory of Nyssa called *epektasis* and Maximus the Confessor as an "ever-moving rest" (e.g., *Opuscule* 16 [PG 91:185A]).

nature; indeed, if glory means sharing in the divine nature—a nature that belongs properly to God alone and to which human beings therefore have no intrinsic claim—then it can hardly be understood in any other terms. But if glory is also understood as the "natural" end of human existence, then it would seem by definition no longer to be a matter of grace. Contrariwise, if the truly gracious, "superadded" character of glory is preserved, then it seems necessary to conclude that it can be distinguished from the essence of what it means to be human in a way that renders it an ultimately unnecessary supplement to a human nature and thus not its "natural" end at all.

Addressing this tension has been a focus of much Catholic theology over the last century. A key feature of the *nouvelle théologie* pioneered by figures like Henri de Lubac and Yves Congar, for example, was the claim that human nature was always already infused with grace. This position was formulated in opposition to the neo-Scholastic category of "pure nature" (*natura pura*) according to which human life could be conceived in terms of purely immanent, this-worldly processes and ends without any reference to God's gift, thereby rendering grace anthropologically superfluous.[9] Yet the theological problems associated with affirming that grace is not an ontologically optional *donum superadditum* but rather inherent in created human nature are evident in Karl Rahner's oxymoronic category of the "supernatural existential": on the one hand, it is "supernatural" because it refers to an orientation to the divine that transcends nature; on the other, it is "an existential of every person" and thus "natural" to human existence.[10] This structure of thought leads to an unstable oscillation between nature and grace that, in the effort to acknowledge the truth of humanity's fulfillment in God, ends up rooting the potential for that fulfillment in the structure of human nature itself.[11]

---

9. The key text is Henri de Lubac, *Surnaturel: Études Historiques* (Paris: Aubier 1946); ET: *Augustinianism and Modern Theology*, trans. Lancelot Sheppard (London: Chapman, 1969).

10. Karl Rahner, *Foundations of Christian Faith: An Introduction to the Idea of Christianity*, trans. William V. Dych (New York: Crossroads, 1992), 127; cf. 39, where Rahner argues that the structure of human beings is such that "the real question of personal existence is in truth a question about salvation," such that salvation is in no sense extrinsic to one's properly human existence but is "rooted in the very nature of freedom."

11. Rahner is, of course, well aware of this tension and attempts to address it. He denies that the universality of divine self-communication renders it "natural," arguing that making the measure of gratuity the idea that the divine gift might equally well be given or withheld is a category mistake: "The gratuity of a reality has nothing to do with the question whether it is present in many or only in a few people," he writes. "Indeed only what is given to everybody reveals the real essence of grace in a radical way. Something gratuitous which is given to one and denied to another is really by its very nature something which falls within the realm of possibility for everyone," and "such an understanding satisfies only the notion of something being unmerited by the individual, but not the notion of something . . . which essentially transcends the natural" (*Foundations of Christian Faith*,

To be sure, Rahner has no intention of arguing that we ascend to God by our own power. On the contrary, he insists that God's offer of grace is not simply the condition of the possibility of our accepting it, since even our acceptance "is borne by God himself in his self-communication."[12] The point remains, however, that human beings are understood as inherently oriented to God by virtue of having God's communicative presence within them as the very content of their humanity. In seeking to counter the neo-Scholastic idea of a human nature that has a meaningful end in itself that is independent of life with God, Rahner holds that humanity is always already in relation to God. But if neo-Scholasticism threatened to drive a wedge between creation and redemption, the Rahnerian position risks conflating them.[13] Humanity is envisioned as created with a God-shaped hole, as it were, such that God's failing to fill it would render human beings ultimately less than human and thereby amount to a failure of God to bring to completion the work of creation God had intended. In this way, the problem with Rahner's and other similar proposals is that they equate humanity's *open-endedness* with an *incompleteness* that renders grace ontologically indispensable if human beings are to be truly human.

AN ALTERNATIVE FRAMEWORK

Over against this way of relating nature and grace, I wish to argue that the open-endedness of human nature does not entail the claim that human nature is incomplete. This perspective allows grace to be understood as that which brings human life to fulfillment without suggesting that human beings have any sort of natural desire for or orientation toward it. Thus, a failure to receive grace would not be inconsistent with the integrity of humanity's created nature.

---

127). For Rahner, the fact that the offer of divine self-communication can be refused or ignored as well as accepted distinguishes it from the "natural" (viz., as something constitutive of human being as such); nevertheless, this claim sits in tension with his assertion that the event of God's self-communication "belongs to all men . . . as something given prior to man's freedom," and as "a modality of his original and unthematic subjectivity" (*Foundations of Christian Faith*, 128, 129).

12. Rahner, *Foundations of Christian Faith*, 129. At the same time, he proceeds to speak of specifically *human* capacity: "The absolutely unlimited transcendence of the natural spirit in knowledge and freedom . . . already implies by itself such an infinity in the subject that the possession [!] of God in absolute self-communication does not really fall outside the infinite possibility of transcendence" (*Foundations of Christian Faith*, 129–30).

13. This is evident in, e.g., Rahner's willingness to view the experience of forgiveness independently of the gospel as possible for any person "who in the forlornness of his guilt still turns in trust to the mystery of his existence which is quietly present" and therein "experiences himself as one . . . who is forgiven" (*Foundations of Christian Faith*, 131).

In order to see how one might speak of nature as having its own integrity without succumbing to the problem of superfluity identified in relation to the category of "pure nature," it is important to note that de Lubac's objection to the latter was not to the possibility of considering human nature apart from life with God, or even with the idea of a natural end to human existence, in the sense of concrete goods attainable by human nature within the created order.[14] His objection was rather to the concept of "natural beatitude," defined as a human end not only wholly immanent to created nature but also divinely ordered, and in relation to which the higher, supernatural end secured by grace is an addition that is, from a strictly ontological perspective, unnecessary to genuinely *human* flourishing.[15] But the claim that human nature is open-ended does not commit one to affirming that it possesses a wholly immanent end; on the contrary, positing such an end would contradict the idea of its being open-ended.

But if human nature has no inherent orientation, either to God or to some immanent "natural beatitude," the challenge is to find a means to interpret open-endedness in a way that allows "participation in the divine nature" to be understood as a fully appropriate and God-intended goal of human existence without being "natural" to it. This aim can be achieved when life with God is conceived not as the *completion* of human nature (in the sense of supplementing its intrinsic properties or capacities) but rather as its *reorientation*, such that while the content (or *logos*) of human nature remains unchanged, its mode (or *tropos*) of enactment shifts.[16] My proposal is that this category of vocation provides resources for such an alternative understanding.

Vocation is, of course, Latin for "calling," and its theological deployment is rooted in the use of the Greek verb *kaleō* and its cognates in the New Testament, perhaps most famously by Paul in his Epistle to the Romans:

---

14. The latter is understood as a *finis politicus vel civilis*, in contrast to the *finis ultimus et principalis*, which is found in God; following Thomas, such an end could be identified with the earthly happiness of rational contemplation enjoyed by ancient pagan philosophers. See de Lubac, *Augustinianism and Modern Theology*, 151, 208.

15. De Lubac sees here a fundamental misunderstanding of the low-flying account of humanity's "natural end" found in Thomas: "St Thomas said that man may be considered in his nature independently of his relationship with God. [His later] commentators . . . explain that this [viz., purely 'natural'] man can be considered in his essential relationship with God, the author and end of nature" (*Augustianism and Modern Theology*, 213).

16. The distinction between *logos* and *tropos* is central to the thought of Maximus the Confessor, who uses it precisely to contrast the unchanging substance of human nature with the variability in the mode it is lived out in the transition from creation through fall and redemption to glory.

> We know that all things work together for good for those who love God,
> who are called according to his purpose. For those whom he foreknew
> he also predestined to be conformed to the image of his Son, in order
> that he might be the firstborn within a large family. And those whom
> he predestined he also called; and those whom he called he also justified;
> and those whom he justified he also glorified. (Rom 8:28–30)

As described by Paul in this passage, calling is the most fundamental of
God's acts toward human beings in time: having foreknown and predestined us to life in Christ from eternity, God effects this purpose in history
first by calling us, then justifying us, and finally bringing us to glory. The
result is a movement from a life sustained by our natural connections with
other earthly creatures to one oriented to and sustained by "the upward call
of God in Christ" (Phil 3:14).[17] But the foundational character of calling
does not lie simply in its being first in a sequence; it is also a matter of its
specificity. For vocation is the act by which God defines the particular shape
of an individual's life in a way that reflects the open-endedness of human
nature: a human being might pursue any number of this-worldly ends,
but to have a vocation is to understand oneself as summoned to take up a
unique and unsubstitutable form of life that defines one's identity eternally.

To have a vocation is to thus be called to an end that, while compatible
with one's nature as a human being, is in no sense intrinsic to it. It is to
find one's identity as that which lies ahead of oneself, in the sense of an
outcome that is given in utter freedom from God's side, and which therefore is not predictable by extrapolation from characteristics or tendencies
already present in the individual. Nothing predisposed Paul, the righteous
Pharisee, to be the apostle to the gentiles, or the Moabite Ruth to be the
ancestor of the Jewish Messiah.[18] To be sure, it is important not to exag-
gerate in the other direction either, as though discernment of one's proper
vocation necessarily entailed a radical break with the circumstances of one's
origins or upbringing: there is nothing to prevent the same God that made
of the fisherman Peter an apostle from determining, with equal grace,
that succeeding generations of Bachs should all be musicians or that many
members of the King family should be pastors. The point is simply that

---

17. The NRSV's rendering of the Greek *anō* as "heavenly" is an overtranslation to which the
RSV's "upward" is to be preferred.

18. In addition to noting his own unworthiness to be an apostle (1 Cor 15:8–10), Paul also makes
this point by stressing the objective unsuitability of gentiles as a class to be God's people (Rom
11:17–18).

the determining factor is not anything intrinsic to and thus located *within* the individual, but extrinsic: constituted entirely by God's address *to* the individual. I happen to have been called to be a parent, but I might have been called to be a celibate monk; the difference is not in me, but in God.[19]

One's vocation thus defines a person as the particular subject, the specific someone, she is before God. But to live out one's vocation, to answer God's calling, is not a matter of completing an otherwise incomplete human nature. A person who fails to heed her calling is no less human for all that: there is no hole that remains unfilled, no gap that needs closing, no desire that is left unmet as she (naturally!) pursues her own human ends without attending to God's call. One who rejects her vocation has not been the person God intended her to be, but she is no less fully and completely human for all that. For a vocation, precisely because it is an extrinsic feature of human life—the free and gracious address of God to the individual—does not depend on or correspond to any particular feature of the individual called. It is not a key that fits a particular lock, a piece needed to complete a puzzle. Nor is there any basis for asserting that humanity's natural capacities function imperfectly or deficiently apart from the grace of vocation.[20] To be sure, the category of vocation presumes that human beings *in general* are the sort of creatures that can respond when called. Thus they are agents: "I's" capable of being addressed as "Thous." But it does not presume that there is anything about a *specific* human being that orients her to her particular calling—up to and including the life of glory that is its telos—beyond the fact of the call itself.

---

19. Lest one suppose that being a parent is intrinsically impossible for some, the Bible is replete with stories of vocation overriding a person's seeming natural capacities, most prominently in the case of Sarah (Gen 17:15–21; 18:9–14; 21:1–3; cf. Rom 4:18–19), but no less Hannah (1 Sam 1) and Elizabeth (Luke 1). And even without appeal to miracle, the practices of adoption and oblation show that even those who may lack a "natural" capacity for parenthood can be parents.

20. It is at this point that my proposal differs from Kathryn Tanner's efforts to redress the problems with the anthropology of the *nouvelle théologie* in the third chapter of *Christ the Key*. Tanner rightly critiques the problem of a natural orientation to God but nevertheless maintains that grace is required for "the excellent exercise of our ordinary functions as human beings" (105), such that "we exist well only with it" (129), so that for her, too, grace becomes part of nature: not as that to which it is oriented but that without which "it does not properly exist at all" (134). These claims are based in the idea that we have a desire for God not based in our nature but rather "from the presence of God that forms an essential ingredient of our constitution as the prerequisite for human well being," so that desire for God "arises from what we have that is not our nature—the divinity in which we participate" (126–27). But this idea of God's constant presence as eliciting desire for God sounds very close to the idea of a passive capacity for God that she elsewhere rejects (119). *Contra* Tanner, I maintain that we do not desire God "as a matter of course" (127) or that it is "natural to us" by virtue of our participating in God as a matter of our created nature (131). Such participation is only and always a gift that comes on us extrinsically—we are called to it. As explained below, this is what it means for grace to reorient our nature; that although we continue to live (as always) by God's Word, in redemption and glory we do so in a new way.

NATURE AND *HYPOSTASIS*

At this point, however, something more needs to be said about the relationship between vocation and nature, lest the life of glory to which we are summoned—"the upward call of God"—seem essentially disconnected from what it means to be human in the way criticized by de Lubac. After all, if the grace by which we come to live with God is utterly adventitious, then how can it not be conceived as an unnecessary ontological surplus? To address this problem, it is necessary to explore what I have called the ontological oddity of human nature in greater depth, beginning with human beings' status as agents—creatures with a nature that is open-ended. To be a human agent is to have a nature in which what one does is not reducible to nature, to recognize that I am accountable for myself in a way that disallows my fobbing off my actions as simply outworkings of my nature, and thus as phenomena for which I have no responsibility. So, for example, while it may be true that there are many factors, deeply rooted in human evolutionary biology, that make it "natural" for me to want to have sex with as many women as I can, for me to do so would be to commit adultery: a sin for which *I*—not my nature—am responsible. Thus, to be human is not merely to be some*thing*: a particular kind of creature. It is rather to be some*one*: an entity whose end, while by no means self-constituted, is nevertheless inseparable from its own willing agency.

Another way of putting this is to say that human beings are creatures whose nature it is to be *persons*, or, in more specifically theological language, hypostases. The Greek word *hypostasis* has a long history antecedent to its deployment in the formulation of classical Trinitarian and, later, christological doctrine in the fourth, fifth, and sixth centuries. Even within a specifically Christian context, the term has continued to be used simply to refer to any individual instantiation of a nature—this particular dog or tulip or star in distinction from other members of these species. In this sense, any concrete particular may be understood as the *"hypostasis"* of a nature. In specifically theological usage, however, *hypostasis* came to refer not simply to any concrete particular, but to a particular *kind* of particular: a person or, in the words of Boethius, "an individual substance of a rational nature."[21]

This definition can be seen as Boethius's way of making the point that in certain cases (viz., "rational natures") the concrete instantiation of a nature

---

21. Boethius, *Liber de persona et duabus naturis*, 3.2 (PL 64:1344A).

is not simply some*thing*, but some*one*.[22] In such cases, to specify a *hypostasis* is not only to clarify *which* entity of a given type is under discussion (e.g., this dog versus that one) but also to identify a person—a *who*. And because to be a who—a someone—is to be an agent, to speak of *hypostasis* in this sense is to highlight once again human nature's ontological oddness. Thus, rather than referring to *what* something is (viz., its nature), *hypostasis* names *how* it is—the particular mode or way in which an individual instantiates a nature (i.e., its *tropos*). And, crucially, although personal identity is central to our experience of what it means to be human, it cannot be identified as an attribute or property of human nature like reason, will, personality, or self-consciousness, for my identity—who I am—is not something "I" have, but precisely the "I" who is the subject of such having. Personality, for example, is a characteristic of human nature (precisely as a "rational" or personal nature) through which my identity is displayed, but who I am can neither be identified with or reduced to my personality.[23]

In this context, it is no accident that Boethius presented his famous definition of personhood in a treatise on Christology, for the idea of *hypostasis* as distinct from nature, referring to who rather than what someone is, took definite form in the context of the classical christological controversies. Scripture and tradition alike named Jesus the Word of God incarnate, the only begotten Son made flesh, but what did this mean? In the fourth century, Apollinaris of Laodicea had been condemned precisely for equating Jesus's divine identity with a natural property, by teaching that in the incarnation the Word took the place of Jesus's intellect, thereby undermining the confession that Jesus was fully human, "like his brothers and sisters in every respect" (Heb 2:17).[24] Half a century later (and from the opposite side of the christological battle lines of those days), Nestorius also effectively viewed *hypostasis* as an attribute of human nature when he denied that Jesus could not be identified directly with the *hypostasis* of the divine Word on the grounds that this would diminish his humanity. The issue emerged again in the seventh century, when proponents of monothelitism held that

---

22. Of course, there are important differences in the way that rational natures are personal. A human person is not simply hypostatically but also numerically distinct from all other human persons (i.e., she is a separate being); by contrast, the divine persons are not numerically distinct from one another (i.e., they live inseparably one and the same divine life).

23. Although it may seem odd to distinguish *hypostasis* from personality, doing so makes it possible to maintain that a human being who through traumatic brain injury or mental illness experiences massive alteration to their personality does not thereby cease to be who they are.

24. Gregory of Nazianzus famously argued the point on soteriological grounds: "That which [Christ] has not assumed he has not healed" ("To Cledonius against Apollinaris [Epistle 101]," in *Christology of the Later Fathers*, ed. Edward R. Hardy [Philadelphia: Westminster, 1954], 218).

the identification of Jesus's *hypostasis* with God's eternal Word implied that his will must be divine, thereby effectively equating *hypostasis* with will. The contrary position, argued by Maximus the Confessor and ultimately vindicated at the Third Council of Constantinople, followed the same lines as the rejection of Apollinaris three centuries earlier: if Jesus was to be confessed as fully human, then his divine identity could not be equated with any part of his human nature.[25]

The upshot of these debates was a theological settlement, rooted in the christological definition produced by the Council of Chalcedon, in which a clear distinction between nature and *hypostasis* served to secure the point that Jesus of Nazareth, though possessed of a fully human nature, was with respect to his *hypostasis* fully and exclusively divine: the eternal Word of God, the second person of the Trinity.[26] *What* he was as a human, "born of a woman, born under the law" (Gal 4:4), was not determinative of *who* he was—the only begotten Son of the Father. Jesus's human nature, like that of any other created entity, subsists in time and space only as it is "hypostatized" as a particular mode of being; but in the case of Jesus alone among all other created entities, the one in whom and as whom the nature is hypostatized is divine.

Because Jesus's *hypostasis* is confessed to be none other than the eternal Word, he may be said to "preexist" his humanity in a way that is not true of any other human being. All other human beings come into being as (human) hypostases with their (human) natures, in such a way that their natures may be said to sustain their hypostases (so that I am a person by virtue of being human). This is not to say that the nature causes the *hypostasis*, for that claim would effectively make the *hypostasis* a part of the nature (and thus some *thing*—one property of the nature alongside others). It is simply to register the fact that I am the *hypostasis* I am as the one who has this particular body, with this personality, will, intellect, and so forth.[27]

---

25. Following in the footsteps of Gregory of Nazianzus (see n24 above), Maximus maintained that if Jesus lacked a human will, then he could not heal it—yet the human will, as the source of human sin and thus of human estrangement from God, is that element of human nature supremely in need of healing. See Maximus, *Opusculum* 16 (PG 91:196D); cf. *Disputation with Pyrrhus* (PG 91:325A).

26. The definition of Chalcedon speaks of "One and the Same Christ, Son, Lord, Only-begotten . . . One and the Self-same Son and Only-begotten God, Word, Lord, Jesus Christ." Heinrich Denzinger et al., eds,. *Compendium of Creeds, Definitions, and Declarations on Matters of Faith and Morals*, 43rd ed. (San Francisco: Ignatius, 2012), §301.

27. "To the question, 'What is your person?' I cannot answer 'my body, my soul, my reason, my will, my freedom, my spirit.' All this is not as yet the person, but, as it were, the stuff of which it is made." Romano Guardini, *The World and the Person* (Chicago: Regency, 1965), 118, cited in John F. Crosby, *The Selfhood of the Human Person* (Washington, DC: Catholic University of America Press, 1996), 60.

But insofar as my identity persists in spite of the most radical changes to any of these features, it cannot be identified with any of them.[28]

Therefore, the question of how I come to be the *hypostasis* I am does not admit of any answer, precisely because *hypostasis* does not refer to some *thing*. The definition of person offered by Richard of Saint Victor some centuries after Boethius illustrates this point especially clearly. Richard spoke of the person as "the individual existence of a rational nature"—which is just to define *hypostasis* as that which has no common essence across cases and thus incapable of being defined.[29] In the words of Roman Guardini, "The person eludes being uttered."[30]

HYPOSTASIS AND VOCATION

And yet if it is impossible to say how I become (or what makes me to be) a *hypostasis*, it is certainly possible to talk about how I come to *experience* myself as the *hypostasis* I am. I do so gradually over time, in and through my relationships with other human beings (and with my external environment more generally), so that my sense of my personhood can be spoken of as the precipitate of these relations.[31] My vocation names one of these relations, albeit the most important, in that it provides ultimate context for my self-understanding as a *hypostasis* called to a life with God that begins now and culminates in eternal glory. All who respond to this call do so as agents and thus through an act of the will, but, again, it is not their willing that constitutes their hypostatic identity since the capacity to will (which pertains to the nature) must be distinguished from the agent who wills, even if the latter is only ever visible through (and never exists apart from) the former. For although it is in my (human) willing that my (human) *hypostasis* is disclosed, my hypostatic identity remains distinct from my willing, as is implicit in the basic fact that my (personal) response to God's call is and must be subsequent to God's prior address to me as a person.

---

28. For example, although belief in the resurrection evidently binds personal identity closely to the body (and thus to a particular feature of human nature), the belief that individual identity endures in God's sight (as the presupposition for resurrection at the eschaton) even when the earthly body decays to the point of no longer being identifiable suggests that the association of *hypostasis* with body is, strictly speaking, a matter of grace rather than ontological necessity.

29. Richard of St. Victor, *De Trinitate* 4.23.

30. Romano Guardini, *Welt und Person* (Würzburg: Werkbund, 1962), 128; cited in Crosby, *The Selfhood of the Human Person*, 61.

31. The language of precipitate is taken from Alistair I. McFadyen, *The Call to Personhood: A Christian Theology of the Individual in Social Relationship* (Cambridge: Cambridge University Press, 1990).

The principle that my identity before God is not reducible to my willing can be seen as just another way of stating a basic principle of the Christian gospel, namely, that our ultimate status is not determined by what we do but rather by what God has done for us. Acting by the power of our (fallen) wills, we invariably turn away from God, but the gospel is that our lives are sustained not by our natural capacities but by the power of God's forgiving Word, spoken to us freely, for Christ's sake. Thus, although we are ultimately vindicated as beloved children of God in our humanity, and thus with and through our human natures, this vindication is not grounded in any capacity or achievement of our natures but solely by God's gracious word of forgiveness, spoken to us as hypostases. In this way it is God's Word, which comes to us from outside of our natures rather than anything intrinsic to our natures that sustains us in being in the face of the threats of death and damnation to which our actions would otherwise doom us.

This movement toward life with God culminates in glorification. And while glory is rightly confessed to have always been God's intention for human beings, when conceived in terms of vocation it need not be seen as implicit in or necessary to human nature, as though our humanity would be incomplete without it. To be sure, our vocation comes to us as those who have already been called into being by God's Word as creatures with a particular nature. And insofar as human nature is open-ended, it may be said to be patient of divine vocation. But such vocation is not required for human nature to function properly, nor can our nature be said to be oriented to vocation as that which completes it—a claim that makes no more sense than the idea that humanity's sin is oriented toward forgiveness. In both justification and glorification alike, God's Word may rightly be said to bring human nature to a fortunate and, indeed, appropriate end, but it remains a word of utter grace: were it lacking, there would be no evident deficiency in the nature itself, no suggestion from the perspective of human ontology that any natural capacity had been left unfulfilled.

At the same time, the correlation of vocation with *hypostasis* entails no commitment to the idea of a self-contained "pure nature" of the sort criticized by de Lubac, for to speak of humanity's end as defined by vocation does not presuppose that there exists a different sort of divinely intended end (viz., natural blessedness) alongside the supernatural blessedness of glory. A vocation—like any address—comes to us freely. If we disregard it, we reject the life with God to which we are called and thereby move toward death. In so doing, we do not fail to live fully human (and thus, at least from the perspective of this-worldly teleology, open-ended) lives, but those lives do not culminate in the end to which God has invited them.[32] Instead, they remain bound by mortality, and their openness terminates in nonexistence. One may, of course, speak of this as humanity's "natural" end as a mortal creature (see Gen 6:3; Ps 90:10), but it is certainly not a matter of beatitude, whether natural or otherwise.[33]

In this way, vocation is properly understood as the reorientation rather than the completion of human nature. God relates to human beings always and everywhere as Creator, sustaining them in existence in the same way as every other creature. Yet this relationship—the divine omnipresence whereby God sustains every creature in existence in every aspect of its existence at every moment of its existence—is fundamentally hidden and thus, however much rooted in the undivided action of the three divine hypostases, essentially impersonal in character. However one chooses to interpret Paul's words in Romans 1:19–20, there is no question in this controverted text of knowing *God* but only *the things of God*—"his eternal power and divine nature"—of knowing *that* God is, not what (let alone who) God is. In creation, then, God is present *in* the world (indeed, intimately so, as the one in whom we "live and move and have our being"; Acts 17:28), but not in such a way as to be present *to* the world (or to us in it). Our natures are at every moment upheld by God in existence and enabled by God to pursue the various sorts of this-worldly ends intrinsic to that existence, but all this happens quite independently of any recognition or acknowledgement or response on our part—behind our backs, so to speak.

In the work of creation, then, God establishes human nature for life in the world, sustained by interaction with other creatures under God's providential rule. Made for life in time and space, as creatures amid other creatures, we live through our natures, using our natural capacities, including especially our bodies, intellects, and wills, to sustain our lives by establishing those relationships with other human beings necessary not only to meet our basic physiological needs for water, food, and shelter but also to achieve our fulfillment as agents. In this way, considered from the

---

32. According to the grammar of Paul's teaching in Romans, it must be allowed that some human beings may not be predestined, and so not called (Rom 8:30; cf. Acts 2:39). Why (and, for that matter, whether) this possibility obtains is not open to our inspection, but the point remains that in such cases there is nothing incomplete about the natures of any who are not called.

33. That human beings, along with all material creatures, are naturally mortal seems firmly grounded in biblical teaching. Alongside passages like Eccl 3:1–2, the fact that the tree of life is put in the garden of Eden (Gen 2:9) suggests that even apart from sin humans receive eternal life as a gift rather than a right (cf. Rev 22:2, 19).

standpoint of creation, it is our natures that sustain our hypostases. We exist under God, since it is God who sustains our natures, along with every other created nature. But if God relates to us directly in upholding our being so that we are in our creaturehood always immediately present to God, we relate to God only indirectly: God's work is not visible to us; on the contrary, we find it possible (as modern science has shown) to understand the world and our place in it in terms of the operation of created natures without reference to the God who sustains them.[34] While as creatures we have always lived by God's power, apart from vocation, the operation of this power, which sustains us by sustaining our natures, remains hidden from us (Isa 45:15).

As we pursue the "upward call" of God, by contrast, our mode of being human, and thus our relation to the Creator, changes. In speaking to us as Christ, the Word made flesh, God is present to us, summoning us to live precisely in God. This call comes to us as hypostases, thereby setting our existence on a new footing by summoning us to life that is sustained not by our natural capacities and relationships but by God's Word. In short, while in creation the nature sustains the *hypostasis*, vocation reorients human life such that God now sustains our natures directly through our hypostases in a process that takes concrete form in the present in justification, where our status as children of God is defined by God's Word rather than our deeds, and reaches its culmination in glory, when our lives will be lived entirely in God: sustained not by the capacities of our created natures, but by God's Word alone (Matt 4:4 and par.; cf. Deut 8:3).

The process of becoming participants in the divine nature that begins with vocation is thus one in which God no longer engages us merely impersonally and anonymously, as Creator, but also personally and directly as Savior. This shift in relation comes entirely from God's side, as calling. It has no ground in human beings: it is not a matter of filling a preexisting God-shaped hole; it is a summoning of human beings to a form of life that they did not seek and that otherwise would have been unknown to them.

That this word should come to us is therefore nothing that can be anticipated on the basis of our natures' structure alone. It is grace and,

---

34. Of course, human beings may (and, as a matter of historical fact, generally do) raise questions about the ultimate origin and goal of the natural order that provides the context for their and other creatures' existence, and they may (and, again, do) use the word "God" to name the absolutely unconditioned reality that provides an answer to these questions. But the God so named is a postulate, however unavoidable: the God "*des philosophes et des savants*" (Pascal), not of Abraham, Isaac, and Jacob.

as such, is neither necessary nor predictable, let alone something owed to us. We are creatures who, by virtue of their natural open-endedness, are capable of being addressed in this way. And since apart from that address, our natures are incapable of sustaining who we are in the long term, and our lives end in death, our being called can hardly be viewed as superfluous to our flourishing. But because the grace by which we are called, justified, and glorified is not to be conceived quasi-substantially, it does not pose the problems that bedevil the Catholic proponents of the *nouvelle théologie*. Grace is neither the addition of some sort of ontological surplus that is either unnecessary to our natures' proper function or, alternatively, necessary for it; rather, it is to be understood as *address* and thus as a matter of reorientation rather than either addition or completion. In short, and insofar as it takes the form of vocation and thus a call to rest in God, grace does not change *what* we are (the content of our natures) but rather *how* we are.

In taking flesh God does not change God's fundamental commitment to sustain creation. What changes is the *mode* in which God relates to creatures. In this process our natures are in no sense left behind. To say that God addresses and thereby sustains us as hypostases is not to suggest that *hypostasis* can be conceived independently of nature. *Hypostasis* is an instantiation of nature and thus does not subsist—and cannot be conceived—apart from nature in the way that, for example, a soul might be conceived as existing apart from the body. So in the process that leads from vocation to glory, our nature is not abandoned, but the manner in which it subsists is profoundly transformed. For example, although in the resurrection we continue to have bodies (indeed, the resurrection affirms the ultimate significance of our lives as embodied), our bodies no longer depend, for their continued flourishing, on the other creaturely realities (air, water, food, etc.) in the way they do at present. Rather than being upheld "from below," so to speak, through a range of interdependent relations with other creatures, they are sustained "from above," through the power of God's Word, which, in calling, the *hypostasis* affirms and upholds the nature so hypostatized. In Jesus in particular this change is one in which God claims a creaturely life as God's own, and in so doing God also transforms the divine relation to all other creatures through Jesus, because in living as a creature God confronts creatures no longer impersonally or anonymously but as actively present to human beings and thus able to call them to live with Jesus (and thereby with the God whose Word Jesus is). To have a vocation is to be called to live life in conscious relationship with God and thus to be sustained by God's Word not just implicitly, as in creation, but explicitly—that is, to live from the Word in the mode of gracious response that sees one's life as ultimately constituted and sustained by that Word.

Apart from that life, human beings would not come to the end that God intended for them. But insofar as human nature is odd—not having a "natural" outcome—the form of the life that God intends for us cannot be read off the structure of nature in the same way one can intuit the shape of a missing puzzle piece by the contours of those already in place. Without the grace of vocation, human nature functions, but it moves on a trajectory that ends in death. Human beings may adopt all manner of projects along the way; they can perfectly well become competent, even exemplary, butchers, bakers, or candlestick makers quite apart from the "upward call of God in Christ Jesus"—but none of these intrahistorical ends will terminate in life with God. That end is achieved only as human beings contextualize the various proximate, intrahistorical projects that they adopt in terms of their experience of being called by God to live their lives in a particular way. That is what it means to be a participant in the divine nature: to be sustained by God's own life as God is, by living in the Word spoken by the Father in the power of the Spirit.

CONCLUSION

It has been a perennial struggle within Christianity to affirm, on the one hand, that our created nature is good in itself and, on the other, that we are destined for an end that transcends that nature. If the latter point is denied, then glory seems in itself unrelated (and so, formally speaking, superfluous) to our created being; but if our natures are viewed as somehow incomplete apart from glory, then our elevation to life with God is seemingly reduced to a matter of fulfilling our natures (on analogy with progressing from infancy to adulthood) rather than a gift of grace. In this chapter I have proposed the category of vocation as a means of reconciling these two seemingly incompatible convictions.

Crucial to this effort at reconciliation has been a rejection of the idea that the process that moves (according to the Pauline *ordo salutis* defined in Romans 8) from vocation through justification to glorification is properly conceived as a matter of completing our natures. It therefore does not entail conceiving human distinctiveness in terms of what de Lubac called "the soul which is open to the infinite."[35] As argued above, the soul may be said

---

35. De Lubac, *Augustinianism and Modern Theology*, 189.

to be "open to the infinite" only as human sin is open to forgiveness, that is, in the sense that it is so structured so as to be able to receive it but not in the sense that it is in any sense oriented toward it. Quite the contrary, apart from the fact of vocation (and the divine works of justification and glorification that follow on from it), human beings remain oblivious to God, as they do to the reality of the sin by which they are alienated from God.

In this context, it is necessary to revisit Augustine's claim that "our heart is restless until it rests in" God. If the "restless heart" is understood to refer to the kind of active orientation toward or desire for God that the proponents of the *nouvelle théologie* ascribed to human nature, then Augustine's claim must be rejected on two grounds. First, it seems hard to see how it could be established empirically that human beings who have not found their rest in God necessarily experience a restless heart in this sense, especially given that some people who seem to be eminently self-reflective insist that they do not.[36] Second, there seem good, specifically theological reasons to reject any such account of a "God-shaped hole" in human nature that relate to the logic of divine transcendence. If God is not one thing among others, then there seems no basis for positing any sort of ontological correlation between human (or, for that matter, any created) nature and God. Thus, if Augustine's account is to be accepted, it must be understood as a retrospective or *a posteriori* description, so that it is only in light of the experience of having heard and answered God's call that it is possible for human beings to recognize that their hearts can find rest in God alone.

This account seems *prima facie* consistent with what can be observed empirically about the character of human life. After all, in this life human beings evidently live in and by their natures, seeking out those conditions, both physical and psychosocial, that will sustain them as the persons they are. With respect to the particular details of how their lives will play out—the ensemble of relationships with other human beings and the world more generally—that a given human being will realize, human nature is open-ended, such that a variety of possible ends is consistent with and, indeed, characteristic of earthly human existence. In every case, however, that which sustains the person is the total set of relationships, rooted in the structure of our natures as material creatures, that tie us to other creatures

---

36. One advantage to my position is thus that it takes the testimony of atheists seriously. If grace is integral to human life, then absent grace we are bound to be unhappy, incomplete, frustrated. But this is not the inevitable testimony of those who see no need for reference to God.

and thereby to the created order as a whole. For though our natures are open-ended, in their open-endedness they are nevertheless firmly tied to worldly realities. From the perspective of our experience as creatures living in the world of time and space, it is an incontrovertible fact that we live by bread (viz., in dependence on other created entities) alone.

That this is not the final word on human existence, that we are called to live "not by bread alone, but by every word that comes from the mouth of God" (Matt 4:4 and par.; cf. Deut 8:3) is believable—indeed conceivable—only as we find ourselves addressed by that Word. And such address is a matter of grace rather than nature. As vocation—calling—it comes to us through special revelation—that is, not through the impersonal processes of providential care whereby God sustains our natures within the world but through the contingent and particular act of God's speaking to each of us as hypostases.[37] Through this address we are called to understand ourselves—who we are—as upheld not by our natures but simply by that Word of address itself. So it is that according to the gospel our lives are ultimately defined and sustained not by our natural capacities or incapacities but solely by God's Word so that, contrary to all appearances, even while we live now, we "have died, and [our] life is hidden with Christ in God" (Col 3:3).

Calling does not entail any substantive addition to our natures (in the sense of the provision of new attributes or abilities) but only its reorientation: it is we who continue to live as the human beings we are, but we now live by the power of God's Word in Christ rather than by our natural capacities. Yet if this model of human life avoids the charge of conflating grace with nature, it may seem to do so at the price of positing a typically Protestant discontinuity between human existence as created and redeemed. For if the only basis for our existence before God is God's Word, which is entirely extrinsic to us, then it seems difficult to explain how our lives are continuous across the divide between life in the present and life eternal. To say that our lives in glory are sustained by God's Word alone is to say that it is all a matter of grace; thus, there is nothing in our natures (e.g., the quality of our wills, or the convictions of our intellects) that serves as the pivot point between the present and the eschatological future and that thereby guarantees that the beings we are now, however otherwise

---

37. To be sure, God's calling is mediated to us through created forms—as creatures we could not apprehend it otherwise—but this happens entirely because of God's appropriation of those forms and not by virtue of any capacity for the divine intrinsic to them.

transformed, somehow continue to subsist across that divide. And in that case, our coming to glory can seem like a "new creation" in too radical a sense, in which there is nothing in common between the created self that subsists by its natural capacities and the glorified self that lives by God's Word alone.

The answer to this worry is simply to affirm that in being reoriented our natures are not destroyed or left behind but rather put on a new footing. It is we, body and soul, who live with God in glory, but we do not do so because of the qualities of our souls and bodies.[38] The upshot of this chapter is that the distinction between nature and *hypostasis* provides a way of making this point by helping to clarify the character of human ends. Vocation is not the fulfillment of an inner telos, for the essentially open-ended character of human nature means that there is no such telos. It is rather a manifestation of freedom insofar as it is realized by every individual willingly, as a matter of personal responsibility. Nevertheless, although mediated by the will in its freedom, it is not the will's achievement. Instead—and as the very term "calling" implies—it comes to us from without. In this calling the person is summoned to immediate relationship with God that constitutes a new mode of existence: an upward calling (Phil 3:14) that signifies a birth from above (John 3:7) in which we become children of God "born, not of blood or of the will of the flesh or of the will of man, but of God" (John 1:13). To invoke the technical language of the patristic period, humanity remains unchanged with respect to the *logos* of its nature (that is, human beings remain ineluctably and irreducibly human), but the *tropos* of their being—*how* they are human—is crucially different. In creation the nature sustains the *hypostasis*, with the result that the *hypostasis*, bound to the nature's mortality, is subject to death. In redemption and glory, the converse is the case: it is through the *hypostasis*, called to share in God's immortal life, that the mortal nature is sustained, with the result that this nature too puts on immortality (1 Cor 15:53–54). Ultimately, then, we are called to live by God's Word alone, but the good news is that by the grace and glory of God, the Word alone is sufficient.

---

38. Cf. Augustine's view that the resurrected saints "will be spiritual not because they will cease to be bodies, but because they will be sustained by a quickening Spirit." Augustine, *City of God against the Pagans*, trans. and ed. R. W. Dyson (Cambridge: Cambridge University Press, 1998), 13.22 (569).

Scripture Index

SUBJECT INDEX

AUTHOR INDEX